Briefcase on Equity and Trusts

Gary Watt, MA (Oxon), Solicitor
Senior Lecturer in Law
The Nottingham Trent University

First published in Great Britain 1996 by Cavendish Publishing Limited
The Glass House, Wharton Street, London, WC1X 9PX
Telephone: 0171-278 8000 Facsimile: 0171-278 8080

**British Library Cataloguing in Publication Data. A catalogue record for
this book is available from the British Library.**

ISBN 1 85941 249 1

Printed and bound in Great Britain

Preface

In spite of its mediaeval origins the trust concept boasts a multiplicity of modern uses. Accordingly, the aim of this volume has been to focus upon a number of recent developments within the law of equity and trusts, while not neglecting their historical (mostly Victorian) background.

The present volume is divided into six parts. Part 1 is an introduction to equity and trusts. Part 2 considers the setting up of express trusts. Part 3 details the ways in which an express trust may be varied. Part 4 examines the role of trustees, and of fiduciaries whose positions are analogous to those of trustees. Part 5 looks at resulting and constructive trusts and part 6 considers tracing and equitable remedies. Each part is further sub-divided into chapters, which reflect headings found in larger textbooks and typical subject areas on modern law degrees. Each chapter contains sub-headings within which the case summaries are arranged in chronological order, the most recent cases appearing last.

Although this volume is primarily a collection of case summaries, it has been necessary to include extracts of certain crucial statutes. Where possible these extracts have been included in paraphrased form, in which case they will appear in square brackets. The reader will also note that the text is interspersed with guidance notes and questions, with a view to prompting reflective thought upon the materials. A book of this size cannot, however, hope to cover everything that might be covered in a longer book. As to which, my personal favourites are Graham Moffat's *Trusts Law: Text and Materials* (2nd edn) Butterworths (1994) and Parker and Mellows' *The Modern Law of Trusts* (6th edn) Sweet & Maxwell (1994).

I hope that the reader will find this volume a useful aid to understanding this area of law, and an inspiration to undertake further study. You might even conclude, as I have done, that the flexibility and utility of equity goes beyond that of any other area of the law. After all, in which other area could the reader find Shakespeare and 'Star Wars', the composer Delius and the pop-star Gilbert O'Sullivan, Arthur Scargill and Robert Maxwell, all within the covers of a single book? They are all to be found within the pages that follow, so pick up your briefcase and go to work!

Gary Watt
March 1996

Contents

Part 6 Tracing and equitable remedies

Table of cases

Table of statutes

Part 1 Introduction to equity and trusts

---

1 Defining equity and trusts

1.1 Understanding equity

Note ──

Equity will not suffer a wrong without a remedy, so where the common law does not provide a remedy, equity will. Thus it is said that equity is a 'gloss' on the common law. Equity is not, however, a mere 'gloss', for equity looks to substance rather than form, thus enabling it to give effect to the true intentions of parties to a transaction where the strict legal position does not reflect those intentions.

──

Equity is said to act between persons (*in personam*), so that it will award a remedy to party B against party A. The classic instance of this is the trust, where equity will require A to hold property for the benefit of party B, even where A is the legal owner of the property. However, the fact that trusts have always existed in relation to specific property added (to B's rights against A personally) certain property rights (rights *in rem*) against the assets held by A. These rights in the property could be enforced against any third party, C, who came into possession of the property, except where C had purchased the legal title in good faith and without notice of B's claim, for in such a case no wrong had been committed and equity would grant no remedy.

1.2 Defining a trust

Kinloch v Secretary of State for India (1882) HL

By Royal Warrant Queen Victoria 'granted' certain spoils of war to the defendant 'in trust' for specified members of her armed forces, to be divided amongst them. The plaintiff brought this action on behalf of himself and other persons entitled under the Royal Warrant, claiming that the defendant should be made to distribute the property to those entitled.

Held Lord O'Hagan stated that 'there is no magic in the word "trust".' Here, although the defendant might properly be said to be a 'trustee' for the Crown, he could not be said to be a trustee for the persons entitled under the Royal Warrant. There had been no transfer of the 'booty' from the Crown to independent trustees, merely a transfer from the Queen to one of her servants. Only the defendant, as agent of the Queen, could actually divest the Crown of the property. This he had not done, and a court of equity would not require him to do so.

Re Williams (1897) CA

W, a testator, left his residuary estate to his wife under the terms of his will, 'in the fullest trust and confidence' that she would carry out his detailed 'wishes' with regard to certain monies. These 'wishes' included W's desire that his wife, on her death, would leave the proceeds of W's life insurance policy to their daughter. W appointed his wife as one of the executors of his estate. W's wife sought a declaration that she held W's residuary estate absolutely, unfettered by a trust.

Held a person is entitled to leave their property to another subject to imperative, binding conditions which would be enforced by a court of equity, but the words used by W in this case were merely 'precatory' in nature (that is, 'by way of request') and did not subject his wife's inheritance to a trust. The fact that W had not indicated any duties that his wife should perform as a trustee was further evidence that a trust had not been intended.

Trustee Act 1925 s 68(17)

The expressions 'trust' and 'trustee' extend to implied and constructive trusts, and to cases where the trustee has a beneficial interest in the trust property, and to the duties incident to the office of personal representative, and 'trustee', where the context admits, includes a personal representative.

Note ———

The following is a modern definition of an express trust (ie a trust which has been expressly created, as opposed to one which has come about automatically, or by order of a court).

The Hague Convention on the Law Applicable to Trusts and on their Recognition (incorporated into English law by the Recognition of Trusts Act 1987)

For the purposes of this Convention the term 'trust' refers to the legal relationship created – *inter vivos* or on death – by a person, the settlor, when assets have been placed under the control of a trustee for the benefit of a beneficiary or for a specified purpose. A trust has the following characteristics – *a* the assets constitute a separate fund and are not part of the trustee's estate; *b* title to the trust assets stands in the name of the trustee or in the name of another person on behalf of the trustee; *c* the trustee has the power and the duty, in respect of which he is accountable, to manage, employ or dispose of the assets in accordance with the terms of the trust and the special duties imposed upon him by law. The reservation by the settlor of certain rights and powers, and the fact that the trustee may himself have rights as a beneficiary, are not necessarily inconsistent with the existence of a trust.

Note

The trustee nearly always holds the legal title to the property, although it is theoretically possible for a trustee to hold merely an equitable title.

1.2.1 Trusts compared to contracts

Harmer v Armstrong (1934) CA

The defendant, A, agreed to purchase the copyright to certain publications from V Co. The plaintiff, H, asserted, *inter alia*, that A had entered this agreement as trustee for H, which A denied. V Co, with notice of the plaintiffs' claim, purported to rescind the contract with A. H brought an action for a declaration that A held the benefit of the agreement as trustee for H. H also sought an order for specific performance of the agreement, which is a form of order which would oblige V Co to complete the sale to A for the benefit of H (see 19.1).

Held A had acted in the capacity of trustee for H. Therefore specific performance of the contract was ordered, with the result that A would hold the benefit of the contract on trust for H. Under contract law H would be unable to claim the benefit of the contract because he had not been privy to it, but because H was the beneficiary of a trust of which A was the trustee, H would be able to claim the benefit of the contract made between A and V Co.

Note

Whereas a contract is a private relationship between the parties to the contract, it is of the essence of a trust that a settlor can give property to his trustee on trust for a third party (see *Beswick v Beswick* (1968) at 19.1).

Swain v The Law Society (1982) HL

By a document circulated in 1975 the Society detailed proposals for a professional indemnity insurance scheme to which all solicitors would be obliged to subscribe under s 37 of the Solicitors Act 1974. By a subsequent letter all solicitors were asked whether they approved of the scheme in its proposed form. Most solicitors who replied were in favour of the scheme and in due course the Society drew up the Solicitor's Indemnity Rules 1975. According to the Rules the insurers would agree to indemnify all solicitors participating in the scheme. In May 1976 the Society contracted with insurance brokers to obtain insurance for the scheme, the brokers agreeing to pay part of their commission (received from the insurers) to the Society. From September 1976 solicitors' participation in the scheme was compulsory. The plaintiffs, two practising solicitors, were unhappy with the scheme and communicated their displeasure to the Society in January 1979. In October 1979 they took out an originating summons seeking a declaration that the Rules were void as being *ultra vires* ('outside the scope of') s 37 of the Act. They also asked whether the Society was entitled to keep the commission it had already received from the brokers, or whether it was obliged to account to individual solicitors under an express or implied trust.

Held in exercising its powers under s 37 of the Act the Society was carrying out a public function for which there could be no equitable liability to account. Further, the Society had not, by express or implied trust, constituted itself a trustee of the 1975 contract, nor had it constituted itself a constructive trustee of the commissions received under the contract. Accordingly there would be no liability to account for the commissions received. The Society had entered a contract, not a trust. The courts will generally be slow to imply a trust where the facts can be analysed as giving rise to a contract, and especially reluctant to imply a trust in the present case, for if any persons could be expected to make clear their intentions to set up a trust, such persons must include 'a society of lawyers'.

1.2.2 Trust compared to debt

Note ─────────────────────
See Asset Protection Trusts at 8.2.

1.2.3 Trusts compared with powers

Re Hay's Settlement Trusts (1981)

Trustees of a settlement made in 1958 held the trust fund subject to a power to allocate it for the benefit of 'such persons or purposes' as they should in their discretion appoint. If they made no such appointment the trust fund would pass to the settlor's nieces and nephews. Only the settlor, her husband and the trustees could not be appointed to benefit from the fund. Questions arose as to how the court should supervise the exercise of such a wide discretionary power and how such a power differed from a trustee's duties under a trust.

Held whereas a trustee is bound to carry out the obligations of a trust, and if the trustee fails to do so the court will intervene to ensure that the trust is fulfilled, a mere power is very different. A trustee does not have to exercise a mere power, and will not be compelled to do so by the court, but the trustee must periodically consider whether or not to exercise the power. If the power is actually exercised the trustee must ensure that he or she acts in accordance with the terms of the power, and must consider both the range of potential beneficiaries and whether each individual appointment is appropriate.

1.2.4 Trusts compared with absolute gifts

Note ───────────────────────────────────────

Gifts 'in trust', which place strict temporal or conditional limitations on the donee's ownership of the subject matter of the gift, must be contrasted with absolute gifts. The donee of an absolute gift will, in general terms, be free to use the subject matter of the gift as they wish.

Re Diggles (1888) CA

A testatrix left all her real and personal property to her daughter whilst expressing her 'desire' that her daughter should pay an annuity of £25 to a named relative and allow that relative to use whatever household furniture her daughter did not need. For a number of years the annuity was paid, but was eventually discontinued. Thereafter the annuitant applied to court claiming that the daughter had been constituted a trustee by the wording of the will, and was therefore obliged to pay the annuity.

Held There was no trust imposed upon the daughter requiring her to pay the annuity to her relative. The expression of the testatrix's 'desire' was merely precatory, that is, in the nature of a request. Construing the will as a whole it could not be said that she had intended to create a trust of the annuity.

Re Osoba (1979) CA

A testator, O, made a bequest to his wife of the rents from certain leasehold properties for her maintenance and for the training of his daughter 'up to University grade'. O's wife died and shortly thereafter his daughter completed her university education. O's son claimed a share of the residue which had not been used for the daughter's education.

Held the gift of residue was an absolute gift to the wife and daughter in equal shares, the expression of the purposes for which the gift was to be used being merely an indication of O's motive for making the gift. Further, as there had been no words of severance of the gift as between the wife and her daughter, they were deemed to hold the residue as joint tenants. Accordingly, ever since her mother's death, the daughter had held the whole of the fund absolutely for her own benefit.

Note ───────────────────────────────────────

Contrast the above case with the case of *Re Abbott* (1900) at 3.2.1 below.

1.2.5 Trusts engrafted onto gifts

Hancock v Watson (1902)

The testator left his residuary estate on trust for his wife for her life, directing that after her death a gift of two-fifths of the estate should be made to SD, a married woman, for her own use during her lifetime. After the death of SD the two-fifths were to pass to her children, and if she had none, to the children of C. In the event SD died without having had a child. The appellants in the case represented the children of C, the respondents represented SD's personal representatives, each claimed to be entitled to the two-fifths portion of the testator's estate.

Held the gift of the two-fifths to SD would take effect as an absolute gift to her, and judgment was therefore awarded in favour of her personal representatives. The trust which had been engrafted onto the gift in favour of the children of SD had failed outright for lack of issue, and the trust which had been engrafted in favour of C's children failed for perpetuity (see 5.1). Where engrafted trusts failed the original absolute gift would take effect.

1.2.6 Trusts compared with agency

Note ──

An agent owes fiduciary duties (duties of good faith) to their principal, and will often have some degree of managerial control of the principal's property. Crucially, however, a trustee's holding or control of the trust property is more fundamental than that of an agent, and is in the nature of entitlement, albeit merely legal entitlement. Further, whereas an agency is founded upon agreement between the agent and principal, there is generally no agreement between trustee and beneficiary.

Part 2 Setting up a trust

2 Capacity and formality requirements

2.1 Capacity

2.1.1 Mental incapacity

Simpson v Simpson (1992)

The testator's mental well-being had become increasingly impaired after an operation to remove a tumour from his brain. After the operation he transferred 70% of his estate into the joint names of himself and his wife, and sent a letter to his solicitor expressing his intention to sell his cottage in due course and to make a gift to his wife of half the proceeds. After the testator's death his children by an earlier marriage sued his widow. They questioned, *inter alia*, whether the testator had possessed sufficient capacity to transfer his beneficial interests into his and his wife's joint names, and whether the letter to his solicitor could have amounted to a declaration of trust in favour of his wife.

Held on the basis of the evidence, including that of medical experts, it was clear that a patient with the testator's medical complaint would deteriorate to a point where a lack of mental capacity must be presumed. In the absence of evidence to rebut the presumption the purported dispositions to the testator's wife were ineffective to transfer his beneficial interests in the various properties. In particular, he had not had capacity to declare a trust by the letter to his solicitor. In any event the letter had not shown an intention to make an *immediate* gift to his wife and consequently could not take effect as a declaration of trust.

2.1.2 Infancy

Edwards v Carter (1893) HL

A husband agreed, one month before attaining his majority, that he would vest his future inheritance, upon his father's death, in a trust set up by his father. The trust was expressed in terms to benefit the husband, his wife and their future issue. The husband's father died four years later, and a further year later the husband purported to repudiate the settlement. The Court of Appeal held that he was bound by the settlement he had entered into as a minor. Certain of his creditors appealed to the House of Lords, the respondents were the trustees of the settlement.

Held the decision of the Court of Appeal was affirmed. The husband's settlement was not void. It was voidable, on account of his infancy at the time that the settlement was made, but he had failed to repudiate the settlement within a reasonable time and it would therefore stand.

Family Law Reform Act 1969 s 1
A person shall attain full age (majority) at the age of 18, instead of the previous age of 21. Before attaining the age of 18 a person shall be an 'infant' and 'minor' for the purposes of any rule of law which uses those terms.

Law of Property Act 1925 s 1(6)
A legal estate is not capable of subsisting or of being created in an undivided share in land or of being held by an infant.

2.2   Formalities

Note ───
A trust may be declared *inter vivos* of pure personalty (not land) without the need to satisfy any formal requirements. So, for example, X could declare 'see this pen of mine, I henceforth hold it on trust for the benefit of Y'. Assuming that X had intended to create a trust these words would be sufficient to move the beneficial (equitable) ownership of the pen from X to Y. X would be a trustee of the pen for Y.

2.2.1   Statutory formality requirements of an express trust

Law of Property Act 1925 s 53

(1) ...

    (b) a declaration of trust respecting any land or any interest therein must be manifested and proved by some writing signed by some person who is able to declare such trust or by his will;

    (c) a disposition of an equitable interest or trust subsisting at the time of the disposition, must be in writing signed by the person disposing of the same, or by his agent thereunto lawfully authorised in writing or by will.

(2) This section does not affect the creation or operation of resulting, implied or constructive trusts.

2.2.2 *Inter vivos* trusts

Note ───

An *inter vivos* trust is one which is effective during the lifetime of the settlor.

───

Grey v Inland Revenue Commissioners (1960) HL

Between 1949 and 1950 H executed six settlements in favour of his grandchildren. Grey was one of the trustees of those settlements. On 1 February 1955 H transferred 18,000 £1 shares to the trustees. On 18 February H orally and irrevocably directed that the shares should be held on the trusts of the six settlements, 3,000 shares to each settlement. On 25 March the trustees made written declarations of trust in accordance with H's directions. The instruments declaring the trusts were assessed to *ad valorem* stamp duty (a tax charged 'according to the value' of an instrument) as voluntary dispositions, in accordance with the Finance Act 1910. The trustees appealed against the assessment.

Held H's oral direction would have constituted a 'disposition' of his equitable interest in the shares, but was ineffective for failing to satisfy the requirement of writing within s 53(1)(c) of the Law of Property Act 1925. Accordingly only the later formal declarations by the trustees were effective to transfer H's equitable interest in the shares. Those formal declarations constituted 'instruments' for the purposes of the Stamp Act 1891 and had been rightly assessed to *ad valorem* stamp duty.

Oughtred v Inland Revenue Commissioners (1960) HL

Two hundred thousand shares in WJ & Son Ltd were held upon trust for Mrs O for life, thereafter to her son, P, absolutely. Mrs O also owned 72,700 shares absolutely. By an oral agreement, and in order to avoid estate duty payable on the shares in the event of Mrs O's death, the parties determined to exchange their interests. Mrs O promised to transfer the 72,200 to P, and P promised to transfer his remainder interest in the 200,000 shares to Mrs O. Written documents of transfer were later executed in accordance with the terms of the oral agreement. The Inland Revenue brought the present action claiming *ad valorem* stamp duty on the document which recorded the transfer of the equitable interest in the 200,000 shares. Mrs O argued that no value had passed by virtue of the later documents, the equitable interest having been transferred by the earlier oral agreement, and accordingly that there was no basis on which to charge *ad valorem* stamp duty on the later document.

Held (Viscount Radcliffe and Lord Cohen dissenting) Mrs O did not have a beneficial interest in the 200,000 shares until the execution of the later documents. It followed, therefore, that the later document was an instrument transferring value, and that it should be subject to *ad valorem* stamp duty at £663. Mrs O had argued that inasmuch as the oral agreement was an agreement of sale and purchase it gave rise in equity to a constructive trust of the remainder interest in her favour, subject only to Mrs O performing her side of the agreement to transfer the 72,700 shares to P (as to the equitable requirement of mutuality of performance, see *Beswick v Beswick* 19.1). She argued, in other words, that the oral agreement had transferred the equitable ownership of the 200,000 shares to her, and that P had thereafter held those shares as constructive trustee for her. The formality requirements laid down in s 53(1)(c) did not enter into the case, she argued, because of the provision in s 53(2) that constructive trusts were not subject to any formality requirements. The majority of their lordships rejected this submission. By analogy with the 'simple case of a contract for sale of land' they pointed out that the deed which comes after the contract and completes the sale has never been regarded as 'not stampable *ad valorem*'. It followed, on this reasoning, that the later instrument of transfer to Mrs O had transferred real value and was stampable *ad valorem* as the Inland Revenue had contended. Dissenting, Viscount Radcliffe, observed that Mrs O need never have called for the subsequent written instrument of transfer, and that she could have simply called upon the trustees of the settlement of the 200,000 shares to transfer the bare legal title to her. For Viscount Radcliffe the subsequent written transfer by P was nothing more than a transfer of the bare legal title to Mrs O, it did not transfer any equitable interest at all and should not have been assessed to *ad valorem* stamp duty.

Note

It is important, here, to read the summaries of *Vandervell v IRC* (1967) and *Re Vandervell's Trusts (No 2)* (1974) (see 16.3). Having completed the reading for this section consider the following questions.

Q Is it necessary to comply with s 53(1)(c) where a new equitable interest is being created, or only where an existing equitable interest is being disposed of?

Q What are the formality requirements where a beneficiary, B, directs their trustee, A, to hold B's equitable interest on trust for C?

2.2.3 'Testamentary' or 'will' trusts

Wills Act 1837 s 9

No will shall be valid unless –

(a) it is in writing, and signed by the testator, or by some other person in his presence and by his direction; and

(b) it appears that the testator intended by his signature to give effect to the will; and

(c) the signature is made or acknowledged by the testator in the presence of two or more witnesses present at the same time; and

(d) each witness either –

(i) attests and signs the will; or

(ii) acknowledges his signature,

in the presence of the testator (but not necessarily in the presence of any other witness),

but no form of attestation shall be necessary.

Re Danish Bacon Co Ltd Staff Pension Fund Trusts (1971)
An employee of the Danish Bacon Co Ltd nominated (by signed writing) his wife to receive his pension entitlement in the event of his death. Later he sent a letter to the pension fund trustees amending his nomination in favour of another relative. After his death the question arose whether the original or the subsequent nomination was valid. It was argued on behalf of the wife that the amended nomination could not be valid, either because it failed the requirements of s 53(1)(c) of the Law of Property Act, the amended form of nomination having never been signed, or because it failed to satisfy s 9 of the Wills Act 1837 governing testamentary dispositions.

Held no statutory rule of formality applied directly to nominations of this sort, they were *sui generis* ('in a class of their own') and governed by the rules of the pension fund. Section 53(1)(c) would not apply because even the amended nomination was revocable up until the testator's death. However, even if s 53(1)(c) had been applicable, the original form of nomination and the letter to the trustees could be read together as satisfying the formality requirements of that section. The Wills Act 1837 had no application to this case. The pension entitlements had never entered the deceased's estate and the nomination of them in favour of another could not, therefore, be seen as a testamentary disposition. Despite certain testamentary characteristics the nomination took effect under the rules and trust of the pension fund, the nominee claimed through those rules and not through the deceased. The wife's arguments failed, the later nomination was valid.

2.2.4 Secret trusts

Note ──
Secret trusts are a means by which a testator is able to by-pass the formality requirements laid down in the Wills Act. As Dankwerts J put it in *Re Young* (1951), 'the whole theory of the formation of a secret trust is that the Wills Act has nothing to do with the matter'. Typically, though largely historically, the reason for wanting secrecy arose where the testator wished to make a testamentary gift to a mistress or illegitimate child (the latter concept does not now exist, see Family Law Reform Act 1987 s 1).

2.2.5   fully-secret trusts

Note ───
This is where X formally leaves property by his will to Y in circumstances where Y is informally made aware by X during X's lifetime (and Y expressly or impliedly accepts) that Y is to hold the property as trustee for the benefit of Z. On the face of the will Y will appear to be the beneficial owner of the property.
───

McCormick v Grogan (1869) HL

The testator, M, left all his estate to G by a will in the briefest of terms. On his death bed M instructed G that his will and a letter were to be found in his desk. The letter named various intended beneficiaries and the intended gifts to them, and concluded with the words: 'I do not wish you to act strictly on the foregoing instructions, but leave it entirely to your own good judgment to do as you think I would, if living, and as the parties are deserving'. G accepted the secret trust. Later, an intended beneficiary, whom G thought it right to exclude, sued.

Held their lordships did not doubt that in an appropriate case they could enforce the terms of a secret trust against the alleged trustee. However, it had not been shown on the facts of the present case that G should be held to any trust. The jurisdiction to enforce a secret trust was aimed at preventing equitable fraud on the part of the alleged trustee. No *malus animus* (bad conscience) was shown on G's part in the present case, and the secret trust would not be enforced against him.

Re Boyes (1884)

B made an absolute gift to his executor by his will. The executor accepted that he was to hold the gift on trust for other persons, but the names of those persons were not communicated to the executor during B's lifetime. Only after B's death were informal letters found which detailed the intended objects of the gift.

Held this was not a valid fully-secret trust. To be valid the precise objects of the trust must have been communicated, and the trust accepted, during the testator's lifetime. However, if B had placed a sealed envelope of detailed instructions into the executor's hands before B's death, this would have constituted constructive notice of the trusts to the executor, and the executor would have been deemed to have accepted the trusts as detailed in the letter.

Ottaway v Norman (1972)

By his will H left his bungalow to his housekeeper together with a legacy of £1,500 and half the residue of his estate. On her death the housekeeper left her property to strangers. O sued her executor, N, alleging that the housekeeper had orally agreed with H to leave the various assets to O in her will.

Held there had been an arrangement between H and the housekeeper under which the latter had agreed to pass on the bungalow, furnishings and fixtures to O. It followed that N now held the bungalow under a constructive trust for the benefit of O. The essential elements which had to be proved were (1) the intention of H to subject the housekeeper to an obligation in favour of O; (2) communication of that intention to the housekeeper; and (3) the acceptance of that obligation by her either expressly or by acquiescence. It was immaterial whether the informal agreement had come before or after the execution of the will. Nor was it necessary to show that the housekeeper had committed a deliberate and conscious wrong. However, Brightman J did hold that clear evidence would be needed before the court would assume that the testator had not meant what he said in his will and that the standard of proof was analogous to that required before a court would rectify a written instrument. (But see the following note.)

Note

In *Re Snowden* (1979), Sir Robert Megarry VC expressed some doubt about how far rectification was a fair analogy to secret trusts when determining the appropriate standard of proof. Apart from in cases where fraud had been alleged against the trustee, he preferred to apply the ordinary civil standard of proof, namely, proof 'on a balance of probabilities'.

2.2.6 Half-secret trusts

This is where X formally leaves property by his will to Y *expressly* 'on trust' for another, but where Y is only informally made aware of the identity of that other. It will be clear on the face of the will that Y is not the beneficial owner of the property. It is clear, then, that with a half-secret trust there is not the risk of fraud which is found in the case of a fully-secret trust. It would seem to follow that the prevention of equitable fraud is an inadequate rationale for the enforcement of half-secret trusts, and that some other justification is required.

Blackwell v Blackwell (1929) HL

The testator, B, left a legacy of £12,000 to five persons by a codicil to his will, and directed them to apply the income 'for the purposes indicated by me to them', with power to apply two-thirds of the capital 'to such person or persons indicated by me to them'. The beneficiaries of the trusts (a mistress and her illegitimate son) were communicated orally by B to the intended trustees, with detailed instructions being given to one of the intended trustees. The intended trustees accepted the trusts before the execution of the codicil. B's widow challenged the validity of the half-secret trust and claimed the £12,000 for herself.

Held The evidence of the oral arrangement was admissible and proved a valid half-secret trust in favour of B's mistress and illegitimate son. Viscount Sumner saw no relevant distinction between fully-secret and half-secret trusts. 'In both cases', he observed, 'the testator's wishes are incompletely expressed in his will. Why should equity, over a mere matter of words, give effect to them in one case and frustrate them in the other?' For his Lordship the 'fraud' to be prevented was the same in both cases.

Re Keen (1937) CA

K, the testator, left £10,000 in his will to his friends, H and E, 'to be held upon trust and disposed of by them among such person, persons or charities as may be notified by me to them ... during my lifetime'. In advance of the execution of his will K handed a sealed envelope to E. The envelope contained the name of a lady to whom K had not been married. E was aware of the contents of the envelope but did not actually open it until after K's death.

Held this was not a valid half-secret trust. The communication via the envelope had preceded the execution of the will and was inconsistent with the terms of the will, the will would therefore take effect as read and the legacy would fall into residue. Further, the clause in K's will purported to reserve to K the power to make future testamentary dispositions by simply notifying the trustees during his lifetime of his intentions. The intended effect of the clause, therefore, was to exclude the requirement of the Wills Act that a duly executed codicil be used to amend a will. The clause would not be permitted to have that effect and must fail.

Re Bateman's WT (1970)

The testator, B, directed his trustees to set aside £24,000 from his estate and to pay the income thereof 'to such persons and in such proportions as shall be stated by me in a sealed letter in my own handwriting addressed to my trustees'. The trustees received a sealed letter after B's will was executed, but before B's death. There was no evidence to show that the letter had been written before the execution of the will.

Held the direction to the trustees was invalid. Pennycuik VC held that 'once one must construe the direction as admitting of a future letter then the direction is invalid, as an attempt to dispose of the estate by a non-testamentary instrument'.

Note ──────────────────────────────────────

A rationale for half-secret trusts appears to be emerging from these cases, which is quite distinct from the policy of fraud prevention which underpins the cases on fully-secret trusts. The rationale is that directions to trustees in the nature of a half-secret trust take effect only when they precede the execution of the will and can be treated as having been incorporated in the will by reference. Inconsistency with the later will renders the half-secret trust invalid.

Q Does the distinction made in modern cases between the rationales underlying fully-secret and half-secret trusts appear to you to be a logical one?

Q Are the modern cases on half-secret trusts consistent with the statement, with which we started this topic, that 'the whole theory of the formation of a secret trust is that the Wills Act has nothing to do with the matter'?

3 Certainty requirements

3.1 General

Note

According to Lord Langdale MR in *Knight v Knight* (1840) the courts will not acknowledge that an express trust has been created unless the 'three certainties' are shown. These are (1) a certain intention to create a trust; (2) certainty as to the object (beneficiaries or purposes) of the trust; and (3) certainty as to the subject (property) of the trust. When construing an instrument to discover whether these certainty requirements have been satisfied, the trust must be given its natural construction.

Rabin v Gerson (1986) CA

The plaintiffs took out a summons for the court's directions as to the proper construction of a charitable trust deed. During the proceedings the plaintiffs sought to refer to the written opinions of the barristers who had originally drafted the trust deed. The opinions having being written before the drafting of the deed, the plaintiffs hoped that they might provide evidence of the settlor's intentions in setting up the trust.

Held it had not been disputed that the words used in the trust deed had been the words the testator had intended to use, accordingly the deed fell to be construed according to the natural meaning of the words used. Counsel's written opinions could not be admitted as evidence that the settlor had intended to achieve a specific legal effect, when such an effect did not otherwise flow from a natural reading of the deed.

3.2 Certainty of intention

Jones v Lock (1865) CA

J, an ironmonger, returned home from conducting some business in Birmingham. When criticised by his family for failing to bring a present for his nine month old son, he produced a cheque in the sum of £900 made payable to himself, said, 'I give this to baby for himself' and placed the cheque in the baby's hand. He then took the cheque and said, 'I am going to put it away for him'. Six days afterwards, J died, and the cheque was found among his possessions. At issue was whether the baby was entitled to the cheque.

Held there had been no gift or valid declaration of trust. Accordingly, the baby was not entitled to the cheque. The Lord Chancellor refused to find an intention to declare a trust in 'loose conversations of this sort'. He observed that, had the father not died, he would have been very surprised to discover that he was not able to use the £900, but was bound to hold it in trust for his baby son.

Lambe v Eames (1871) CA

The testator, L, left his entire estate to his widow 'to be at her disposal in any way she may think best, for the benefit of herself and her family'. On her death she left part of the testator's estate to an illegitimate son of one of the testator's own sons.

Held the gift was valid. Whereas words similar to those of the testator's will might, in previous cases, have been held to create a trust, the will fell to be construed, not by precedent, but according to the testator's actual intention on a true construction of the will. In the present case the court held that the testator had not intended to impose a trust upon his widow's inheritance. Such a construction would have made invalid a gift to illegitimate 'family' members.

Re Adams and the Kensington Vestry (1884) CA

The testator provided by his will that all his property real and personal should pass to his wife, her heirs, personal representatives and assigns, 'in full confidence that she would do what was right as to the disposal thereof between his children, either in her lifetime or by will after her decease'. The question arose whether this amounted to an absolute gift in favour of the wife, or whether the words of the will had imposed a trust in favour of her children.

Held the words created an absolute gift in favour of the widow, unfettered by any trust. The reference to the children had been made merely to call to his widow's attention the moral obligations which had weighed upon the testator in making an absolute gift to her. His intention was merely to make express his motivation for making the gift. A testator's 'confidence' in his donee might suggest a trust in some contexts, but in the present case, on a proper construction of the whole will, no trust had been intended.

Comiskey v Bowring-Hanbury (1905) HL

H, the testator, left to his wife, by his will, 'the whole of my real and personal estate and property absolutely in full confidence that she will make such use of it as I should have made myself and that at her death she will devise it to such one or more of my nieces as she may think fit and in default of any disposition by her thereof by her will or testament I hereby direct that all my estate and property acquired by her under this my will shall at her death be equally divided among the surviving said nieces'.

Held upon a true construction of the words of the will the disposition took effect as an absolute gift to the wife subject to a gift over in favour of the nieces should the wife not provide for them in her will.

Paul v Constance (1977) CA

Mrs P and Mr C lived together as man and wife. C received £950 in settlement of an action for personal injuries, which they decided to deposit in a bank account. The account was opened in C's sole name so as to avoid any embarrassment in view of the fact that C and P were unmarried. C frequently assured P that the money in the account was as much hers as his and that she could make withdrawals with C's written authority. In fact only one withdrawal was ever made from the account, the sum withdrawn being then divided equally between C and P. On the other hand, further monies were paid into the account, notably their joint winnings from playing 'bingo'. C eventually died intestate and his executors closed the bank account, the balance being then roughly equivalent to the original deposit of £950. P claimed that the money in the account had been held by C in trust for P and C.

Held the words frequently used by C to assure P of her joint entitlement to the monies in the account were sufficient to constitute a declaration of trust. The absence of the word 'trust' was not fatal to the finding of an express declaration of trust, taking into account the 'unsophisticated character of the deceased and his relationship with the plaintiff'. The Court of Appeal acknowledged that this was a 'borderline' case, but found a trust on the facts. The plaintiff's claim succeeded.

Q was this case decided on the right side of the borderline? Was it correct to find an express trust on the basis of 'loose conversations' (compare *Jones v Lock*, above). If C had intended to declare a trust, at which precise point in time did he declare it?

3.2.1   Intention to create a trust or a gift?

Re The Trusts of the Abbott Fund (1900)

Dr Fawcett of Cambridge collected £500, from various subscribers, for the maintenance and support of two elderly, deaf sisters. No arrangement was made as to the disposal of any sums surplus to their needs. In the event they died leaving a surplus of £367.

Held the surplus in the 'Abbot Fund' account was held on a resulting trust for the subscribers to the fund in proportion to their contributions thereto. The money had never been the property, absolutely, of the ladies 'so that they should be in a position to demand a transfer of it to themselves, or so that if they became bankrupt the trustee in bankruptcy should

19

be able to claim it'. Rather, the monies in the fund had been held to benefit the ladies in a particular way, that purpose having failed, a resulting trust arose.

Re Andrew's Trust (1905)
The Bishop of Jerusalem had died and a fund was set up to finance the education of his children. When all the children had grown up and their education had been completed, there remained a surplus of monies in the fund.

Held the surplus should be divided equally between the Bishop's children. It should not be held on resulting trust for the subscribers to the fund. The donations were treated as a gift to the children, albeit for the primary purpose of their education.

Q How can the decision in *Re Andrew's* be reconciled with the decision in *Re Abbott*? Is it enough to point to the fact that the beneficiaries in *Re Abbott* had died? What if the beneficiaries in *Re Andrew's* had died before completing their education, what would have happened then? (See, also, *Re Osoba* at 1.2.4.)

3.2.2 The effect of precedent

Re Hamilton (1895) CA
H, a testatrix, left certain legacies to her nieces 'for their sole and separate use', adding, 'I wish them to bequeath the same equally between the families [of certain named individuals]'. The question was whether the additional words imposed a trust on the gift to the nieces.

Held the legacies belonged to the nieces absolutely and were not impressed with any trusts. Lindley LJ determined that in each case the wording of the will should be construed to find its proper meaning 'and if you come to the conclusion that no trust is intended, you say so, although previous judges have said the contrary on some wills more or less similar to the one which you have to construe'. Precedent should not be conclusive of the question of construction.

Re Steele's Will Trusts (1948)
S, the testatrix, left an heirloom to her son, to be held by him for his eldest son and so on 'as far as the rules of law and equity will permit', adding 'I request my said son to do all in his power by his will or otherwise to give effect to this my wish'. The phrasing of the gift *exactly* reproduced the wording of a similar gift in a previous reported case. In that case the trust had been held to be effective.

Held in choosing to adopt the precise wording used in a previous reported case the testatrix had made clear her intention to achieve the result which was achieved in that previous case, namely a trust binding on the son. Accordingly the wording of the present gift would take effect as a valid trust of the heirloom.

Q How can the decisions in *Re Hamilton* and *Re Steele's WT* be reconciled?

Re Endacott (1960) CA

E, a testator, left his residuary estate to his local parish council 'for the purpose of providing some useful memorial to myself'.

Held the gift failed. It could not be construed as an absolute gift to the parish council for its own use. The words 'for the purpose of providing some useful memorial' showed E's imperative intention to create a trust. Such a trust, being a trust for a purpose, and not for a human beneficiary, must fail. The only exceptions to this rule were charitable purpose trusts (see Chapter 7) and certain recognised 'anomalous' purpose trusts (see 6.2). The trust in the present case was not saved as being within these exceptions and no new exception would be created.

3.3   Certainty of subject matter

Re Thomson's Estate (1879)

The testator, T, left realty and personalty to his wife by his will 'for the term of her natural life to be disposed of as she may think proper for her own use and benefit', providing further that, 'in the event of her decease should there be anything remaining of the said property or any part thereof', the said remainder should pass to certain named persons.

Held the widow took a life interest with a power to dispose of the property during her lifetime, but the provision as to the testamentary gift of the remainder would be void for uncertainty of subject matter.

Re Golay (1965)

The testator directed his executors 'to let Tossy ... enjoy one of my flats during her lifetime and to receive a reasonable income from my other properties ...'. The issue was whether the direction to allow a 'reasonable' income was void for uncertainty.

Held the words 'reasonable income' invited an objective determination by the court, which the court was quite capable of carrying out. As the judge said, 'the court is constantly involved in making such objective assessments of what is reasonable'.

Re London Wine Co (Shippers) Ltd (1975)

LW Ltd was a wine merchant which ran its business on the basis that wine ordered by customers was held on trust by the company from the date of each customer's order and until delivery to the customers. However, the bottles representing each order were not physically separated from the company's stocks until delivery. So, in the present case, where the customer had ordered 20 bottles of Lafite 1970 out of the company's 80 bottle holding, the question arose whether the subject matter was sufficiently certain for the company to be treated as trustee of the customer's order.

Held there was no trust of the 20 bottles. An express trust had certainly been intended by the company but the subject matter had not been removed from the company's general stock and there was therefore insufficient certainty of subject matter. To have achieved certainty of the trust of 20 bottles the company could have declared itself trustee of 'one-quarter' of the general stock of 80 bottles.

Hunter v Moss (1994) CA

The defendant was the registered owner of 95% of the issued share capital of a limited company. The trial judge held that the defendant had orally declared a valid trust of 50 of his shares (being 5% of the total issued share capital of the company). The defendant applied by motion to have the judgment set aside, on the ground, *inter alia*, that there could not have been a valid declaration of trust because the subject matter of the trust was uncertain. The deputy judge dismissed the motion whereupon the defendant appealed.

Held the appeal was dismissed. All the shares in the company were identical in nature, it was therefore quite valid to declare a trust of 50 shares without specifying which 50 shares were intended to form the subject matter of the trust. *Re London Wine Co (Shippers) Ltd* (1975) was distinguished.

3.4 Uncertain subject matter may indicate uncertain intention

The Mussoorie Bank Ltd v Raynor (1882) PC

A testator left the whole of his estate to his widow by his will stating that he felt 'confident' that she would 'act justly to our children in dividing the same when no longer required by her'. The question was whether his widow was obliged to hold the estate on trust for their children.

Held uncertainty of subject matter was one factor which suggested that a trust had not been intended. Thus, certainty of intention and certainty of subject matter being absent the widow took the estate absolutely, free from any trust.

Re Last (1958)

The testatrix, L, left all her property to her brother, directing that upon his death 'anything that is left' should pass to her late husband's grandchildren. When L's brother died intestate, and without issue or relations, the grandchildren applied to court claiming the residue of L's estate. The Treasury Solicitor argued in response that on a true construction of her will

L had made an absolute gift of her property to her brother and that the Crown was therefore entitled now to the residue as *bona vacantia.*

Held on a proper construction of the will L's brother had been entitled only to a life interest in the property and accordingly the applicants would be entitled to equal shares of the residue of L's estate. The judge was impressed by the absence of any words indicating the absolute nature of the gift to L's brother.

Note ───

The decision in *Re Last* can be criticised as an instance of a judge finding a trust because the words of the will did not suggest sufficient certainty of intention to make an absolute gift of the estate. The orthodox approach, as we have seen, is just the opposite. Namely, to presume an absolute gift in the absence of certainty of intention to create a trust. However, can the decision be justified because the last thing the testatrix would have intended was that the property should have passed to the Crown?

3.5 Certainty of object

Note ───

See generally, Purpose Trusts (Chapter 6) and Charitable Trusts (Chapter 7).

3.5.1 Class ascertainability

Inland Revenue Commissioners v Broadway Cottages (1955) CA

A settlor settled £80,000 on trust to apply the income therefrom for the benefit of the members of a class of beneficiaries in such shares as the trustees in their absolute discretion saw fit. It was not possible to list all the members of the class at any one time but it was possible to say with certainty whether any particular claimant was or was not a member of the class. Two charities who had received monies from the trustees under the terms of the trust claimed to be exempt from income tax thereon.

Held the trusts of the income were void for uncertainty of object and accordingly the monies which the charities had received could not qualify as income of the charities for which they could claim exemption from income tax. A trust for members of a specified class was void for uncertainty, unless every individual member of the class could be listed at a given time. This is the so-called 'class ascertainability' text. The reason given for the fixed list rule was that there are circumstances when a trust might fall to be carried out by the courts, and the courts, according to the orthodox view, must effect an equal division of the fund on the basis that 'equality is equity'. Equal division obviously necessitates a complete fixed list of the members of the class of potential beneficiaries.

3.5.2 Individual ascertainability

McPhail v Doulton (Re Baden's Deed Trusts No 1) (1970) HL
Mr B settled a trust for the benefit of certain persons connected with a company controlled by him. The deed granted the trustees an absolute discretion to apply the net income 'to or for the benefit of any officers and employees or ex-officers or ex-employees of the company or to any relatives or dependants of any such persons in such amounts at such times and on such conditions (if any) as they think fit ...'. The first question was whether the deed had (1) granted the trustees a power of appointment among the class, or (2) had subjected them to a discretionary trust. The second question, which flowed from the first, was 'is the gift void for uncertainty'? If the gift was in the form of a power, the trustees would have been able to appoint (distribute part of the fund to) any applicant of whom it could be said with certainty that they were or were not within the class of 'staff, relatives or dependants'. If, on the other hand, the gift was in the nature of a trust, the trustees would only have been able to appoint beneficiaries if every member of the class had been identified (see *IRC v Broadway Cottages* (3.5.1)).

Held the deed created a trust, not a power. However, the trust would not fail for uncertainty of object, even though it would not be possible to draw up a complete fixed list of every potential beneficiary within the class. Lord Wilberforce rejected what he considered to be a narrow and artificial distinction between discretionary trusts and powers of appointment in the context of gifts of this sort. According to his Lordship, 'such distinction as there is would seem to lie in the extent of the survey which the trustee is required to carry out ... a wider and more comprehensive range of inquiry is called for in the case of trust powers than in the case of powers'. Nor did his Lordship find himself compelled by the orthodox argument that a fixed list was required in order that the court could make a distribution in the event that the trust might fall to be carried out by the courts: 'Equal division is surely the last thing the settlor ever intended: equal division among all may, probably would, produce a result beneficial to none. Why suppose that the court would lend itself to a whimsical execution?' Rather, 'the court if called upon to execute the trust power, will do so in the manner best calculated to give effect to the settlor's or testator's intentions'.

In a move away from the orthodox approach his Lordship held that the test of certainty of object which had hitherto been applied to powers (laid down by the House of Lords in *Re Gulbenkian's Settlements* (1970)) should henceforth apply to discretionary trusts. That test, known as the 'individual ascertainability test' is whether it can be said with certainty that any individual potential beneficiary is or is not a member of the class of potential beneficiaries. 'Certainty' here was of two types: 'linguistic uncertainty' (where the class of beneficiary is not susceptible of legal definition) would render the gift void, whereas 'evidential uncertainty' (which is uncertainty as to the practical identification of individual beneficiaries) would not render the gift void. His Lordship also referred to a third case where the meaning of the words is clear but the definition of beneficiaries is so hopelessly wide as not to form 'anything like a class' so that the trust is 'administratively unworkable'.

Note ──

An example of administrative unworkability is illustrated on the facts of *R v District Auditor, ex parte West Yorkshire Metropolitan County Council* (1986), where the council, before its abolition, purported to set up a trust 'for the benefit of any or all or some of the inhabitants of the county of West Yorkshire'.

Re Baden's Deed Trusts (No 2) (1973) CA

Having considered the Baden's Deed Trusts in *McPhail v Doulton* (see above) the House of Lords remitted the case to the High Court to apply the individual ascertainability test to the deed, to determine, *inter alia*, whether the class 'relatives' was sufficiently certain. The judgment of the High Court was appealed.

Held the term 'relatives' was conceptually certain and the trust was therefore valid. However, their Lordships did differ in their conception of 'relatives'. Sachs LJ took 'relatives' to mean any persons who could 'trace legal descent from a common ancestor', whereas Stamp LJ took it to mean 'legal next-of-kin' of the employees.

Q Do you agree that the term 'relatives' is conceptually certain?

3.5.3 Absolute gift subject to a condition precedent

Re Barlow's Will Trusts (1979)

A testatrix died leaving a collection of paintings in her will. Having made some specific bequests she gave the remainder of the paintings to her executor on a trust for sale but subject to a direction that 'any members of my family and any friends of mine who may wish to do so' should be allowed to purchase any of the paintings at far below their market values. The executor took out a summons for a declaration as to whether the gift to the 'friends' was void for uncertainty. He also sought a direction as to the proper meaning of 'family' in the context of this gift.

Held the direction did not fail for uncertainty. If it could be said with certainty that a particular claimant qualified as a 'friend' a sale of paintings to that person would be valid under the terms of the will. This was because uncertainty as to whether other persons may or may not be 'friends' could have no effect on the quantum of the gift to those persons who clearly qualified as 'friends'. In the same way that it was unnecessary to establish a precise definition of 'friend' for the gift to be effective, it was also unnecessary to restrict the meaning of family to 'statutory next-of-kin'. For the purposes of the present gift it was sufficient to define family as 'blood relations'.

4 Perfecting gifts and constituting trusts

4.1 Perfecting a gift

Note ─────────────────────────────────────

An absolute gift to X from Y is perfected by effecting a transfer of the property to X, being careful to use the mode of transfer required by law for that particular type of property (as to which see 4.3, below), or by Y's execution of a valid legal deed of gift in favour of X. The Rule in *Strong v Bird*, and the rules governing a *donatio mortis causa*, are notable equitable exceptions to these legal rules.

───

4.1.1 The rule in *Strong v Bird*

Strong v Bird (1874)

B borrowed the sum of £1,100 from his step-mother. She lived in his house and paid rent quarterly and so it was agreed that B would repay the loan by deducting £100 from each quarter's rental payment. The deduction was made on two consecutive quarter days but on the third quarter day the step-mother insisted upon paying her full rent without deduction. She continued to make full payments of rent on every quarter day until her death, four years later. B was appointed as his step-mother's sole executor. This action was brought by S, the step-mother's next-of-kin, alleging that B should be charged with a debt of £900, representing the unpaid portion of the loan.

Held B owed no debt to the step-mother's estate. The appointment of B as executor released the debt at law, while the step-mother's continuing intention (up until her death) to make a gift of the £900 to B released the debt in equity. Her continuing intention to make such a gift was amply evidenced by her making nine quarterly payments of the full rent without deduction.

Re Stewart (1908)

The testator, S, by a codicil to his will, left all the monies in a certain bank account to his widow. The will appointed the widow to be one of his executors. A few days before S's death he purchased, through agents, some valuable 'bearer bonds'. In the event the bonds were not delivered until after his death, at which time they were delivered to S's executors. S's widow brought this action against the other executors to determine whether she was entitled to the bonds in addition to the monies in the bank account.

Held the rule in *Strong v Bird* was not restricted to the release of a debt and it was irrelevant that the intended donee might not be the sole executor, but one of many. The widow was entitled to claim the bonds under the rule because S had expressed an *inter vivos* intention to make a gift to his widow of his personal estate and that intention had continued until his death.

Re James (1935)

J senior, the deceased, died intestate in 1924. His son, J junior, died intestate in 1933. Mrs J had been employed by J senior as a housekeeper. She had received no payment for her services, but had been regularly assured By J senior that his house and furniture would be hers upon his death. After the death of J senior, J junior had left the house taking only a few small articles with him. He left Mrs J in occupation of the house and left the deeds to the house in her possession. After the death of J junior letters of administration were granted to Mrs J, constituting her administratrix of the estate of J junior. The question arose whether the rule in *Strong v Bird* should be extended to perfect an otherwise imperfect gift to a donee who had not been appointed by the testator to be his executor, but had only fortuitously been appointed his administratrix by the court.

Held the otherwise imperfect gift to the housekeeper was perfected by her appointment as administratrix to the estate of J junior. She had thereby acquired the legal estate to the property, while the equitable estate was hers by virtue of J junior's intention to give the property to her, which intention continued up until his death.

Q Does the decision in *Re James* represent an extension too far of the rule in *Strong v Bird*?

4.1.2 *Donatio mortis causa*

Wilkes v Allington (1931)

A widow mortgaged a farm, in which she held a life interest, to her late husband's brother, A. After the widow's death he passed the deeds to the farm, apart from the mortgage deed, to the widow's executors (his nieces). It later transpired that A was dying of an incurable disease and so, in anticipation of his death, he passed a sealed envelope to his nieces, which turned out to contain the mortgage deed. Some short time later A caught a chill and died of pneumonia. This action was brought by his executors, claiming that the mortgage was a subsisting security which could be enforced against the nieces.

Held the mortgage could not be enforced. The otherwise imperfect gift of the mortgage to the nieces was made perfect by a valid *donatio mortis causa* (DMC). A DMC is a gift made in contemplation of death where part of the means of acquiring the subject matter of the gift has been passed to the donee in circumstances where it was clear that the gift was only to become binding on the donor's death. In order for a DMC to take effect it was not necessary for the donor to have died from the same disorder as that from which he had been suffering when contemplating death.

Sen v Headley (1991) CA

Mrs S had lived with a man for several years. On his death-bed he gave her the keys to a box containing the deeds to his house and told her that the house was hers.

Held this was a valid DMC. The court rejected the orthodox assumption that DMC could not apply to gifts of land.

4.2 Constitution of a trust

Note ───

A valid will automatically constitutes any will trust contained within it. *Inter vivos* trusts, however, must satisfy certain constitutional requirements. Thus an *inter vivos* trust may be constituted where the owner of property, X, declares himself, or herself, to be a trustee of it for the benefit of Y (a declaration of trust) or where X transfers the trust property to Z for the benefit of Y (a trust by transfer).

4.3 Constitution by transfer of legal title to trustees

4.3.1 Where the trust property consists of shares

Milroy v Lord (1862)

A settlor owned shares in a bank which he purported to transfer to L by deed, to be held by L on trust for M. The settlor later passed the share certificates to L. L was the settlor's attorney and was therefore authorised to transfer the shares to M, but ultimately there could only be a valid transfer of the shares by registration, at the bank, of M as owner of the shares. This registration was never carried out. The issue was whether M could claim the shares under a trust created by the settlor.

Held on the facts no valid trust had been created. M had not provided consideration for the shares, he was therefore a mere 'volunteer'. Applying the maxim that 'equity does not assist a volunteer', it followed that the settlement would not be binding on the settlor (even if he had wished it to be so) unless the settlor had 'done everything which, according to the nature of the property comprised in the settlement, was necessary to be done in order to transfer the property'. The settlor could have transferred the property to M by way of gift, or transferred the property to L upon trust for M, but neither method of constituting the settlement had been effective on the facts of the present case, because there could be no valid transfer of the shares without registration. Further, if the settlement was intended to take place by transfer the court would not give effect to it by finding a valid declaration of trust. The court will, on a proper reading of the facts, construe every settlement as either an attempted outright gift, an attempted trust by transfer to trustees or an attempted declaration of trust constituting the settlor trustee. If the settlor's chosen mode of donation fails, the court will not perfect the donation by allowing it to take effect by another of the modes.

Note ─────────────────────────────────────

The effect of valid constitution of a trust is to transfer beneficial ownership of the trust property from the settlor to the beneficiaries of the trust. Until the trust is validly constituted it will not bind the settlor, after it is validly constituted the settlor will no longer be able to claim the trust property as his own.

Re Fry (1946)

F, a resident of the United States, owned shares in an English company which he transferred by way of gift in favour of his son. By reason of wartime restrictions imposed upon the transfer of securities the English company was prohibited from registering, and refused to register, the transfer without Treasury consent. The forms necessary to obtain consent were sent to the donor to sign, which he duly did and he returned them to the company. F died, however, before consent was obtained from the Treasury.

Held the transfer being ineffective, the intended gift was incomplete. The shares passed into F's residuary estate.

Re Rose (1952) CA

In March 1943 R transferred 10,000 shares in an unlimited company to his wife and on the same day transferred a further 10,000 shares in the same company to trustees to hold upon the terms of a settlement. The transfers were in an authorised form. In the event the transfers were not registered by the company until June 1943. R died in 1947 after which, in accordance with certain tax regulations, the Inland Revenue claimed estate duty on the shares because the gift had not been completed before April 1943.

Held R had done everything in his power to transfer his legal and equitable interest in the shares on the date of the transfer in March 1943. The factors which delayed the registration of the legal title until after April

1943 were beyond R's control. Counsel for the Inland Revenue had argued that the purported transfer must have been entirely ineffective according to *Milroy v Lord*, but the court held that *Milroy v Lord* would not invalidate a transfer in a case such as the present where the donor, after the purported transfer, would not be permitted to assert any beneficial ownership in the shares at all. R had divested himself entirely of his equitable interest in the shares and accordingly his estate would not be liable to pay tax thereon. This result was not effected by the fact that, between March 1943 and the date when the legal title was registered with the company, R continued to hold the legal title as a nominal trustee.

4.3.2   Where trust property comprises land

Richards v Delbridge (1874)
D, the tenant of certain premises and the owner of a business which he carried on at those premises, purported to make a gift of his lease and business to his grandson R. R was an infant at the time. In order to give effect to the gift D endorsed and signed the following memorandum on the lease: 'This deed and all thereto belonging I give to R from this time forth, with all the stock-in-trade.' He then delivered the deed to R's mother to hold for R. D later died, making no reference to the gift in his will. At issue was whether the lease and the business should pass to R, by gift or trust, or whether the property should pass to other persons under D's will.

Held the property passed under the will, there being no valid gift or declaration of trust in favour of R. R had not given any consideration for the property and was, therefore, a mere 'volunteer', whom equity would not assist. Accordingly R would only be entitled to take the property if there was evidence of a valid gift or a trust of the property. On the facts there had not been a perfect gift because there had not been a formal legal conveyance to R. There could not be a validly constituted trust imposed upon R's mother because there had not been a formal legal conveyance to R's mother. Further, there could not be a validly constituted trust binding on D, because D had not expressed with sufficient certainty his intention to constitute himself a trustee by declaration of trust. The court would not spell out a trust from a failed gift. *Milroy v Lord* followed.

Law of Property Act 1925 s 52(1)
All conveyances of land or of any interest therein are void for the purpose of conveying or creating a legal estate unless made by deed.

Land Registration Act 1925 s 19(1)
Transfer of the registered estate in land shall be completed by the registrar entering the transferee on the register as the new proprietor of the estate.

4.3.3   Where the trust property is an ordinary chattel

Re Cole (1964) CA

A husband bought a house in London while his wife and family were living elsewhere. Some time later his wife came to London and he took her to the house and showed her round. The wife was particularly impressed by certain chattels, namely a silk carpet and a card table. After the tour of the house the husband announced to her 'it's all yours'. Some 16 years later the husband was declared bankrupt. In the year after the bankruptcy the wife sold the moveable contents of the house. This action was brought by the trustee in bankruptcy to recover from the wife the proceeds of sale of the chattels.

Held words of gift were not in themselves enough to perfect a gift of chattels. In order to assert title to the chattels the wife must also prove some act of delivery as would unequivocally show the husband's intention to transfer title to the wife. In the absence of evidence of such an act legal title to the chattels must be said to have remained with the husband and to have vested in his trustee in bankruptcy. Judgment accordingly for the trustee in bankruptcy.

> Note ───────────────────────────────
>
> In *Jaffa v Taylor Galleries Ltd* (1990) it was held that a trust of a painting had been validly constituted where the trust had been declared formally in a document, of which the trustees each had a copy, even though the painting had not been physically transferred to the trustees (one of whom lived abroad).

4.3.4   Where the trust property is a *chose* in action

Law of Property Act 1925 s 136(1)

> Any absolute assignment by writing under hand of the assignor ... of any debt or other legal thing in action, of which express notice has been given to the debtor ... or other person from whom the assignor would have been entitled to claim such debt or thing in action, is effectual in law ... to pass and transfer from the date of such notice ... the legal right to such debt or thing in action ...

4.4   Constitution by transfer where the subject of the gift or trust is an equitable interest

> Note ───────────────────────────────
>
> See s 53(1)(c) Law of Property Act 1925 (2.2.1).

Re McArdle (1951) CA

The testator, M, left his residuary estate upon trust for his widow for life remainder to his five children in equal shares. During the lifetime of M's widow, one of the children, MM, carried out improvements to a property forming part of the testator's residuary estate. The testator's other children signed a document in these terms: 'To MM ... in consideration of your carrying out certain alterations and improvements to the property ... at present occupied by you, we the beneficiaries under the will of M hereby agree that the executors ... shall repay to you from the said estate when so distributed the sum of £488 in settlement of the amount spent on such improvements'. Accordingly, when the widow died MM claimed the £488. However, the other children of M objected to the claim. The questions which arose for consideration were, first, whether the signed document could take effect as a binding contract, and secondly, in the alternative, if it failed as a contract could the document constitute an effective assignment of an equitable interest to MM?

Held the document did not constitute an enforceable contract, because the works of improvement had been completed before the execution of the document and therefore the consideration for the agreement was wholly past. Nor could the document constitute a perfect gift of the equitable interest. The document had been expressed in the form of a contract for valuable consideration and it would therefore be artificial to construe it as being a valid equitable assignment. Accordingly MM had no entitlement in law or equity to receive the £488. To remedy this the beneficiaries would have had to have authorised the executors to pay the £488. Until this had been done the beneficiaries had not done all within their power to dispose of their interest in the £488.

Note

The above case is authority for the proposition that a transfer of an equitable interest is not complete until the trustees of the trust have been given notice of the transfer.

4.5 Constitution of a trust by declaration

Note

See s 53(1)(b) (2.2.1); *Jones v Lock* (3.2); *Paul v Constance* (3.2); *Simpson v Simpson* (2.1.1).

4.6   Constitution of a trust by contract

Re Plumtre (1910)

P and his wife executed a marriage settlement to which the trustees were also parties. In the deed the wife covenanted to settle her after-acquired property on trust for herself, her husband, their prospective children and ultimately for her next of kin. Some years later the husband made a gift to his wife of certain valuable stock. The wife sold this and re-invested the proceeds in other stock which remained registered in her sole name right up until her death. She died not having had children. After her death letters of administration were granted to her husband and the stock was, accordingly, placed in his name. This action was brought by the deceased's next-of-kin, claiming to be entitled to the stock under the terms of the marriage settlement.

Held the next-of-kin did not fall within the marriage consideration and therefore were mere volunteers. As such they were not entitled to enforce the contract to settle. A voluntary contract to create a trust under which the next-of-kin might get an interest must be distinguished from a declaration of trust in favour of the next-of-kin. The next-of-kin were not beneficiaries under the settlement and in the result the husband could keep the stock.

> **Note**
>
> The result in *Re Plumtre* may have been different if there had been children of the marriage. Such children would have fallen within the marriage consideration and accordingly would not have been mere volunteers. They would have been entitled to enforce the covenant to settle, with resulting benefit, not only for themselves, but also for prospective beneficiaries such as the next-of-kin in that case. The judgment of the Court of Appeal in the 1880 case *Re D'Angibau* acknowledged the possibility that volunteers might benefit indirectly in this way.

Pullan v Koe (1913)

By a marriage settlement of 1859 a husband and wife covenanted to settle the wife's after-acquired property upon trusts for the benefit of the husband, the wife and their future children. In 1879 the wife's mother made a gift to her of £285 which the wife paid into her husband's bank account. A portion of this money was later invested in two bearer bonds which remained at the bank (gathering interest) until the husband's death in 1909. The trustees of the marriage settlement brought the present action against the husband's estate claiming that the bonds should be held for the benefit of the beneficiaries of the marriage settlement.

Held under the Statute of Limitations the trustees were far too late to sue at common law for damages on the covenant. However, the husband had received the bonds with notice of the trusts of the marriage settlement and had given no valuable consideration for the bonds. Being, therefore, a mere volunteer, he took the bonds subject to the trusts of the marriage settlement. Accordingly, even though their legal action had been time-barred, the trustees were able to claim the bonds in equity on behalf of the beneficiaries. A person can contract (whether or not for value and whether or not by deed) to assign property which is to come into existence in the future, and when it comes into existence, equity treats as done that which ought to be done and will insist upon the specific performance of the contract. It is true that the court will not assist a volunteer, but here the plaintiffs (the trustees) were parties to the contract and were acting on behalf of persons within the marriage consideration.

Re Pryce (1917)

On facts in other respects similar to those in *Re Plumtre* (above) trustees sought directions as to whether they should take proceedings to enforce, for the benefit of statutory next-of-kin, a covenant to settle after-acquired property.

Held the trustees were directed not to take steps to enforce the covenant for the benefit of the next-of-kin. The next-of-kin, being mere volunteers, had no direct means of enforcing the covenant, either by an action at law for damages for breach of contract, or as beneficiaries under a trust declared in their favour. As they could not enforce the covenant by direct means the court would not permit them to enforce it by indirect means.

Note ───

In *Re Kay's Settlement* (1939), which applied *Re Pryce*, the judge directed the trustees not to take steps to enforce a covenant on behalf of volunteers, but added a further direction that the trustees should not sue for damages for breach of the covenant.

Re Gillott's Settlement (1934)

G executed a marriage settlement under which property was settled upon his wife if she survived him. By the terms of the settlement the wife had the power to appoint the settled property in favour of any new husband she might marry, but the new husband would forfeit any entitlement to the property if he assigned it to a third party. After G's death his widow remarried. An agreement for a loan was made between the widow, the new husband and a lender. The agreement provided that the husband and wife should apply income received under the marriage settlement in discharge of the loan, any surplus income to be handed to the husband and wife. A further agreement in similar terms provided that any surplus should be held by the lender in trust for the husband and wife and certain other named parties. The wife died and by her will appointed an interest in the income of the settlement in favour of her husband until he should assign it.

Held although not intended to have that effect the loan agreements constituted an equitable assignment of the income by the husband, and accordingly the husband had forfeited his equitable interest. A contract for consideration to convey future property to a person upon trust was valid. After the wife's death her husband became a trustee of the settlement income for the benefit of those persons with interests under the loan agreements.

Re Haynes WT (1949)

The testator, H, by his will directed his trustees to hold his residuary estate on protective trusts for his sons. The trusts provided, *inter alia*, that the sons' interests should vest in possession when the sons reached 21, but only if at that time the sons interests had not already been committed to pay some other person. Before reaching 21 one of the sons executed a marriage settlement in which he covenanted to settle, when he became entitled to it, one-third of his interest in his father's residuary estate in favour of his wife.

Held the covenant to settle after acquired property upon the terms of the marriage settlement constituted an equitable assignment of part of the son's interest under his father's will. Accordingly the son had forfeited his interest in the residue under his father's will. *Re Gillott's Settlement* followed.

Cannon v Hartley (1949)

H and his wife, their marriage having broken down, executed a deed of separation. Their daughter, C, was also a party to the settlement. By the terms of the deed H covenanted to settle after-acquired property in the following terms: 'If and whenever during the lifetime of the wife or [C] ... [H] shall become entitled ... under the will ... of either of his parents to any money exceeding in net amount or value £1,000 he will forthwith ... settle one-half of such money or property upon trust for himself for life and for the wife for life after his death and subject thereto in trust for the daughter absolutely.' In due course H became entitled to a valuable share of his mother's estate. Shortly thereafter H's wife died. H refused to execute a settlement in accordance with his covenant to settle. C brought this action claiming damages for breach of the covenant.

Held because C had been a party to the deed and a direct covenantee of the covenant to settle she was entitled to a significant award of compensatory damages at common law. Although equity will not assist a mere volunteer, in the present case C did not require the assistance of equity, she was entitled, as a party to the covenant, to enforce directly her common law right to the benefits of that covenant. When a person executes a deed any covenants within the deed are deemed, at common law, to have been made for legal consideration. Accordingly, as valid consideration had been given at common law the problems associated with C being a mere volunteer in equity did not arise.

Re Ralli's Will Trusts (1963)

The testator, R, left his residuary estate to trustees on trust for his wife for life, remainder to his daughters H and I. H, by a marriage settlement, covenanted to settle her share on trustees for the benefit of her own children and ultimately for the children of I. A clause of the marriage settlement declared that all property within the terms of the covenant should be subject to the terms of the trusts pending assignment to the trustees. H died childless. Later, a trustee who had been a party to H's marriage settlement was additionally appointed trustee under the will of R. That trustee, who happened also to be I's husband, brought the present action, seeking directions as to whether H's share of her father's residuary estate should be held by him on the trusts of the marriage settlement, or under the terms of H's will. He claimed that the property should be held on the trusts of the marriage settlement. H's personal representatives claimed that H's estate should be entitled, in accordance with H's will.

Held the plaintiff held H's share of R's estate on the trusts of the marriage settlement. Those trusts had become fully constituted when the legal title to the property had vested in the plaintiff in his capacity as trustee of R's will trusts. The fact that the constitution had been purely fortuitous did not matter. In the alternative, assuming the reversionary interest under R's will to be 'vested' and not 'after-acquired' property, H held that property as trustee, because the execution of the marriage settlement had constituted a declaration of trust binding upon her pending transfer to the trustees of the settlement. According to either view the property must be held upon the trusts of the marriage settlement. If it had been necessary to enforce performance of the covenant equity would not have done so at the request of the beneficiaries under the settlement, as they were mere volunteers. In the present case, however, there had been no need to invoke the assistance of equity to enforce performance of the covenant. On the contrary, it had been for the defendants to invoke equity to show that it would be unconscientious for the plaintiff to perform the covenant. In the present case it had not been unconscientious for the plaintiff to exercise his legal authority to perform the covenant and to carry out the settlement trusts.

Re Cook's Settlement Trusts (1965)

In 1934 HC and his son FC (great grandchild of Sir Francis Cook) executed a settlement which provided that FC's reversionary interest under a will should be exchanged for other property of equal value. The settlement also provided that some of the new property should be settled by FC on trust for certain named beneficiaries. That part of the new property which was not required to be so settled (primarily comprising valuable paintings) was to be held by FC for his own benefit, but it was agreed that the proceeds of the sale of any of the paintings, if sold during FC's lifetime, should be paid to the trustees of the settlement to be held by them on the trusts of the settlement. FC later made a gift of one of the paintings (a Rembrandt) to his wife and she later expressed her intention to sell it. The trustees took out a summons for directions from the court as to what action the trustees should take if the painting were sold during FC's lifetime and the proceeds not paid to them.

Held the covenant to settle constituted a contract to settle after-acquired monies which did not exist at the time of the settlement and might never come into existence. The beneficiaries under the settlement had not been parties to the contract and accordingly they would not be permitted to sue on it. Nor had the beneficiaries provided consideration for the covenant to settle, either by providing valuable consideration or by falling within marriage consideration, therefore, being mere volunteers, equity would not assist them. Nor would the beneficiaries be entitled to require the trustees to enforce the covenant on their behalf.

5 Perpetuities and public policy limitations on the formation of trusts

5.1 The rules against perpetuities

Note ──────────────────────────────────────

The law has always resisted attempts by persons to keep property tied up indefinitely for private purposes. There are a number of reasons for this. One reason is the desire to keep societal wealth in the open market, where it can assist in financial enterprise to the greater public good. Another is the perceived need to restrict the aggrandisement, over generations, of families and other private institutions. Whether such policy considerations are thwarted by the immortal modern corporation is a moot point, but they are certainly not defeated by the trust institution. A number of rules against perpetuity have seen to this. We will be considering the content of each of these rules throughout the remainder of this section.

5.2 The rule against remoteness of vesting

Note ──────────────────────────────────────

This rule provides that where a gift is made to X subject to a contingency (a condition which may or may not be met, such as 'upon X attaining a university degree' or 'reaching the age of 25') the gift must vest in the donee of the gift (ie the contingency must be met) within the 'perpetuity period'. The perpetuity period for the purpose of this rule ends 21 years after the death of all 'lives in being'. 'Lives in being' are any persons alive or in their mother's womb at the *effective date of the gift*, the duration of whose lives might effect the date of the vesting of the gift. *Inter vivos* deeds of gift or trust are effective at the date of their execution. Testamentary gifts or trusts are effective, not at the date of the execution of the will, but at the date of the testator's/testatrix's death. If there are no 'lives in being' the perpetuity period will be a straightforward 21 years from the effective date of the gift.

5.2.1   Common law rules

Note ───

At common law the rule has always been strictly applied. Because the property must vest within the perpetuity period, a gift will be declared void for perpetuity if it might vest outside the perpetuity period, no matter how improbable the likelihood of it so doing. The common law rule against remoteness of vesting is said to be concerned with possibilities, not probabilities.

───

Re Dawson (1888)

The testator, D, left all his estate to trustees upon trust to pay an annuity to his daughter, M, for her life, and directing that after his daughter's death the trustees should hold the estate for those of M's children and thereafter for those of M's grandchildren who should attain 21 or (in the case of females) should marry under that age. When D died M was over 60 years of age and had one son and five daughters living.

Held the gift in favour of the grandchildren was subject to a contingency and subject therefore to the rule against remoteness of vesting. At common law the rule must be applied strictly and would render void any gift which might vest outside the perpetuity period, no matter how remote the possibility might be of it vesting so late. Accordingly, evidence was not admissible to show that at D's death M had passed the age of childbearing and was, as a result, highly unlikely to produce any further children. Because there was a remote possibility of later-born children of M (who would not, of course, have been lives in being at D's death) there was a remote possibility that a later-born child of M might produce grandchildren of M outside the perpetuity period. (The perpetuity period being 21 years after the death of the last survivor of the lives in being, ie M, M's daughter and M's five sons living at D's death.)

Re Hargreaves (1889) CA

H, a testatrix, left certain freehold properties to trustees for their own use but upon trusts to pay the rents therefrom to her sister, M, for life, then to M's children successively for their lives, then to her sister, E, for life, then to E's children successively for their lives. Finally the rents were directed to be paid to whoever might be appointed by the last survivor of M, E and their children. The last survivor (the LS) eventually executed a will in which she purported to appoint the property in favour of a certain person. H's heir at law claimed to be entitled to the property.

Held the power of appointment could not be exercised by the LS because it fell foul of the rule against remoteness of vesting. This was because at the time of H's death, which was the effective date of the gift, it could not be said with certainty that the LS would be asertainable within the perpetuity period.

Note

Lives in being in the case of *Re Hargreaves* would have been those persons living at H's death whose life-spans could have a bearing on the date at which the power of appointment would ultimately vest in the LS. Therefore, M, E and their children would all have been lives in being.

Re Moore (1901)

The testatrix, M, bequeathed £500 to trustees upon trust to apply the income thereof towards the maintenance and repair of her brother's tomb in Zambesi, Africa, 'for the longest period allowed by law, that is to say, until the period of 21 years from the death of the last survivor of all persons who shall be living at my death'.

Held it would be impossible to state with certainty when the last life in being had died, therefore the gift must fail for uncertainty of lives in being.

Re Wilmer's Trusts (1903) CA

W, a testatrix, devised her residuary real estate on trustees upon trust to pay the income therefrom to M for life and thereafter to M's sons successively in tail male (which means that the land must pass from male heir to male heir). W died in October 1880 at which time M had not given birth to any sons who could qualify as beneficiaries under the trust. She was, however, pregnant with a son, S, who was born in February 1881. The question was whether S could take the property absolutely, or whether he merely held a life interest in accordance with the limitations specified in the trust.

Held the limitations coming into effect after S's life estate did not infringe the rule against remoteness of vesting. A child *en ventre sa mere* (in its mother's womb) at the effective date of the gift, who is subsequently born, must be treated as having been a life in being at the effective date of the gift. Accordingly, S, who had been alive at the testatrix's death, was a life in being. Because the tail male limitations would certainly have been satisfied within 21 years of S's death (in fact they would have come into effect immediately upon S's death) those limitations fell within the perpetuity period and did not infringe the rule against remoteness of vesting.

Re Gaite's Will Trusts (1949)

A testatrix, G, gave £5,000 to trustees upon trust to pay the income to HG for her life, and thereafter to pay the income and capital to such of HG's grandchildren as should be living at G's death or within five years of it, provided that such grandchildren reached 21 or (in the case of females) married earlier. At the death of the testatrix, HG was 67 and had two children and one grandchild. On the question whether the gift to HG's grandchildren infringed the rule against remoteness of vesting because of the possibility that HG might produce children more than 21 years after G's death.

Held quite apart from any question of physical impossibility it would be a legal impossibility for HG to produce a child who could produce legal issue after the end of the perpetuity period. This is because the Marriage Act 1929 provided that a child under the age of 16 could not lawfully marry. Accordingly the gifts to the grandchildren were valid.

Note ───

In 1949 the law did not recognise illegitimate children and so the gift in *Re Gaite* could not have been said to infringe the common law rule against perpetuities. Ever since 1969 the law has drawn no distinction between legitimate and illegitimate children (Family Law Reform Act 1969 s 1).

5.2.2 Class gifts

Note ───

Gifts and trusts are often made to a class, an example would be a gift or trust 'to all my nephews who reach the age of 25'. A 'class' for this purpose comprises persons who 'come within a certain category or description defined by a general or collective formula, and who, if they take at all, are to take one divisible subject in certain proportionate shares' – *per* Lord Selborne LC, *Pearkes v Mosely* (1880). The basic common law position is that the gift or trust will be void unless all potential members of the class *must* satisfy the contingency within the perpetuity period. Thus if (taking the example given at the beginning of this note and assuming that the gift has become effective today) there are three nephews in being and a fourth nephew is born a year from now, none of the nephews will take under the gift. The lives in being *might* all die tomorrow, in which event the fourth nephew will not reach 25 within the remaining 21 years of the perpetuity period.

Note ───

The rule in *Andrews v Partington* (1791) was created to address the clear hardship of the basic common law treatment of class gifts. The Rule allows a member of the class to take their share if they have already satisfied the contingency at the effective date of the gift. And if members of the class living at the effective date of the gift have not at that time already met the contingency, the rule permits the trustees to wait until the first member of the class satisfies the contingency, and to give that beneficiary their share at that time. Shares are worked out by closing the class of potential beneficiaries to include all members of the class living at the date when the first member of the class satisfies the contingency. Any later born members of the class will be excluded from taking any part of the fund.

Re Clifford's Settlement Trusts (1981)

C settled a fund on trustees for the benefit of his son's children 'born in C's lifetime or after his death who before the expiration of the period of 21 years from the death of the survivor of C and the said son shall attain the age of 25 years and the other children of the said son living at the expiration of such period'. When C died his son was 32 and had two children of his own. At the hearing of this case those two children had attained 25. However, since C's death the son had fathered another two children who had not yet attained 25. The question arising for consideration was whether the son's eldest child had become entitled to a quarter share of the fund when he attained 25 or whether the gift was void for perpetuity.

Held the rule in *Andrews v Partington* (1791) applied to save the gift. In the present case, the Rule applied to allow a gift of a quarter of the fund to the eldest child. Also, the other three members of the class living when the eldest child reached 25 would be entitled to a quarter share upon satisfying the contingency. Any later born members of the class would be excluded from the gift. It was held that in order to exclude the effect of the rule the words of the gift must be inescapably incompatible with the application of the rule. The fact that in the present case the rule could not apply to save the gift to part of the compound class of beneficiaries (namely those 'other children of the said son living at the expiration of such period') did not suffice to show an intention to exclude the effect of the Rule upon the gift to the principal beneficiaries.

Note ──

If any of the members of the closed class in *Re Clifford's* had died before satisfying the contingent age of 25 their shares would have been distributed amongst the members of the class who had satisfied the contingency.

──

5.2.3 The Perpetuities and Accumulations Act 1964

Note ──

The 1964 Act has the effect of saving a number of gifts which would otherwise have been void for perpetuity under the strict common law rules. It applies only to gifts coming into effect after 15 July 1964. Unfortunately, however, even after 1964, the common law rules must be applied first, and only if a gift is void for perpetuity at common law will it be permissible to apply the more generous provisions of the Act. If the gift is valid at common law the gift will be subject to the common law rules, and not to the rules under the Act. A notable exception to this 'double jurisdiction' is the statutory perpetuity period contained in s 1 of the Act. Where a statutory period is specified in an instrument the common law perpetuity period will have no application.

──

Perpetuities and Accumulations Act 1964 s 1

... Where the instrument by which any disposition is made so provides, the perpetuity period ... shall be of a duration equal to such number of years not exceeding 80 as is specified ... in the instrument.

Perpetuities and Accumulations Act 1964 s 2

(1) Where in any proceedings there arises on the rule against perpetuities a question which turns on the ability of a person to have a child at some future time, then –

    (a) ... it shall be presumed that a male can have a child at the age of 14 years or over, but not under that age, and that a female can have a child at the age of 12 years or over, but not under that age or over the age of 55; but

    (b) in the case of a living person evidence may be given to show that he or she will or will not be able to have a child at the time in question.

(4) ... these provisions (except subsection (1)(b)) shall apply in relation to the possibility that a person will at any time have a child by adoption, legitimation or other means.

Note ───

The next section contains the so-called 'wait and see' principle. Where a gift would have been automatically void at common law because of the *possibility* that it might vest outside the perpetuity period, the Act treats the gift as valid until such time as it is clear that their is *no possibility* of it vesting within the perpetuity period. So, the Act will not save a gift where, at the very end of the perpetuity period, the contingency has still not been met. In most cases it vastly decreases the likelihood that a gift will be void for perpetuity.

Perpetuities and Accumulations Act 1964 s 3

(1) Where ... a disposition would be void on the ground that the interest disposed of might not become vested until too remote a time, the disposition shall be treated, until such time (if any) as it becomes established that the vesting must occur, if at all, after the end of the perpetuity period, as if the disposition were not subject to the rule against perpetuities; and its becoming so established shall not affect the validity of anything previously done in relation to the interest disposed of by way of advancement, application of intermediate income or otherwise.

(4) Where this section applies to a disposition and the duration of the perpetuity period is not determined by virtue of s 1 ... of this Act, it shall be determined as follows:

    (a) where any persons falling within subsection (5) below are individuals in being and ascertainable at the commencement of the perpetuity period the duration of the period shall be determined by reference to their lives

... [unless] ... the number of such persons ... is such as to render it impracticable to ascertain the date of the death of the survivor;

(b) where there are no lives ... the period shall be twenty-one years.

Perpetuities and Accumulations Act 1964 s 3

(5) The said persons are as follows:

(a) the person by whom the disposition was made;

(b) a person to whom or in whose favour the disposition was made, that is to say –

(i) in the case of a disposition to a class of persons, any member or potential member of the class;

(ii) in the case of an individual disposition to a person taking only on certain conditions being satisfied, any person as to whom some of the conditions are satisfied and the remainder may in time be satisfied; ...

(c) a person having a child or grandchild within ... paragraph (b) above, or any of whose children or grandchildren, if subsequently born, would by virtue of his or her descent fall within [that paragraph];

(d) any person on the failure or determination of whose prior interest the disposition is limited to take effect.

Note

The next section, s 4, reduces contingent ages specified in gifts, and reduces the membership of class gifts, to whatever extent is necessary to save the gift. However, the provisions of s 3 must first be applied before reliance is placed upon the provisions of s 4. In practice this will mean that s 4 is only applied as a last resort, when the gift would otherwise have no possibility of vesting within the perpetuity period.

Perpetuities and Accumulations Act 1964 s 4

(1) Where a disposition is limited by reference to the attainment by any person or persons of a specified age exceeding twenty-one years, and it is apparent at the time the disposition is made or becomes apparent at a subsequent time –

(a) that the disposition would ... be void for remoteness [under the common law rules]; but

(b) that it would not be so void if the specified age had been twenty-one years, the diposition shall be treated as if, instead of being limited by reference to the age in fact specified, it had been limited by reference to the age nearest to that age which would, if specified instead, have prevented the disposition from being so void.

Q Consider s 4(1) of the Act, in what way, when combined with s 3 of the Act, is it more generous than the rule in *Andrews v Partington*?

Perpetuities and Accumulations Act 1964 s 4

(3) Where the inclusion of any person, being potential members of a class or unborn persons who at birth would become members or potential members of the class [would cause the disposition to be void for remoteness] those persons shall thenceforth be deemed for all purposes of the disposition to be excluded from the class, and the said provisions shall thereupon have effect accordingly.

(4) Where ... it is apparent at the time the disposition is made or becomes apparent at a subsequent time that ... the inclusion of any persons, being potential members of a class or unborn persons who at birth would become members or potential members of the class, would cause the disposition to be treated as void for remoteness, those persons shall, unless their exclusion would exhaust the class, thenceforth be deemed for all purposes of the disposition to be excluded from the class.

Perpetuities and Accumulations Act 1964 s 5

Where a disposition is limited by reference to the time of the death of the survivor of a person in being at the commencement of the perpetuity period and any spouse of that person, and that time has not arrived at the end of the perpetuity period, the disposition shall be treated for all purposes, where to do so would save it from being void for remoteness, as if it had instead being limited by reference to the time immediately before the end of that period.

5.3 The rule against excessive accumulation of income

5.3.1 General

Law of Property Act 1925 s 164(1)

No person may ... settle or dispose of any property in such manner that the income thereof shall ... be ... accumulated for any longer period than one of the following, namely:

(a) the life of the grantor or settlor; or

(b) a term of twenty-one years from the death of the grantor, settlor or testator; or

(c) the duration of the minority or respective minorities of any person or persons living or *en ventre sa mere* at the death of the grantor, settlor or testator; or

(d) the duration of the minority or respective minorities only of any person or persons who under the limitations of the instrument directing the accumulations would, for the time being, if of full age, be entitled to the income directed to be accumulated.

(e) the period of 21 years from the date of making the disposition;

(f) the duration of the minority or minorities of any person in being at the date of making an *inter vivos* disposition.

In every case where any accumulation is directed otherwise than as aforesaid, the direction shall (save as hereinafter mentioned) be void; and the income of the property directed to be accumulated shall ... go to and be received by the person or persons who would have been entitled thereto if such accumulation had not been directed.

Note ───

Paragraphs (e) and (f) were added by the 1964 Act. They apply therefore only to gifts taking effect after 15 July 1964.

5.3.2   An exception to restrictions on accumulations

Law of Property Act 1925 s 165

Where accumulations of surplus income are made during a minority under any statutory power or under the general law [see 14.1], the period for which such accumulations are made is not ... to be taken into account in determining the periods for which accumulations are permitted to be made by [s 164] and accordingly an express trust for accumulation for any other permitted period shall not be deemed to have been invalidated or become invalid, by reason of accumulations also having been made as aforesaid during such minority.

5.4   The rule against inalienability of capital

Note ───

A gift or trust will be void for perpetuity if it has the effect of rendering capital inalienable for a period longer than the perpetuity period. Property is inalienable if it cannot be disposed of. See Unincorporated Associations (6.5).

5.5   The rules against perpetuity and charities

Re Tyler (1891) CA

A testator gave a fund to the trustees of a certain charity and as a condition of the gift he directed them to keep his family vault at Highgate Cemetery 'in good repair, and name legible, and to rebuild when it shall require'. If the trustees failed to comply with his request the monies were directed to pass to another charity.

Held the condition for the maintenance and repair of the vault was valid and binding on the first charity. Further, that the gift over to the second charity on failure to comply with the condition was good. The rule against perpetuities has no application to a transfer, on a certain event, of property from one charity to another.

5.6 Public policy

5.6.1 Trusts intended to defraud creditors are void

Re Butterworth (1882) CA

A trader, B, before embarking upon a new business, made a voluntary settlement (that is, without legal 'consideration') for the benefit of his wife and children. His business eventually became insolvent, his liabilities far exceeding his assets.

Held irrespective of whether or not B had been solvent at the date of the settlement, the settlement was void as against the trustee in the liquidation. The settlement had clearly been executed with the intention of putting the settlor's property out of the reach of his creditors. A person is not entitled to go into a hazardous business, and immediately before doing so settle all his property voluntarily, the object being this: 'If I succeed in business, I make a fortune for myself. If I fail, I leave my creditors unpaid. They will bear the loss.' Accordingly the settlement was void for public policy reasons as an attempt to defraud creditors.

Q Why were the trusts in *Re Kayford Ltd* and *Barclays Bank Ltd v Quistclose Ltd* (8.2) not void as attempts to defraud creditors?

6 Purpose trusts

6.1 Pure purpose trusts

Morice v Bishop of Durham (1804) CA

A bequest was made to the Bishop upon trust for 'such objects of benevolence and liberality as the Bishop of Durham in his own discretion shall most approve'.

Held this was not a charitable trust, as it failed the requirement that such a trust be exclusively charitable (See 7.1). The bequest was not a gift to the bishop personally, it was a gift to be held by him on trust for an uncertain and unspecified purpose. Every non-charitable trust must have a definite object: 'There must be somebody, in whose favour the court can decree performance.' In the present case the human object of the trust was uncertain and so the benefit of the trust resulted to the testator's estate.

Re Astor (1952)

Non-charitable trusts were declared of substantially all the issued shares of 'The Observer Limited' for purposes including the 'maintenance ... of good understanding .... between nations' and 'the preservation of the independence and integrity of newspapers'.

Held the trusts were invalid because they were not for the benefit of individuals, but for a number of non-charitable purposes which no one could enforce. The trusts would, in any event, have been void for uncertainty.

Re Shaw (1957)

George Bernard Shaw left his residuary estate on trust to apply the income therefrom for 21 years for, *inter alia*, the following purposes: (1) to ascertain the number of persons currently using the 26 letter English alphabet, and (2) to ascertain how much effort could be saved by replacing the 26 letter alphabet with a 40 letter British alphabet proposed by Shaw.

Held the trust was not charitable (see Chapter 7). It failed, therefore, as being for the benefit not of an individual but of a mere purpose or object. Harman J noted that 'an object cannot complain to the court, which therefore cannot control the trust'. A trust, such as the present, which would not have been susceptible to control by the court would not be upheld. He approved Lord Greene in *Re Diplock* (1948) who had said that 'in order for a trust to be properly constituted, there must be a beneficiary'. This has come to be known as the 'beneficiary principle'.

6.2 Anomalous purpose trusts

Note ————————————————————
The following class of cases are anomalous, and will not be added to (*Re Endacott* (1960) (3.2.2)). They will be valid, despite the absence of any ascertainable human beneficiary. The are sometimes classified as 'trusts of imperfect obligation', this is because the trusts are valid even though there is nobody in a position to 'actively enforce' the trust obligations against the trustees.

6.2.1 The erection or maintenance of tombs or monuments

Re Hooper (1932)
A testator made a bequest and declared that the income therefrom should be used for the care and upkeep of certain graves, a vault, certain monuments, a tablet and a window.

Held the upkeep of the tablet and window was valid as a charitable purpose. The trust for the upkeep of the graves, vault and monument in the churchyard would take effect as a trust of imperfect obligation and income could be applied for this purpose for 21 years.

6.2.2 The maintenance of specific animals

Re Dean (1889)
A testator set up a will trust for the maintenance of his horses and hounds for a period of 50 years. He declared that the trustees should not be bound to render any account of expenditure.

Held the trust was valid. It was not a perpetuity and would take effect as a trust of imperfect obligation.

6.2.3 Fox-hunting

Re Thompson (1934)
A legacy was bequeathed to a friend of the testator to be applied by him as he should in his absolute discretion think fit towards the promotion and furtherance of fox-hunting.

Held this was a valid trust of imperfect obligation.

6.3   A device for avoiding the rule against pure purpose trusts

Note

The following case illustrates how a private purpose trust might be enforced by indirect means.

Re Chardon (1928)

A clause of C's will was in the following terms: 'I give unto my trustees the sum of £200 free of duty upon trust to invest the same upon any of the investments hereinafter authorised and pay the income thereof to the South Metropolitan Cemetery Company West Norwood during such period as they shall continue to maintain and keep the graves of my great grandfather and the said Priscilla Navone in the said Cemetery in good order and condition with flowers and plants thereon as the same have hitherto been kept by me'.

Held the gift was valid. One of the principles underlying the rule against the validity of pure purpose trusts is that purposes are often perpetual and thus funds applied for such purposes might be rendered inalienable (see 5.4). In the present case, however, the fund given to the company was not inalienable, but could be disposed of by the company at any time that a purchaser or donee could be found. Nor did the gift offend the rule against remoteness of vesting (see 5.2), here the gift had vested absolutely in the company (at law a person theoretically distinct from its members) within the perpetuity period.

6.4   Purpose trusts with indirect human beneficiaries

Re Bowes (1896)

A bequest was left on trust to expend the same in planting trees on certain settled estates. It so happened that the tenant for life and the tenant in tail in remainder were between them able to bring to an end the settlement of the estates.

Held the tenant for life and the tenant in tail in remainder were absolutely entitled to the bequest. North J held that 'there clearly is a valid trust to lay out money for the benefit of the persons entitled to the estate' and accordingly the expressed purpose of planting trees could be dismissed as being a mere motive for making the gift.

Compare *Re Andrew's* (3.2.1) and *Re Osoba* (1.2.4). Contrast with *Re Abbott* (3.2.1).

Leahy v AG for New South Wales (1959) PC

A testator left a freehold property 'upon trust for such order of nuns of the Catholic Church or the Christian Brothers as my executors and trustees shall select'. The residue was directed to be applied to build a new convent or to up-date existing buildings.

Held the gift of residue was saved by a statute of New South Wales. However, applying the beneficiary principle, the principal gift was invalid. Their Lordships held that the gift was not intended to benefit the individual nuns or Christian Brothers, but had been intended to further the purposes of their orders, and because the orders were perpetual, the gift must fail. (Due to the closed nature of some of the orders the gift could not be charitable, see Chapter 7.)

Re Denley's Trust Deed (1969)
Land was settled on trustees for use as a sports ground 'primarily' for the benefit of the employees of a company, and 'secondarily' for the benefit of such other persons (if any) as the trustees may allow to use the same. The gift was limited to take effect within 21 years of the death of certain named persons.

Held because of the private nexus between the potential beneficiaries of the trust and a particular company the trust was not sufficiently 'public' to be charitable (see 7.2.9). *Prima facie*, then, it would be void as a non-charitable purpose trust. However, where the trust, though expressed to be for a purpose, is directly or indirectly for the benefit of an individual or individuals, it falls outside the mischief of the beneficiary principle. The rule against enforcing non-charitable purpose trusts should be confined to those which are abstract or impersonal. In the present case there were clearly indirect human beneficiaries and the trust would therefore be valid. Goff J was satisfied that, in contrast with the case of a pure purpose trust, there were persons here who would bring the matter to court if the trustees failed to meet their obligations. (Note: being for present and future indirect beneficiaries the trust would have failed the rules against perpetuity had it not been for the express limitation to the perpetuity period.)

Re Lipinksi (1976)
The testator, L, left one-half of his residuary estate to the trustees of an association for Jewish Youth. The gift was expressly made in memory of his late wife to be used 'solely' in the work of constructing new buildings for the association. The trust was not charitable because it produced insufficient benefit to the general public. The question was whether it was void as a pure purpose trust, being 'solely' for the erection of buildings.

Held the trust was valid for any one of three reasons. First, applying *Re Denley*, because there were indirect human beneficiaries; secondly, because, applying *Re Recher* (6.5.2), the gift should be construed as an outright gift to the members of the association, subject to the rules of the association; or thirdly, applying *Re Turkington* (1937), because the members of the association were both the trustees and the beneficiaries and thus able to vest the capital in themselves according to the rule in *Saunders v Vautier* (9.1.1).

Note ───

None of the reasons given for the decision in *Re Lipinski* is particularly convincing. First, *Re Denley's* is readily distinguishable. In *Re Denley's* the beneficiary principle had been avoided partly by treating the reference to building a sports ground as a mere motive for setting up the trust (applying *Re Bowes*, see above). In other words, the purpose was ancillary to the ultimate human benefit. In *Re Lipinski* the trust was set up in memory of the testator's wife and 'solely' for the purpose of building. It is hard to dismiss such an imperative statement of purpose as an ancillary motive, the expressed purpose appears to be in terms fundamental to the existence of the trust. Oliver J reasoned that the direction to build was not fundamental to the testator's intentions, but had been his attempt to second-guess the current needs, whatever they might be, of the ultimate human beneficiaries. Secondly, to apply *Re Recher* assumes that an absolute gift has been made to the present members of the association, but in the present case the benefiting members are Jewish 'youth', the majority of whom would be precluded by their infancy from taking as an absolute gift that part of the residuary estate which comprised land. Thirdly, the infancy of the beneficiaries means that the rule in *Saunders v Vautier*, and therefore the reasoning in *Re Turkington*, is inapplicable.

6.5   Gifts to unincorporated non-profit associations

Note ───

Speaking in very general terms, the law readily legislates for incorporated associations (eg limited liability companies) and profit-oriented unincorporated associations (ie partnerships), but it struggles to understand the essential nature of unincorporated associations which do not exist primarily with a view to making financial profit (eg clubs and associations). If a gift is made to a club only very rarely will a sensible construction allow it to be divided among the present members in individual shares. How, then, is such a gift to be construed? Is it void as a gift on trust for the impersonal purposes of the club? Or is it valid as a trust for the benefit of indirect beneficiaries? Is it an absolute gift to the present members to be held by them subject to the contractual rules of the club? Is it a gift to the officers of the club to be held by them as agents for the members of the club? We shall consider each possible construction in turn.

6.5.1   Gifts on trust for the purposes of the association or club

See *Re Denley* and *Re Lipinksi*, above.

6.5.2   Absolute gifts to members subject to the rules of the club

Re Recher's Will Trust (1972)

R, a testatrix, left a share of her residuary estate on trust to 'The Anti-
Vivisection Society'.

Held the gift should not be construed as a gift in trust for the purposes
of the society. Rather, the gift should be construed as a legacy to the present members of the society as an accretion to the funds which constituted
the subject matter of the contract by which the members had bound themselves *inter se*. There would be no breach of the rule against inalienability
of capital because if all the members agreed, they could decide to wind up
the society and divide the net assets amongst themselves beneficially. The
only reason the gift failed in the present case was because the society had
ceased to exist by the time of R's death.

Re Grant's WT (1980)

G, the testator, had been financial secretary of the Chertsey Constituency
Labour Party, which had since become the Chertsey and Walton
Constituency Labour Party. The new constituency party was subject to
rules laid down by the National Executive Committee of the Labour Party
and the national annual party conference. By his will, G devised all his real
and personal estate (for the benefit of the Chertsey headquarters of the
new constituency party) to the committee in charge of property at the
headquarters.

Held the gift could not take effect as a gift to the current members of the
new constituency party subject to their contractual rights and duties *inter
se* because the members were not free, under the rules of their association,
to dispose of the property in any way they thought fit. On the contrary, the
rules made it plain that the decisions of the members of the local party
were subject to the control of the national Labour Party. The gift must
therefore fail as infringing the rule against inalienability of capital.

6.5.3   Gift to officers as agents of the members of the association

Conservative and Unionist Central Office v Burrell (1982) CA

Re Grant's WT (above) concerned a gift to a local Labour Party association.
The present case considered gifts to the central office of the Conservative
Party. The central office had been assessed to corporation tax on the
ground that it was a 'company' within the meaning of s 526(5) of the
Income and Corporation Taxes Act 1970. Included within the definition of
'company' were unincorporated associations of two or more persons
bound together for common purposes (not being business purposes) by

mutual undertakings and rules governing the holding and control of property. Appealing against the tax assessment the central office contended that it was not an unincorporated association within this definition.

Held funds held by the central office were not held on behalf of an unincorporated association within the 1970 Act definition. It became necessary to consider, therefore, upon what basis donations were received by the central office. It was held *per curiam* (for the sake of clarity) that when a contributor makes a donation to the treasurer, or other officer, of the central office the officer receives the donation as an agent and subject to a mandate that it be used for the political purposes for which it was given. The law of agency, not of trusts, is applicable. Once the donation has been mixed with the general funds under the officer's control the mandate becomes irrevocable. In other words, it is then too late for the contributor to reclaim the donation. However, the contributor has a remedy against the officials to restrain or make good a misapplication of the mixed fund except where the contributors donation can be shown, on normal accounting principles, to have been legitimately expended before the misapplication of the mixed fund.

6.6 Distribution of surplus donations

Note ────────────────────────────────────
When monies are given for a purpose or to an association what happens if there are surplus funds after the purpose is fulfilled or the association dissolved? The answer depends largely upon the way in which the original gift is construed. If the gift is construed as being a gift 'in trust' for a particular purpose, any surplus of the gift will generally be held on resulting trust for the original donor. If it was originally construed as an absolute gift, whether or not subject to the contractual rules of the donee association, any surplus of the gift will generally belong beneficially to the members of the association in existence at the time of its dissolution. It is crucial, therefore, that trusts (which are made with an *imperative* intention) are distinguished from absolute gifts (which are merely *motivated* by a particular intention).

Note ────────────────────────────────────
See *Re Bowes* (6.4); *Re Abbott* (3.2.1); *Re Andrew's* (3.2.1); *Re Osoba* (1.2.4).

Cunnack v Edwards (1896) CA
A society had been established to raise a fund by members' subscriptions to provide annuities for the widows of deceased members. The last member died in 1879 and the last widow died in 1892, the society having then a surplus or unexpended fund of £1,250.

Held the widows, and not the members, were the beneficiaries of the society's funds, accordingly there would be no resulting trust of the surplus in favour of the estates of the members of the society. As Smith LJ stated 'as the member paid his money to the society, so he divested himself of all interest in this money for ever, with this one reservation, that if the member left a widow she was to be provided for during her widowhood'. The fund would pass to the Crown as *bona vacantia*.

Re Gillingham Bus Disaster Fund (1958) CA

In 1951 a bus careered into a column of Royal Marine cadets, who were marching along a road in Gillingham, Kent. Twenty-four were killed and others were injured. A memorial fund was set up for the purpose of meeting funeral expenses, caring for the disabled, and for such other worthy causes as the trustees may determine. Substantial gifts were made by named donors and money was contributed to the fund anonymously through street collections. The principal question was whether the monies were held on charitable trusts and should be devoted under a *cy près* scheme to other charitable ends. That having been determined in the negative the question arose whether the surplus should be held on resulting trust for the donors or should pass to the crown as *bona vacantia*.

Held the surplus would be held on resulting trust for the donors. *Cunnack v Edwards* was distinguished as being a case were the funds had been held subject to a contractual arrangement. Harman J was not impressed with the Crown's argument that the resulting trust solution should be avoided due to the impracticalities of identifying the anonymous donors. His lordship was convinced that the resulting trust solution was appropriate to the named donors and saw no reason to suppose that the anonymous donor had any larger intention than the named donor as to the ultimate destination of their donation. In the event that the anonymous donors might not be found the surplus should be held in the court's account, but should not pass as ownerless goods (*bona vacantia*) to the Crown.

Re West Sussex Constabulary's Benevolent Fund Trusts (1971)

The fund existed to provide for widows and orphans of deceased members. When the West Sussex Constabulary amalgamated with other forces in 1968 the question arose as to how the funds should be distributed. Sources of the fund were (1) members subscriptions; (2) receipts from entertainments, raffles and sweepstakes; (3) collecting boxes; and (4) donations and legacies.

Held surplus of sources (1), (2) and (3) would pass to the Crown as *bona vacantia*. Surplus of source (4) would be held on resulting trusts for the donors. Equity would 'cut the gordian knot' of accounting difficulties by dividing the surplus in proportion to the sources from which it had arisen. Surplus of source (1) could not be the subject of a resulting trust because the members had received consideration for the payment of their sub-scriptions in the form of the benefits of membership. Surplus of source (2) could not be the subject of a resulting trust because, first, such payments had been made for consideration; and, secondly, they were not direct donations to the fund, but merely donations of net profits after payment out of prizes etc. Surplus of source (3) would not be deemed subject to a resulting trust because donors to collecting boxes are presumed to have intended to part with their monies out and out.

Re Bucks Constabulary Fund Friendly Society (1979) CA
The Society had been established to make provision for widows and orphans of deceased members of the Bucks Constabulary. In 1968 the Bucks Constabulary was amalgamated with other constabularies to form the Thames Valley Constabulary. The trustee of the society applied to court to determine (1) whether the surplus assets should be distributed among the persons who were members of the society at the date of its dissolution or whether they should pass to the Crown as *bona vacantia*, and (2) if the assets were to be distributed among the members whether they should be distributed in equal shares or *pro rata* the members' payment of subscrip-tions. Members voluntary subscriptions had made up the majority of the fund.

Held (1) as there had been members in existence at the time of the dis-solution, the surplus would be held upon resulting trusts for those mem-bers to the total exclusion of any claim on behalf of the Crown. The *Re West Sussex* case (see above) was distinguished (rather artificially) on the basis that it involved a simple unincorporated association, whereas the present case involved a friendly society. (2) claims of members of a friendly soci-ety *inter se* on surplus funds held on trust for their benefit were governed by the contract between them, and where the contract, as here, provided no other method of distribution such funds were *prima facie* to be distrib-uted in equal shares.

6.7 When is an unincorporated association wound up?

Note
In *Re GKN Bolts and Nuts Sports and Social Club* (1982) it was held (1) that clubs do not automatically dissolve through mere inactivity unless the period of inactivity is such that the only reasonable inference is that the club has ceased to exist; (2) in the present case the club had ceased to exist, but only by virtue of the positive resolution of the members to sell the club's sports ground.

Q We usually think of unincorporated associations as an aggregate of human persons, but could it be that the existence of special property (eg the clubhouse) is of more fundamental importance to the identity of an association than the individuals within it?

7   Charitable trusts

Note ───
There are a number of advantages attaching to a trust which has charitable status. First, it is not subject to the beneficiary principle (see 6.1).
This exemption follows logically from the fact that a charitable trust is by
definition a trust for public purposes and not a trust for private persons.
The Attorney General will bring actions against charity trustees to
ensure that they discharge their trust. Secondly, and related to the first
point, a charitable trust will not be void for uncertainty of object.
Provided that the trust was intended to be applied exclusively for charitable purposes it will not fail if those purposes are, or become, uncertain
(see *cy près* at 7.6). Thirdly, a charitable trust is usually not subject to the
rules against perpetuities (5.1). This is because the public policy considerations which prohibit perpetual gifts and trusts should be no bar to the
public benefits which charities bring about. Fourthly, but perhaps most
significantly, charitable trusts enjoy a wide range of fiscal exemptions
and privileges.

7.1   The exclusivity requirement

Salusbury v Denton (1857)

A testator left a fund to his widow for life and directed that after her death
she should leave a part of the fund to certain charities and the remainder
to his relatives. The widow died having failed to make the relevant
appointments.

Held the wording of the trust permitted a severance of the non-charitable from the charitable objects. In accordance with the maxim 'equality is
equity' the court applied half of the fund towards the charitable purposes
and the other half to the testator's relatives.

Chichester Diocesan Fund and Board of Finance (Incorporated) v Simpson (1944) HL

The testator, CD, left the residue of his estate on trust 'for such charitable
institution or institutions or other charitable or benevolent object or objects
as his executors might in their absolute discretion select'. The residue was
distributed amongst several charities. After the distribution the testator's
statutory next-of-kin claimed that the residuary gift was not a valid chari-

table bequest because the words 'charitable or benevolent' had rendered the gift uncertain.

Held upon a true construction of the clause the word 'or' indicated that 'benevolent' was intended to be an alternative to 'charitable'. Accordingly, the gift was void for uncertainty. (This decision meant, of course, that the statutory next-of-kin had to try and recover the misapplied property – see *Re Diplock* (18.2.1).)

Note ───

In *Re Best* (1904) a bequest of residue was made to such 'charitable *and* benevolent institutions' as the trustees shall in their discretion determine. The gift was construed as exclusively charitable and was therefore held to be a valid charitable gift.

Re Coxen (1948)

The testator gave the residue of his estate, some £200,000, to the Court of Aldermen of the City of London upon trust to (1) spend £100 towards an annual dinner for the aldermen upon their meeting together upon the business of his trust; (2) to pay one guinea to each alderman who attended the whole of a committee meeting in connection with the trust; (3) to apply the remainder for the benefit of certain medical charities. On the question whether the trust was valid.

Held all the trusts were valid charitable trusts. The provisions in favour of the aldermen personally were made to ensure the better administration of the main charitable trusts. In any event, even if those provisions had not themselves been charitable, the sums involved were so insignificant in comparison to that part of the fund devoted to the medical charities that the provisions for the benefit of the aldermen personally could be seen as merely ancillary to the principal trust and would take effect on that basis. In cases where the non-charitable allocation was so significant as not to be 'ancillary' the whole trust must fail, unless the non-charitable part could be precisely quantified in which case only that part would fail.

Oxford Group v Inland Revenue Commissioners (1949) CA

The Oxford Group, a company limited by guarantee, claimed to be exempt from income tax on the grounds that the group existed in order to further certain charitable purposes. The objects clause of the company's memorandum of association provided that the company existed to 'advance the Christian religion'; to 'maintain ... the Oxford Group Movement in every way' and to 'establish and support ... any charitable or benevolent associations'.

Held the last provision did not qualify as an exclusively charitable trust. The provision relating to the maintenance of the Oxford Group similarly failed, as it permitted the company to engage in non-charitable activities. Accordingly, even though the first provision was in itself charitable the whole trust must fail as a charitable trust. The latter provision could not be said to merely ancillary to the former. A religious body could engage in subsidiary non-charitable activities, but a trust which permitted the expenditure of income on such subsidiary activities was not a valid charitable trust.

Charitable Trusts (Validation) Act 1954 s 1

A trust provision which could properly be construed as being for exclusively charitable purposes, but which could nevertheless be used for non-charitable purposes, is validated as an exclusively charitable trust by this Act. However, the Act only applies to trusts taking effect before 16 December 1952.

Note ───
See Guild (1992) (7.3).
───

7.2 Definition of charity

7.2.1 General

Note ───
There is no statutory definition of charity, the definition has developed on a case by case basis, courts taking guidance from the preamble to the Statute of Charitable Uses 1601. Even today a trust will only be charitable if it falls within the 'spirit and intendment' of that statute.
───

Charities Act 1960 s 38

(4) Any reference in any enactment or document to a charity within the meaning, purview and interpretation of the Charitable Uses Act 1601 or of the preamble to it, shall be construed as a reference to a charity within the meaning which the word bears as a legal term according to the law of England and Wales.

The preamble to the Statute of Charitable Uses 1601

The following represent the nature of charitable uses in 1601: 'Relief of aged, impotent and poor People ... the maintenance of sick and maimed Soldiers and Mariners, Schools of Learning ... Scholars in Universities ... the Repair of Bridges, Ports, Havens, Causeways, Churches, Sea-Banks and Highways ... the Education and Preferment of Orphans ... Houses of Correction ... Marriages of Poor Maids ... Supportation, Aid and Help of Young Tradesmen, handicraftsmen and Persons decayed ... the Relief or Redemption of Prisoners ...'.

Commissioners for Special Purposes of the Income Tax v Pemsel (1891) HL
On the question whether a particular trust was for 'charitable purposes' according to the legal and technical meaning of those words.

Held per Lord MacNaghten: 'Charity' in its legal sense comes under four principal heads: trusts for the relief of poverty; trusts for the advancement of education; trusts for the advancement of religion; and trusts for other purposes beneficial to the community, not falling under any of the preceding heads.

Note ────────────────────
Each of Lord MacNaghten's four heads is considered in turn below.

Scottish Burial Reform and Cremation Society Ltd v Glasgow Corporation (1968) HL
The appellant was a non-profit making company incorporated in order to promote cremation, which service it had carried out in Glasgow for many years. It provided opportunities for religious observance but had not been incorporated on any religious basis. On the question whether it was a charity and entitled to relief from rates.

Held the objects of the company were for the benefit of the community and fell within the fourth of Lord MacNaghten's heads of charity. It was noted, however, that the 'four heads' were a classification of convenience and not necessarily a comprehensive set of charitable classes, that Lord MacNaghten's words should not be given the force of statute and that the law of charity is a continually evolving subject. The fundamental question was whether the objects of a gift fell, in the light of current social needs, within the 'spirit and intendment' of the preamble to the Act of 1601.

7.2.2 The first head: relief of the poor

Re Gwyon (1930)
The testator directed that the residue of his estate should be applied by his executor to establish the 'Gwyon's Boys Clothing Foundation'. A foundation to provide 'knickers' (a sort of trouser) for boys in a certain district. The boys could replace their old pair for a new pair, provided that the words 'Gwyon's Present' were still legible on the waistband of the old pair. The terms of the gift did not prefer the children of poor parents.

Held the gift was not a valid charitable trust for the relief of poverty. None of the conditions of the gift necessarily imported poverty.

Re Coulthurst (1951) CA
The testator, C, directed that the income from his estate should be applied by his trustees 'to or for the benefit of such ... of the ... widows and orphaned children of deceased officers and deceased ex-officers' of a bank 'as the bank shall in its absolute discretion consider by reason of his, her or their financial circumstances to be most deserving of such assistance ...'.

Held this was a valid charitable trust intended to benefit the poor, in accordance with the meaning of the preamble to the Act of 1601. The fact that the beneficiaries were chosen by reference to their employment with a particular bank did not defeat the charitable nature of a gift for the relief of poverty. Further, poverty need not mean destitution. It might be paraphrased as 'going short', due regard being had to the beneficiaries social status and so on.

Re Young (1951)

The testator, Y, left his estate to his wife with a direction that she should leave it at her death 'for the permanent aid of distressed gentlefolk and similar purposes'.

Held the court accepted *obiter* that a trust of this nature was a valid charitable trust for the relief of poverty.

Re Scarisbrick (1951) CA

The testatrix, S, left one-half of her residuary estate upon ultimate trusts for such of the relations of her son and daughters as the survivor of her son and daughters shall deem to be 'in needy circumstances'. The judge at first instance held that the trust for relations was not a valid charitable trust because the beneficiaries did not constitute a section of the poor, but merely individual poor persons.

Held on appeal. The disposition was a valid charitable trust for the relief of poverty. Gifts or trusts for the relief of poverty were an exception to the rule, which applied to every other form of charitable disposition, that an element of general public benefit must be shown. The true question in a case of this sort was whether the gift was for the relief of poverty amongst a class of persons, in which case it would be valid, or whether it was a gift to individuals motivated by a desire to relieve their poverty, in which case it would not be a valid charitable trust. In the present case the gift was for a class of poor persons. The fact that the survivor of the sons and daughters had the power to elect beneficiaries did not alter this conclusion, that power having been included merely to avoid disputes.

Re Sander's Will Trusts (1954)

The testator directed his trustees, by a codicil to his will, to 'apply one equal third part of my residuary trust fund in ... providing dwellings for the working classes and their families resident in the area of Pembroke Dock, Pembrokeshire, Wales, or within a radius of five miles therefrom (with preference to actual dockworkers and their families employed at the said docks)'. On the question whether this direction constituted a valid charitable trust for the relief of poverty.

Held it did not. The words 'working class' did not indicate a gift to the poor.

Dingle v Turner (1972) HL

The testator, D, gave his residuary estate to trustees upon trust for his wife for her life and thereafter to place £10,000 with trustees upon trust 'to apply the income thereof in paying pensions to poor employees of E Dingle & Co Ltd' who were old or disabled.

Held the terms of the will created a valid charitable trust for the relief of poverty, despite the nexus between the beneficiaries and the named company. (The *Oppenheim* case, see 7.2.10, was distinguished on the basis that the trust there had not been for the relief of poverty.) In the case of trusts for the relief of 'poverty' the distinction between a public charitable trust and a private non-charitable trust depended upon whether, on a true construction of the gift, it was for the relief of poverty amongst a particular description of poor people or was merely a gift to particular poor persons (approving *Re Scarisbrick*, above).

Re Cohen (1973)

The testatrix gave part of her residuary estate to trustees upon trust to apply the same in their absolute discretion 'for or towards the maintenance and benefit of any relatives of mine whom my trustees shall consider to be in special need'.

Held a valid charitable trust was created for the relief of poverty amongst a class, namely, those relations of the testatrix chosen by the trustees.

Re Niyazi's Will Trusts (1978)

The testator provided by his will that his residuary estate should be held by his trustees upon trust to pay the capital and income to a local authority in a needy part of Cyprus 'on condition that the same shall be used for the purposes only of the construction of or as a contribution towards the cost of the construction of a working men's hostel'.

Held this was a valid charitable trust for the relief of poverty. The judge described the case as 'desperately near the border-line', but concluded that only poor persons would be likely to live in a hostel. The word 'hostel', he said, was very different from the word 'dwelling' as used in *Re Sanders' WT* (see above), the former suggested a poor inhabitant, the latter was appropriate to any house. The judge also took into account the depressed nature of the area in which the hostel had been directed to be built.

Joseph Rowntree Memorial Trust Housing Association Ltd v Attorney General (1983)

The plaintiff was a charitable housing association which desired to build individual dwellings for sale to elderly people on long leases in consideration of a capital payment. On the tenant's death the lease would be assigned to the tenant's spouse or a family member, provided that person was also elderly. Failing such an assignment the lease would revert to the association who would pay to the tenant's estate 70% of the then current market value of the lease. The Charity Commissioners objected to the scheme on the grounds, *inter alia*, that it operated by way of contract, benefited private individuals rather than a charitable class and could produce a financial profit for those individuals.

Held the scheme was a valid charitable scheme for the relief of the aged notwithstanding the objections of the Charity Commissioners.

7.2.3 The second head: the advancement of education

Re Shaw (1957)

See 6.1 for the facts and decision in this case. You will recall that Shaw's trust for research into a new English alphabet failed as a charitable trust for the advancement of education. The judge held that 'if the object be merely the increase of knowledge, that is not in itself a charitable object unless it be combined with teaching or education'. Having failed as a valid trust for charitable purposes the trust was necessarily void as a trust for private purposes.

Re Hopkins (1965)

The testatrix, H, left a third of her residuary estate to the Francis Bacon Society by her will. The monies were directed to be 'applied towards finding the Bacon-Shakespeare manuscripts and in the event of the same having been discovered by the date of my death then for the general purposes of the work and propaganda of the society'. The society, which was a registered charity under the Charities Act 1960, existed primarily to study the evidence for Francis Bacon's authorship of plays commonly ascribed to William Shakespeare. On the question whether the bequest created a valid charitable trust.

Held in view of the importance of the research directed to be carried out, the gift would qualify as a charitable one for the advancement of education. For a gift for research to be charitable it must be combined with teaching or education, albeit the education of the researchers themselves.

Note ——————————————————————————————
In *Re Hopkins* the judge held that it did not matter that the charitable purposes might not fall neatly into any one only of the four heads of charity. He considered the possibility that the research might fall within the general head of charities 'beneficial to the community', and stressed that 'benefits' need not be material and would include intellectual or artistic benefits.

The Incorporated Council of Law Reporting for England and Wales v Attorney General (1971) CA

The principal object of the society was 'the preparation and publication ... at a moderate price, and under gratuitous professional control, of Reports of Judicial Decisions of the Superior and Appellate Courts in England'. These reports were used to draw judicial attention to the current state of the law. The society's profits were not distributed to its members, but were applied to the further pursuit of its objects. The society applied for registration as a charity under the Charities Act 1960. The Charity Commissioners refused registration.

Held the purposes of the council were exclusively charitable. Two of the three judges held that its primary purpose was the advancement of education. 'The practising lawyer and the judge must both be lifelong students in the field of scholarship for the study of which The Law Reports provide essential material'. The court also found, unanimously, that the trust would in any event have fallen within the fourth head of charity, that of 'purposes beneficial to the community'.

Barralet v Attorney General (1980)

The objects of the South Place Ethical Society were 'the study and dissemination of ethical principles' and 'the cultivation of a rational religious sentiment'. The society contended that their objects were charitable as being for the advancement of religion, for the advancement of education or for other purposes beneficial to the community. On the question whether the society's purposes were for the advancement of education.

Held the whole of the society's objects were charitable under this head. The advancement of education should be construed widely. The 'dissemination of ethical principles' through the society's lectures, concerts and monthly publication satisfied the need for a public benefit in a charitable educational trust. The 'cultivation of a rational religious sentiment' was also for the advancement of education, for a 'rational' sentiment could be cultivated only through education.

McGovern v Attorney General (1981)

The Amnesty International organisation set up a trust to administer those of its purposes which were considered to be charitable. Its aims included the release of and humane treatment of prisoners of conscience, research into the observance of human rights and the dissemination of the results of such research. It applied to the Charity Commissioners for registration of the trust as a charity under s 4 of the Charities Act 1960. Registration was refused.

Held on appeal to the High Court the commissioners' decision was confirmed, the trust was not a trust for exclusively charitable purposes. The major part of the trust purposes were of a political, and therefore non-charitable, nature (see 7.4). The court did state, however, that had the provisions as to research stood alone they would have been charitable. The subject matter of the research was 'capable of adding usefully to the store of human knowledge'. The judge noted that human rights has become an accepted academic discipline. He also stated that it should be benignly presumed that the trustees would not implement the research in a political manner.

7.2.4 Educative value of art

Re Delius (1957)

The widow of Frederick Delius, the composer, left her residuary estate to trustees upon trust to apply the income therefrom 'for or towards the advancement ... of the musical works of my late husband under conditions in which the making of profit is not the object to be attained and which might be economically impossible by any concert operatic or other organisation ... by means of the recording upon the gramophone or other instrument for the mechanical reproduction of music of those works ... the publication and issue of a uniform edition of the whole body of the works ... and ... the performance in public of the works'.

Held the trusts were valid charitable trusts for the advancement of education. In view of the high quality of Delius' work the judge did not consider what he might have decided had the works been of an 'inadequate composer', although he mused that 'perhaps I should have no option but to give effect even to such a trust'. In the present case the fact that the trust would incidentally enhance the reputation of Delius and incidentally bring pleasure to listeners were not reasons for denying the charitable nature of the trust.

Re Pinion (1964) CA

The testator, P, left his freehold studio, together with his paintings and some antique furniture, silver, china etc to be offered to the National Trust to be kept together as a collection. The income from the residue of his estate was left to be used for the maintenance of the collection. If the National Trust declined the gift, P's executors were directed to keep the collection as a museum. In fact evidence was produced to show that the collection was of low quality and that P's own pictures were 'atrociously bad', and that the National trust had turned down the gift. On the question whether this was a valid trust for the advancement of education.

Held it was not. Expert evidence was admissible to assist the court in determining the educative value of a trust. In the present case the experts concluded that the collection had no value as a means of education. The judge took the view that P's aim had been, not to educate, but to enhance his own reputation and that of his family.

7.2.5 Educative value of sport

Re Dupree's Trusts (1944)

At issue was the charitable nature of a gift of £5,000 for the promotion of an annual chess tournament for boys and young men under 21 resident in the City of Portsmouth. The trustees included the chairman of the Portsmouth Education Committee and the headmaster of Portsmouth Grammar School.

Held chess is something more than a game, it is an historic institution which encourages foresight, concentration, memory and ingenuity. The trust was therefore a valid charitable trust for the advancement of education, although the judge acknowledged that the case 'may be a little near the line' and could put the courts on a 'slippery slope'. The identities of the trustees assisted the judge in reaching his conclusion in the present case.

Inland Revenue Commissioners v McMullen (1980) HL

The Football Association created the FA Youth Trust in 1972. The objects of the trust were 'to organise or provide or assist in the organisation and provision of facilities which will enable and encourage pupils of schools and universities in any part of the United Kingdom to play Association Football or other games or sports and thereby to assist in ensuring that due attention is given to the physical education and development of such pupils as well as to the development and occupation of their minds'. The Charity Commissioners agreed to register the trust as a charity. The Crown appealed against the registration.

Held on the proper construction of the objects of the trust the word 'thereby' showed that the purpose of the trust was not merely to organise the playing of sport, but to promote physical education. Regard being had to the need for a balanced education and the fact that the benefits were limited to students, this was a valid charitable trust for the advancement of education. A majority of their Lordships held that a benign construction should be given to ambiguity in the wording of a purportedly charitable trust. The possibility that the trust might be charitable under the Recreational Charities Act 1958 was left open (see 7.3 below).

7.2.6   The third head: the advancement of religion

7.2.7   Churches and churchyards

Re Douglas (1905)

The testatrix, D, left the whole of her estate to her husband for his life. After his death certain specific legacies and bequests were directed to be made, with the residue to be used for the maintenance of a churchyard.

Held this was a valid charitable gift for the advancement of religion, and by analogy to the provision with regard to the repair of churches contained within the preamble to the Act of 1601 (7.2.1).

Re King (1923)

The testatrix left the residue of her estate to provide for the erection, to the memory of the testatrix and her relations, of a stained-glass window in a parish church.

Held this was a valid charitable trust of the whole fund. The surplus after the provision of the window was applied *cy près* (see 7.6) in the provision of a second window.

Note ───────

Contrast the last two cases with the case of *Re Hooper* (6.2.1).

7.2.8 Recognising religion

Thornton v Howe (1862)

A gift of land was made to assist in the promotion and publication of the 'sacred writings of the late Joanna Southcote', whom the then Master of the Rolls described as 'a foolish ignorant woman'. She had claimed that she was with child by the Holy Spirit and would give birth to a Second Messiah.

Held the gift was held to be a charitable gift for the advancement of religion. The court would not make any distinction between one sect and another, provided, as here, that there was nothing in its preachings which would make persons immoral or irreligious. The decision, however, must be read in the context of its consequences. Being a charitable gift of land the gift failed under the Statute of Mortmain (now repealed) and passed to the donor's heir.

Yeap Cheah Neo v Ong Chen Neo (1875) PC

A trust was set up to promote ancestor worship. On the question whether it was a valid charitable trust for the advancement of religion.

Held it was not. It failed for two reasons. First, worship of human ancestors did not involve the worship of a deity and could not, therefore, be described as being a religion. Secondly, on the terms of the particular trust there was no assurance that the worship would produce a sufficient public benefit (see *Gilmour v Coats* (7.2.11)).

Re Watson (1973)

The testatrix, W, left her estate to H 'for the continuance of the work of God as it has been maintained by [H] and myself since 1942 by God's enabling ... in propagating the truth as given in the Holy Bible'. H predeceased the testatrix, but had written a number of religious tracts during his lifetime. His publications were regarded by experts as being unlikely to extend the knowledge of the Christian religion, but quite likely to confirm, in the group who had produced the publications, their own religious opinions.

Held the trust was a valid charitable trust for the advancement of religion. Public benefit could be presumed through the publication of the tracts because the court would not prefer one religion to another unless it was shown that its doctrines were adverse to the foundations of all religion and subversive of all morality. *Thornton v Howe* followed.

Re Barralet v Attorney General (1980)
For the facts and result see 7.2.3, above. On the question whether the objects of an agnostic, although not atheistic, 'ethical society' could be said to be for the advancement of religion.

Held 'religion' is concerned with mankind's relations with God or gods, whereas ethics is concerned with relations between humans only. Without belief in a supernatural entity faith could not properly be described as religious, no matter how sincerely held. The view held in America that a religion is any belief occupying in the life of the possessor a place parallel to that occupied by belief in God prompted the judge to remark that 'parallels, by definition, never meet'. The judge suggested, further, that worship of God or gods was essential to religion, and worship in that sense had no place between humans, and accordingly no place in a humanist ethical system of belief.

7.2.9 The public benefit requirement

Note
We noted above that trusts for the relief of poverty will be charitable even if they are not shown to benefit the general public. In contrast, trusts for the relief of the aged and impotent (7.2.13), for the advancement of education and for the advancement of religion must produce a sufficient public benefit in order to be charitable.

7.2.10 The public benefit requirement in educational trusts

Oppenheim v Tobacco Securities Trust Co Ltd (1951) HL
A settlement directed trustees to apply the income from the trust fund 'in providing for ... the education of children of employees or former employees of the British-American Tobacco Co Ltd ... or any of its subsidiary or allied companies in such manner ... as the acting trustees shall in their absolute discretion ... think fit'. The employees referred to numbered over 110,000. The issue was whether the class of potential beneficiaries constituted a sufficient section of the general public.

Held (Lord MacDermott dissenting). Despite the huge number of potential beneficiaries, they were identified by the personal nexus between them and the employer company. Accordingly, the trust did not satisfy the requirement that it produce a benefit to a sufficient section of the community. The words 'section of the' community have no special meaning, but they indicate, first, that the possible beneficiaries must not be numerically negligible, and secondly, that they must not be distinguishable from other members of the public by reason of a relationship to a particular individual.

Q What would be the result of a case where the description of the occupation and employment is in effect the same? As counsel, in *Oppenheim* asked, is there a difference between 'soldiers' and 'soldiers of the King'? Would a trust to educate soldiers fail because of their personal nexus to the Crown?

7.2.11 The public benefit requirement in trusts for the advancement of religion

Note ——————————————————————————
See *Yeap v Ong* (7.2.8).

Gilmour v Coats (1949) HL

The sum of £500 was settled upon trust to pay the income therefrom for the purposes of a community of strictly cloistered nuns. The nuns devoted themselves to prayer, meditation, fasting, penance and self-sanctification. They conducted private religious services, but were not engaged in any good works outside of the convent.

Held the trust for the purposes of the cloistered community did not satisfy the public benefit requirement. Accordingly this was not a valid charitable trust for the advancement of religion. The potential for religious edification of others through the example set by the nuns was said to be too vague. Nor did their Lordships accept the argument, made by analogy to educational trusts, that the public benefit requirement had been met through the fact that membership of the community was potentially open to any woman in the whole world. (Lord Simonds made the following general observation on the law of charities and the four heads of charity: 'the law of charity ... has been built up not logically but empirically ... To argue by a method of syllogism or analogy from the category of education to that of religion ignores the historical processes of law'.)

Neville Estates Ltd v Madden (1962)

NE Ltd claimed specific performance of a contract for the sale of land owned by a synagogue. The trustees of the synagogue claimed that the synagogue existed for charitable purposes and that the consent of the Charity Commissioners would be required before sale could proceed.

Held the synagogue's purposes were charitable. *Gilmour v Coats* being distinguished on the basis that the members of the synagogue 'spend their lives in the world, whereas the members of the Carmelite Priory live secluded from the world'. Cross J held that the court was entitled to assume 'that some benefit accrues to the public from the attendance at places of worship of persons who live in the world and mix with their fellow citizens. As between different religions the law stands neutral, but it assumes that any religion is at least likely to be better than none'.

Re Hetherington (1990)

The testatrix, H, left a legacy to 'the Roman Catholic Church Bishop of Westminster for the repose of the souls of my husband and my parents and my sisters and also myself when I die', and left the residue of her estate 'to the Roman Catholic Church St Edwards Golders Green for Masses for my soul'.

Held the gifts were for charitable purposes. However, to be valid the gift must be construed as a gift for the purpose of saying masses in public. The celebration of a religious rite in private would not contain the necessary element of public benefit.

7.2.12   The fourth head: other purposes beneficial to the community

Note ───

See *Barralet v AG* (7.2.3); *Joseph Rowntree v AG* (7.2.2); the *Scottish Burial Reform* (7.2.1).

───

Re Grove-Grady (1929) CA

The testatrix left her residuary estate to her trustees upon trust to found an institution called 'The Beaumont Animals Benevolent Society', provided that all officials of the society should be declared anti-vivisectionists and opponents of all blood-sports, including angling. The objects of the society included the acquisition of land 'for the purpose of providing a refuge or refuges for the preservation of all animals birds or other creatures not human ... and so that all such animals birds or other creatures not human shall there be safe from molestation or destruction by man'.

Held at first instance Romer J (as to whom see, further, *Re Moss*, below) had held that the gift was a valid charitable trust for purposes beneficial to the community. His decision was reversed by the majority of the Court of Appeal. The present gift lacked the required element of public benefit. It did not seek to diminish the cruel treatment of animal life generally, but only those within the society's compound. The public does not come into the matter at all.

Re Moss (1949)

The testatrix, M, made a gift to a Miss H of one-half of the proceeds from the sale of her leasehold house, 'for her use at her discretion for her work for the welfare of cats and kittens needing care and attention'. The residue of M's estate was given in the same way. Miss H had for many years taken in stray cats, having them painlessly destroyed if they were badly injured, and finding good homes for the others. M's next-of-kin claimed that the gifts were void as being trusts for a private purpose.

Held the gifts were valid charitable trusts for purposes beneficial to the community. Romer J stated that the 'care of and consideration for animals which through old age or sickness or otherwise are unable to care for themselves are manifestations of the finer side of human nature'. Accordingly, gifts made in furtherance of such acts were for the benefit of mankind.

7.2.13 Trusts for the aged or impotent

Re Mead's Trust Deed (1961)
Membership of The National Society of Operative Printers and Assistants, a trade union, was confined to persons employed in the printing trade, but not every person engaged in the trade was necessarily a member. The society executed a deed of trust for the provision of a convalescent home for its aged and ill members. No means test was used to select residents of the home.

Held the trust was not exclusively for the relief of poverty. Accordingly it was necessary for the trust to benefit a sufficient section of the community. Residents of the home were restricted to members of the society, accordingly the trust could not take effect as a valid charitable trust. *Oppenheim* (see 7.2.10) followed.

7.2.15 Trusts for private hospitals

Re Resch's Will Trusts (1969) PC
The testator left his residuary estate (then valued around $8m) to trustees upon trust to pay two-thirds of the income 'to the Sisters of Charity for a period of 200 years so long as they shall conduct the St Vincent's Private Hospital'. The hospital did not seek to make a commercial profit, but its charges for treatment, while not necessarily excluding the poor, were not low. On the question whether this was a valid charitable trust.

Held it was a valid charitable trust for purposes beneficial to the community. The requisite public benefit had been satisfied because evidence showed that the public needed accommodation and treatment of the type provided by the hospital. A gift for the purposes of a hospital is *prima facie* a good charitable gift, but the presumption could be rebutted if evidence showed that the hospital was carried on commercially for the benefit of private individuals.

7.3   Recreational trusts

Note ───────────────────────────────
See *Inland Revenue Commissioners v McMullen* and *Re Dupree* (7.2.5).
────────────────────────────────────

Re Hadden (1932)
The testator left the residue of his estate to trustees upon trust to provide 'places of the working people such as playing fields, parks, gymnasiums or other plans which will give recreation to as many people as possible' in the cities of Vancouver and Nottingham.

73

Held this was a valid charitable trust within 'the meaning, purview and interpretation' of the preamble to the Charitable Uses Act 1601.

Inland Revenue Commissioners v Baddeley (1955) HL

Land including a mission church, lecture room and store was given to trustees on trust to permit the leaders of the mission to promote thereon 'the religious, social and physical well-being of persons resident in the county boroughs of West Ham and Leyton ... by the provision of facilities for religious services and instruction and for the social and physical training and recreation of such aforementioned persons who for the time being are in the opinion [of the leaders of the mission] members of or likely to become members of the Methodist Church'.

Held the trust was not for the relief of poverty, for 'relief' implied the meeting of a need or quasi-necessity, such as the provision of a dwelling. Nor could the trust be charitable as being for a purpose beneficial to the community. The trust did not benefit a sufficient section of the public because the beneficiaries had been selected not only by reference to a particular geographical area, but by the further condition that they share a particular creed. Further, promotion of 'religious, social and physical well-being' was too wide a statement of the trust's objects, and accordingly the trust would be void for potentially including non-charitable purposes.

Recreational Charities Act 1958 s 1

(1) the provision of facilities for recreation or other leisure-time occupation shall be charitable if the facilities are provided in the interests of social welfare and for the public benefit.

(2) the 'social welfare' requirement shall not be satisfied unless –

(a) the facilities are provided with the object of improving the conditions of life for the persons for whom the facilities are primarily intended; and

(b) either –

(i) those persons have need of such facilities as aforesaid by reason of their youth, age, infirmity or disablement, poverty or social and economic circumstances; or

(ii) the facilities are to be available to the members or female members of the public at large.

(3) Subject to the said requirement, subsection (1) of this section applies in particular to the provision of facilities at village halls, community centres and women's institutes, and to the provision and maintenance of grounds and buildings to be used for purposes of recreation or leisure-time occupation, and extends to the provision of facilities for those purposes by the organising of any activity.

Re Guild (1992) HL

The testator, G, left the residue of his estate 'to the town council of North Berwick for the use in connection with the sports centre in North Berwick or some similar purpose in connection with sport'. The IRC claimed that the transfer of value was liable to capital transfer tax. The executor appealed, claiming that the gift was for charitable purposes and therefore exempt from the tax.

Held on a proper construction of s 1(2)(a) of the Recreational Charities Act 1958 a gift for the provision of recreational facilities could be charitable notwithstanding the fact that the intended beneficiaries were not in a position of social disadvantage and did not suffer from any particular deprivation. Accordingly, the gift in the present case was a charitable one, the facilities having been provided in the interests of social welfare. In construing the second part of the gift, 'or some similar purpose in connection with sport', it should be presumed that G had intended those other purposes to share the aspects of social welfare provision and public benefit which had been present in the first part of the gift. Such a benignant construction should be applied to deeds whose wording was ambiguous and susceptible to two constructions, one which would render the trust void, the other which would render it a valid charitable trust.

7.4   Trusts for political purposes

Note ───────────────────────────────

In *Bowman v Secular Society Ltd* (1917), Lord Parker stated that '... a trust for the attainment of political objects has always been held invalid, not because it is illegal ... but because the court has no means of judging whether a proposed change in the law will or will not be for the public benefit ...'. The prime reason for refusing charitable status to trusts for political purposes is that courts, whose role it is to enforce the law of Parliament, cannot sanction organisations whose role it is to change the law of Parliament.

Q Is this reasoning valid as an objection to charitable status where an organisation is seeking to alter the law of a foreign state? (See *McGovern v AG*, below.)

National Anti-Vivisection Society v Inland Revenue Commissioners (1947) HL

The society claimed to be exempt from income tax as being 'a body of persons established for charitable purposes only'.

Held the overriding test of charitable status was whether the purposes of the organisation existed for the public benefit. The society failed that test as, on balance, the object of the society was detrimental to the public benefit (Lord Porter dissenting). Further, a prime object of the society was political, namely, to secure the repeal of the Cruelty to Animals Act 1876 and to see it replaced by an enactment absolutely prohibiting vivisection. The court could not award charitable status to a trust for a political purpose. Lord Simonds stated *obiter* that the concept of what is charitable may change from age to age, and that a trust which was once held to be charitable might one day cease to be so, in which case the trust fund should be applied *cy près* (7.6).

Re Hopkinson (1949)

The testator, H, gave his residuary estate to four well-known members of the Labour Party 'as trustees of the educational fund hereinafter mentioned upon trust that they shall stand possessed of the same as an educational fund and shall apply the same ... for the advancement of adult education with particular reference to the following purpose (but in no way limiting their general discretion in applying the fund for adult education), that is to say, the education of men and women of all classes (on the lines of the Labour Party's memorandum headed 'A note on Education in the Labour party', a copy whereof is annexed to this my will and signed by me) to a higher conception of social, political and economic ideas and values and of the personal obligations of duty and service which are necessary for the realisation of an improved and enlightened social civilisation'. The object of the memorandum was to promote the cause of the Labour Party.

Held the trust was not charitable. The direction to refer to the memorandum was the dominating purpose of the trust and was not merely intended to guide the administration of the trust. The judge acknowledged that without the reference to the memorandum the trust would have been a valid charitable trust for the advancement of adult education generally. However, he would not allow what he described as 'political propaganda' to 'masquerade' as education.

Re Strakosch (1949) CA

A testator directed his trustees, by his will, to apply monies 'to a fund for any purpose which in their opinion is designed to strengthen the bonds of unity between the Union of South Africa and the mother country, and which incidentally will conduce to the appeasement of racial feeling between the Dutch and English speaking sections of the South African community'.

Held the expressed purpose of the trust was undoubtedly charitable, but that purpose could be achieved by methods, including the support of political parties, which would not produce charitable benefits in themselves.

Note ————————————————————

The Court of Appeal of 1949 appears to have ignored entirely the fact that Dutch and English speaking sections of the South African community were the ruling minorities of an apartheid regime!

McGovern v Attorney General (1981)

For the facts see 7.2.3.

Held the trust in this case was not a valid charitable trust. A trust for the relief of human suffering was capable of being charitable, but not where a direct and main object of the trust was to secure such relief through attempting to change the laws of a foreign country. Such a trust would be a trust for a political purpose and as such would not be capable of being a valid charitable trust. The judge stated that an English court has 'no adequate means of judging whether a proposed change in the law of a foreign country will or will not be for the public benefit' of the foreign community. The judge also pointed out the risk of prejudicing relations between the United Kingdom and foreign states if English courts passed judgment on foreign regimes. The judge did acknowledge, however, that if the main objects of a charitable trust are non-political it will not cease to be charitable if the trustees have the power to use political means to achieve those non-political ends.

Q Bearing in mind the last point made above, do you think that *Re Strakosch* would be decided differently if it fell for consideration today?

Re Koeppler (1985) CA

The testator, K, came to England from Germany in 1933. After World War II he ran conferences, known collectively (and rather confusingly) as the 'Wilton Park' project, for politicians, academics, civil servants, industrialists and journalists. By his will K left a large part of his estate to 'Wilton Park' for 'as long as Wilton Park remains a British contribution to the formation of an informed international public opinion and to the promotion of greater co-operation in Europe and the West in general ...'. The will provided that, in the event of Wilton Park ceasing to exist, there should be a gift over to a named Oxford college. The Wilton Park conferences were private, unofficial and not intended to follow any party political line. In fact, the law had never acknowledged Wilton Park as an entity, rather it was a sort of movement, or body of thought. Accordingly the gift was bound to fail outright unless it could be shown to be a gift for a charitable purpose. The judge at first instance decided that the gift must fail for vagueness of purpose. The Attorney General appealed.

Held because Wilton Park was not a legal entity K's gift must have been intended to be for purposes of one sort or another. Those purposes must be taken to be the purposes of the Wilton Park project, namely for the advancement of education through the provision of conferences. It followed that this was a valid charitable gift for the advancement of education. The persons attending the conferences would benefit themselves and pass on the benefits of their education to the general public. So far as the conferences touched upon political matters they were merely genuine attempts to objectively ascertain and disseminate truth. The trust was entitled to a 'benignant construction'. In other words, it should be assumed that the trustees would act in accordance with their duties, and would not use the funds to propagate tendentious political opinions.

7.6   Cy près

Note ───
Where a charitable trust cannot be carried out, or is fulfilled leaving a surplus of charitable funds, the doctrine of *cy près* might enable an application of the funds to charitable purposes as near as possible to the purposes intended by the settlor.

Where money has been successfully dedicated to charity the next-of-kin will never be able to assert a claim to it, the *cy près* doctrine will apply even if the particular charitable purpose is subsequently impossible or impracticable to carry out. However, different considerations apply where there is initial failure of the gift.

7.6.1   Initial failure

Note ───
Where a gift fails from the outset the *cy près* doctrine will only save the gift where the donor, in making the gift, had a 'general' or 'paramount' charitable intent. In other words, did the donor desire a charitable outcome by whatever means, or was the particular means specified essential to the donor's intention in making the charitable gift. If the donor's intention is restricted to making a gift for a particular purpose in a particular way, the gift will fail and the subject matter of the gift will result to the donor.

Re Rymer (1895)
R left £5,000 'to the rector for the time being of St Thomas' Seminary for the education of priests in the diocese of Westminster'. At the date of the will the seminary still existed, but it had ceased to exist at the date of R's death. On the question whether the £5,000 could be applied *cy près*:

Held the gift lapsed and resulted to R's residuary estate. Chitty J held that this was a gift for the particular seminary, and not a general gift for the education of the priests in the diocese of Westminster. It was plain from the language used, which referred to the saying of masses and the choice of candidates, that the choice of the seminary was not mere 'machinery' for the carrying out of a general charitable intent, but was the very substance of the testator's gift.

Re Faraker (1912) CA

F, the testatrix, left £200 to 'Mrs Bailey's Charity, Rotherhithe'. The charity, founded in 1756 for the benefit of poor widows of Rotherhithe, had been amalgamated in 1905 with other charities in the area of Rotherhithe.

Held the amalgamated charities would be entitled to the legacy. Not by the doctrine of *cy près*, but because the original charity continued to exist in a slightly modified form.

Re Wilson (1913)

A testator left money to pay the salary of a school master. He was to teach at a specified school according to a syllabus of the testator's design. In the event the school was never built.

Held there was an initial failure and so the doctrine of *cy près* would not apply to save the gift. The fine details of the testator's gift were not consistent with a general charitable intent.

Note ——————————————————————

Contrast *Re Lysaght* (10.3) where in a case of initial failure of a charitable trust the court was able to find (perhaps artificially) a general charitable intention by making only a peripheral alteration to the donor's expressed intentions.

Re Harwood (1936)

The testatrix, H, left £200 to the Wisbech Peace Society, Cambridge and £300 to the Peace of Society of Belfast. The former had ceased to exist before the date of H's death, while the latter had never existed at all.

Held the gift to the Wisbech Peace Society failed and would not be applied *cy près* as H had lacked a general charitable intention in making that gift. As regards the gift of £300, it was held that H had shown a general charitable intention to benefit any society connected with Belfast which existed for the promotion of peace. The gift of £300 was applied *cy près*.

Re Finger's WT (1972)

The testatrix, F, left gifts to an unincorporated association, the National Radium Commission, and to an incorporated company, the National Council for Maternity and Child Welfare.

Held the gift to the former institution was valid as a trust for general charitable purposes, whereas the gift to the company was *prima facie* void as being for a particular legal person which had ceased to exist (see *Re Harwood*). However, Goff J thought the present case to be a special one and distinguished *Re Harwood* on the basis that here the major part of F's estate, including the residue, had been specifically devoted to charitable purposes. Accordingly, the gift to the corporations was validated by the operation of the *cy près* doctrine.

Note

Section 14 of the Charities Act 1993 provides that monies donated to collecting boxes, raffles, entertainments and so on, may be applied *cy près* without having to obtain the donor's consent. As regards other donations, the trustees must advertise and take steps to find the donors and, if they are found, return the donation to them or obtain in writing a waiver of the donor's claims to the donation.

7.6.2 The impossibility/impracticality requirement

Note

Prior to the Charities Act of 1960 the *cy près* doctrine would only be applied where the charitable objects of the trust were impossible or impracticable to fulfil. The 1960 Act relaxed these limitations on the application of *cy près*. The law is now to be found in s 13 of the Charities Act 1993.

Charities Act 1993 s 13

(1) Subject to subsection (2) below, the circumstances in which the original purposes of a charitable gift can be altered to allow the property given or part of it to be applied *cy près* shall be as follows –

(a) where the original purposes, in whole or in part –

(i) have been as far as may be fulfilled; or

(ii) cannot be carried out, or not according to the directions given and to the spirit of the gift; or

(b) where the original purposes provide a use for part only of the property available by virtue of the gift; or

(c) where the property available by virtue of the gift and other property applicable for similar purposes can be more effectively used in conjunction, and to that end can suitably, regard being had to the spirit of the gift, be made applicable to common purposes; or

(d) where the original purposes were laid down by reference to an area which then was but has since ceased to be a unit for some other purpose, or by reference to a class of persons or to an area which has for any reason ceased to be suitable, regard being had to the spirit of the gift, or to be practical in administering the gift; or

(e) where the original purposes, in whole or in part, have, since they were laid down –

(i) been adequately provided for by other means; or

(ii) ceased, as being useless or harmful to the community or for other reasons, to be in law charitable; or

(iii) ceased in any other way to provide a suitable and effective method of using the property available by virtue of the gift, regard being had to the spirit of the gift.

(2) Subsection (1) above shall not affect the conditions which must be satisfied in order that property given for charitable purposes may be applied *cy près* except in so far as those conditions require a failure of the original purposes ...

8 Special categories of trust

8.1 Protective trusts

Note ───

The beneficiary of the typical protective trust has a life interest in the trust fund which will determine if ever the income of the fund becomes payable to someone other than the beneficiary. It follows that the most common 'determining event' will be the personal bankruptcy of the beneficiary. When the life interest determines, a discretionary trust 'springs up' under which the original beneficiary, together with certain members of his or her family, has a hope of being re-appointed as a beneficiary by the trustees of the discretionary trust (Trustee Act 1925 s 33). Thus protective trusts are used to protect beneficiaries from their own folly and from their creditors. Note, however, that, whereas a life interest which is limited to take effect *until* bankruptcy will be valid, a *condition* of a protective trust which purports to determine the life interest *in the event of* the bankruptcy of the life tenant will be void.

Re Balfour's Settlement (1938)
B had a life interest in the income of the settled fund until he should 'do or suffer something whereby the same or some part thereof would through his act or default or by operation or process of law or otherwise ... become vested in or payable to some other person'. It was provided, further, that in the event of determination a discretionary trust would spring up. The trustees paid capital of the fund to B in breach of their trust, and later impounded income due to B in order to remedy that breach.

Held the impounding of the income effected a forfeiture of B's life interest under the terms of the protective trust.

Re Baring's ST (1940)
Mrs B had a protected life interest under a family settlement which provided that income should be paid to her 'until some event should happen whereby the income ... would become ... payable to ... some other person'. A discretionary trust was to arise in the event of determination of the life interest. When Mrs B absconded abroad with the children of the family and ignored a court order to return them to England, Mr B obtained a

court order against her property Eventually Mrs B returned and the question arose whether she had forfeited her life interest.

Held she had forfeited her life interest and was left with a mere hope of an interest under the discretionary trust. The court order against her property had deprived her, albeit temporarily, of her interest in the income of the settlement.

Gibbon v Mitchell (1990)

G had a life interest under a protective trust. On the mistaken advice of his accountants and solicitors, he executed a deed purporting to surrender his life interest in favour of his children. In fact, the surrender amounted to a forfeiture of his life interest under the protective trust, accordingly the trust fund became subject to a discretionary trust in favour of certain other beneficiaries. When the true effect of his surrender became apparent he applied to court to have the deed of surrender set aside.

Held the application was granted and the deed of surrender was set aside under the court's 'equitable jurisdiction to relieve from the consequences of mistake'. Millet J noted that G should have applied in the first place for a variation of the trusts under the Variation of Trusts Act 1958 (9.1.3).

Q Do protective trusts defraud creditors? (See 5.6.1).

8.2   Asset-protection trusts

Note ──────────────────────────────

It is not infrequent in commercial transactions for party A to incur a debt to party B. In such a case A will be subject to a *personal* obligation to re-pay the debt to B. But if A becomes insolvent before re-paying the debt to B, B will have to 'join the cue' of all the creditors with personal claims against A's assets. If, however, A is a trustee (and not merely a debtor) of assets held by A for the benefit of B, the situation is quite different. In such a case B, as beneficiary of the trust, will have *proprietary* rights in those assets. B will no longer have to 'join the cue' of A's general creditors. This is because the assets will be treated as never having belonged to A.

Barclays Bank Ltd v Quistclose Investments Ltd (1970) HL

RR Ltd declared a dividend in favour of its shareholders, but being already heavily overdrawn at its bank (BB Ltd) RR Ltd could not afford to pay the dividends. QI Ltd made a loan of £210,000 to assist RR Ltd, the loan being made upon condition that the monies would be used to pay the dividends. The cheque from QI Ltd was paid into a new account with BB Ltd and BB Ltd agreed that the monies should be held for the sole purpose of paying the dividends at the due date. However, RR Ltd went into liquidation before the due date for payment of the dividends. BB Ltd claimed that the £210,000 should be used to clear some of RR Ltd's overdraft. Against this QI Ltd argued that RR Ltd had held the monies on trust, and now that the trust had failed, the monies should return to QI under a resulting trust.

Held first, the monies were held by RR Ltd on trust for its shareholders, and when that trust failed the monies were held by RR Ltd on resulting trusts for QI Ltd. BB Ltd had notice of that trust and therefore held the monies on trust for QI Ltd. Second, the fact that the transaction, had it succeeded, would have given rise to a standard common law debt owed by RR Ltd to QI Ltd did not preclude the co-existence of a trust remedy in equity.

Re Kayford Ltd (1975)
K Ltd ran a mail order business the customers of which paid either a deposit or the full price in advance. Fearing insolvency, the company was advised to set up a 'Customer's Trust Deposit Account' to hold customers' monies until their goods were delivered to them. In fact, K Ltd paid customers' monies into one of its existing, dormant accounts. Only later was the name of the account changed to 'Customers' Trust Deposit Account'. Soon afterwards K Ltd went into voluntary liquidation. The liquidator raised the question whether the monies in the account belonged to the customers or to K Ltd's other creditors.

Held the subject matter and object of the trust being certain, the crucial question was whether a trust had certainly been intended. In the circumstances the intention to create a trust was manifestly clear. The failure to use the separate account and the word 'trust' did not defeat such a finding.

Carreras Rothmans Ltd v Freeman Mathews Treasure Ltd (1985)
CR Ltd, a cigarette manufacturer, had for many years employed FMT Ltd to advertise its products, for which FMT received an annual fee. The annual fee was paid on a monthly basis. FMT eventually fell into financial difficulties and was unable to meet its own monthly debts to third party agents. Fearing it would lose the custom of CR, FMT set up a special account into which CR would henceforth make its monthly payments and out of which FMT would finance advertising on CR's behalf. Ultimately, however, FMT went into a creditor's voluntary liquidation and the special account was frozen. CR was obliged thereafter to pay FMT's agents directly in order to maintain the advertising campaign. CR brought an action against FMT and its liquidators claiming a declaration that the balance of monies in the special account had been held by FMT on trust to pay for CR's advertising and, that trust having failed, the monies were now held by FMT on resulting trust for CR.

Held the monies in the special account had never been held by FMT for its own benefit, but for a specific purpose. Accordingly, the monies were not available to FMT's general creditors, but were held by the liquidator on trust for CR.

Re EVTR (1987) CA

EVTR Ltd was in trouble financially and B (who had just won a small fortune on his premium bonds) agreed to assist it. He deposited £60,000 with EVTR's solicitors and authorised them to release the monies 'for the sole purpose of buying new equipment'. This they did. However, EVTR went into receivership before the equipment was delivered, the receivers recovering a large part of the monies which had been paid to the equipment suppliers. The trial judge held that the sums recovered should be held as part of the general assets of the company. B appealed.

Held allowing the appeal, B had paid the monies to EVTR for the specific purpose of purchasing equipment. When this purpose failed EVTR held the monies on trust for B. Through merely contracting to purchase the equipment EVTR had not fulfilled the purpose for which the monies had been provided, the true purpose had been the acquisition of equipment, and that had failed. As Dillon LJ put it, 'I do not see why the final whistle should be blown at half time'.

Re Multi Guarantee Co Ltd (1987) CA

MG Ltd was a supplier of insurance for domestic appliances. V Ltd, which owned a chain of retail outlets, collected insurance premiums from customers and paid them to MG. MG kept customer's premiums in a special account, the IBA account. The monies in that account were later paid into a new account and could only be withdrawn by MG and V's solicitors acting together. There was no detailed agreement as to when withdrawals could be made. Eventually, it was determined that the monies should be paid to V, but before this could be done, MG went into liquidation. The trial judge dismissed V's claim that MG had held the monies in the IBA account on trust. V appealed.

Held dismissing the appeal. MG had not manifested a sufficient intention to create a trust as no decision had been made regarding the destination of the monies in the account. The monies would, therefore, be held by the liquidator as part of the general assets of MG.

Mac-Jordan Construction Ltd v Brookmount Erostin Ltd (1992) CA

BE Ltd was a property development company. MJC Ltd was a construction company which had been contracted to carry out certain building works for BE. The contract provided that BE should make interim payments to MJC, but that BE should retain 3% of each interim payment in a retention fund. The contract further provided that BE would hold the retained monies as a trustee for MJC. BE retained the monies (over £100,000) but failed to keep them in a separate fund. BE's banker's had taken a floating charge over all BE's assets, and when BE fell into financial difficulties the bank appointed an administrative receiver under the charge. MJC claimed that the retained monies were held on trust for it, whereas the bank argued that the monies were subject to their charge.

Held the retention fund had not in fact been set up, in spite of the contractual requirement that it should be, and therefore there was no fund which could be said to have been fixed with a trust in favour of MJC Ltd.

8.3 Pension fund trusts

Note ────────────────────────────────

Trusts are used as a vehicle for pension provision precisely because (as we saw in the previous section) if the trustee fund holder becomes insolvent, the persons beneficially entitled to the fund will still be able to claim their share of the pension fund by asserting their property rights in it. Use of trust machinery also brings with it the added advantage of subjecting the pension fund holder to strict equitable obligations.

Report of The Pension Law Review Committee, 'The Goode Report', September 1993, recommendation 103
Pension fund trustees should exercise 'in relation to all matters affecting the fund, the same degree of care and diligence as an ordinary prudent person would exercise in dealing with property of another for whom the person felt morally bound to provide and to use such additional knowledge and skill as the trustee possesses or ought to possess, by reason of the trustee's profession, business or calling'.

Davis v Richards and Wallington Industries Ltd (1990)
A group of companies established a pension scheme for its employees. The companies later fell into financial difficulties and terminated the pension scheme. The surplus in the fund, comprising contributions by employer and employees, amounted to £3m. One of the questions which arose was whether the surplus fund should be held on trust for the companies or for the employees, or should pass as *bona vacantia* to the Crown.

Held (having considered *Re West Sussex* (6.6)) the contractual origin of the rights under the pension scheme was relevant to, but not conclusive of, the question whether a resulting trust would apply to the surplus. A resulting trust solution to the question of distribution would only be excluded by the court if such a solution is expressly or impliedly excluded by the trust instrument. The fact that the employer had made contributions to the scheme under a contractual obligation did not preclude it from recovering its contribution under a resulting trust. However, the employees would not be able to recover their contributions because, *inter alia*, each

87

employee had made a different contribution, and a resulting trust could not work to effect a distribution between them.

British Coal Corp v British Coal Staff Superannuation Scheme Trustees Ltd (1995)

The facts of this case are not of direct relevance here.

Held (*per curiam*) the rule of trust law that a person should not be appointed to be a trustee of a discretionary trust under which they are a potential beneficiary does not apply to pension fund trusts. If an employer has the power to amend a pension fund scheme that power may be exercised in any way which is calculated to promote the purposes of the scheme, even if the amendment might be of direct or indirect benefit to the employer.

Note

See, further, *Mettoy Pension Fund Trusts v Evans* (1991) (12.3.3); *Wilson v Law Debenture Trust Corp plc* (1995) (12.3.5); *Cowan v Scargill* (1985) (13.8); and *Mason v Farbrother* (1983) (13.6).

Part 3 Varying a trust

9 Variation of trusts

Note ───
'The general rule … is that the court will give effect, as it requires the trustees themselves to do, to the intentions of a settlor as expressed in the trust instrument, and has not arrogated to itself any overriding power to disregard or re-write the trusts' *per* Sir Raymond Evershed MR in *Re Downshire's SE* (1953) (see below).

9.1 Modes of variation

9.1.1 Variation by adult beneficiaries

Saunders v Vautier (1841) Master of the Rolls
A testator bequeathed certain stock on trust to accumulate the dividends until V should attain the age of 25, and then to transfer the stock and accumulated income to V. Having reached the age of 21 V claimed to have the entire fund transferred to him.

Held the fund would be transferred as claimed. Where a legacy under a trust is deferred for a period the legatee, if he has an absolute indefeasible interest in the legacy, is not bound to wait until the expiration of that period, but may require payment upon attaining majority.

Note ───
The rule in *Saunders v Vautier* was applied in *Re Brockbank* (10.2.7) and in *Stephenson (Inspector of Taxes) v Barclays Bank Trust Co Ltd* (1975). In the latter case Walton J stated some 'elementary principles' of its application: (1) where persons, being *sui juris*, between them hold the entirety of the beneficial interest under a trust they can direct the trustees as to how to deal with the trust property; (2) but they cannot thereby override the existing trusts and at the same time keep them in existence; (3) so, for

instance, they cannot require the current trustees to make particular investments; (4) nor can they deny the trustees' basic right to be indemnified out of the trust fund for any expenses incurred by them in carrying out the trust.

9.1.2   Variation under s 57 Trustee Act 1925

Trustee Act 1925 s 57(1)

Where in the management or administration of any property vested in trustees, [any transaction] is in the opinion of the court expedient, but the same cannot be effected by reason of the absence of any power for that purpose vested in the trustees by the trust instrument, if any, or by law, the court may by order confer upon the trustees ... the necessary power for the purpose.

Re Downshire's SE (1953) CA

A variation (or 're-moulding') of the beneficial interests under a trust was sought under the court's inherent jurisdiction, under s 57 Trustee Act 1925 and/or under s 64 Settled Land Act.

Held neither the court's inherent jurisdiction nor s 64 was applicable. Section 57 could not be used to sanction the re-moulding of the equitable interests under the trusts, as had been requested, but could only be used to vary the administration of the trust. The reference to property in s 57 meant property vested in the trustees, not the equitable interests which the settlor had created in that property.

Anker-Peterson v Anker-Peterson (1991)

A beneficiary under his father's will trust applied to the court for an order extending the trustees' powers of investment. The application was made under s 57 of the Trustee Act 1925 and, in the alternative, under The Variation of Trusts Act 1958.

Held the order was granted. The judge stated that, where the beneficial interests under a trust would remain unaltered by the variation, as here, it was preferable for the variation to be sought under s 57 of the Trustee Act 1925. This was because, by the 1958 Act, trusts were varied on the basis of the consent of individual beneficiaries, and such consent should not be required to authorise that which was in the trustees' domain, namely the administration of the trust.

9.1.3   Variations under s 53 Trustee Act 1925

Trustee Act 1925 s 53

Where an infant is beneficially entitled to any property the court may, with a view to the application of the capital or income thereof for the maintenance, education or benefit of the infant, make an order –

(a) appointing a person to convey such property; or
(b) in the case of stock, or a thing in action, vesting in any person the right to transfer or call for a transfer of such stock, or to receive the dividends or income thereof, or to sue for and recover such thing in action, upon such terms as the court may think fit.

Re Meux's WT (1957)

G was the life tenant of a will trust, G's sons would take in remainder. When his eldest son was still an infant G applied to court for an order varying the trust. The application was made under s 53 Trustee Act 1925, requesting that a person be appointed to convey the infant's interest to G at a fair price. G would then re-settle the sale proceeds on terms similar to those of the original trust, except G would no longer have an interest under the trust and D would have a contingent interest rather than a vested interest.

Held the court could approve of the variation under s 53 Trustee Act 1925 as an 'application ... for ... the benefit of the infant'.

9.1.4 Variation under the court's inherent jurisdiction in cases of salvage and emergency

Re Jackson (1882)

An infant was absolutely entitled, under certain trusts, to the beneficial interest in real estate held by the trustees. The estate became in urgent need of repair and the trustees applied for a variation in the administration of the trust to meet the repairs.

Held the court had an inherent jurisdiction to direct the raising of money to salvage the estate. It would do this by means of a variation in the administration of the trust which would allow the estate to be used as security for a mortgage.

Re New (1901)

The trustees wished to approve a proposal to reorganise a limited company in which the trust owned shares but they had no power to do so. The beneficiaries could not approve the reorganisation because they were not all *sui juris*, but the reorganisation would certainly have been to their benefit. The trustees applied to the court for a variation under the court's inherent jurisdiction.

Held the court could approve the variation under its inherent jurisdiction to alter the administration of a trust in cases of emergency, where circumstances had arisen which the settlor of the trust had not foreseen and had not made provision for. Such variations would be approved only where the variation was desirable in the best interests of the beneficiaries. But the court would not sanction every act desired by the trustees and beneficiaries merely because it may appear beneficial to the estate.

9.1.5 Variation through compromise of disputes

Chapman v Chapman (1954) HL

A variation was sought to achieve certain tax advantages for infant and unborn beneficiaries. The variation was sought under the court's inherent jurisdiction to compromise disputes.

Held the court could vary a trust under that inherent jurisdiction only in cases of genuine dispute, the jurisdiction could not be used to sanction a bargain made by the beneficiaries *inter se*. The general view of their Lordships was that a so-called 'variation' by compromising a dispute was not really a variation at all, because when a genuine dispute is resolved the compromise-solution ought to represent the proper original state of the trusts as the settlor/testator had intended them. As Lord Morton put it, 'the court's jurisdiction to sanction a compromise in the true sense, when the beneficial interests are in dispute, is not a jurisdiction to alter these interests, for they are still unascertained'. Lord Cohen disagreed on this point, stating that 'the very essence of a compromise is that it may give each party something other than that which the will or settlement would, on its true construction, confer on him'.

Note ────────────────────────────────────

Before the decision in *Chapman v Chapman* the courts had used their inherent jurisdiction to compromise disputes in order to effect variations of beneficial interests in cases where there had been no genuine dispute (as to the construction of the trust instrument) at all. *Chapman v Chapman* removed this large jurisdiction and the Variation of Trusts Act 1958 was passed in response.

9.2 Variation under the Variation of Trusts Act 1958

Variation of Trusts Act 1958 s 1

Where property, whether real or personal, is held on trusts arising, whether before or after the passing of this Act, under any will, settlement or other disposition, the court may if it thinks fit by order approve on behalf of –

(a) any person having, directly or indirectly, an interest, whether vested or contingent, under the trusts who by reason of infancy or other incapacity is incapable of assenting;

(b) any person (whether ascertained or not) who may become entitled, directly or indirectly, to an interest under the trusts as being at a future date or on the happening of a future event a person of any specified description or a member of any specified class of persons, so however that this paragraph shall not include any person who would be of that description, or a member of that class, as the case may be, if the said date had fallen or the said event had happened at the date of the application to the court; or

(c) any person unborn; or

(d) any person in respect of any discretionary interest of his under protective trusts where the interest of the principal beneficiary has not failed or determined,

any arrangement (by whomsoever proposed ...) varying or revoking all or any of the trusts, or enlarging the powers of the trustees of managing or administering any of the property subject to the trusts: provided that except by virtue of paragraph (d) of this subsection the court shall not approve an arrangement on behalf of any person unless the carrying out thereof would be for the benefit of that person.

Note ────────────────────────────────

'The court does not itself amend or vary the trusts of the original settlement. The beneficiaries are not bound because a court has made the variation. Each beneficiary is bound because he has consented to the variation' *per* Lord Reid, *IRC v Holmden* (1968).

Q Can you see why the 1958 Act is said to operate by analogy to the rule in *Saunders v Vautier*?

Re Druce's ST (1962)

The facts of the case are not of central importance here.

Held (*per curiam*) when an application is made to vary the beneficial interests under a trust, the beneficiaries should ordinarily bring the application. The trustees should bring the action only where the application is in the beneficiaries' best interests and no beneficiary can or will make the application.

Re Suffert's Settlement (1960)

An application was made to vary a settlement. Under the original terms of the settlement the applicant had a life interest in the fund under a protective trusts and her children were to take in remainder upon their attaining 21. If she had no children she could exercise a general power of appointment over the remainder in favour of persons of her choosing. In default of exercising the power of appointment the fund would pass to her statutory next-of-kin. At the date of the application her statutory next of kin were three adult cousins. One of these cousins had been joined as a respondent to the application and had given his approval to the proposed arrangement to vary the trusts. The applicant was, in fact, a childless spinster aged 61.

Held the court made an order approving the variation and gave consent on behalf of persons unborn and unascertained who might have become entitled under the terms of the original settlement. However, the judge stated that the order would not be effective to bind the applicant's two adult cousins who had not joined in the application. The court could not consent to the arrangement on their behalf as they fell within the proviso to s 1(1)(b) of the 1958 Act, and they must give their own consent before the arrangement could be binding upon them. The two cousins came within the proviso to s 1(1)(b) because they would have been the applicant's 'next-of-kin' (a 'specified class of persons') had the applicant died (had 'the said event ... happened') at the date of her application to court.

Re Moncrieff's ST (1962)

An application was made to vary a settlement. Under the original terms of the settlement the applicant had a life interest in the fund. On her death the fund was to be held on trust for any of her children that she might appoint under a general power of appointment. In default of such appointment the fund was to be held on trust for purposes or persons appointed by her will. In default of such appointment the fund was to be held for her statutory next-of-kin. The applicant was a widow and her only child was an adopted son; he was joined as the first respondent to the application. Other respondents were four adult cousins of the applicant and the trustees of the settlement.

Held approval was given for the arrangement varying the trusts. The court was able to consent on behalf of the adopted son because he was an infant and the variation would be for his benefit (s 1(1)(a) VTA 1958). The court was also able to consent on behalf of the cousins under s 1 (1)(b), as they were persons who 'may' have become entitled in the future as being the applicant's 'next-of-kin'. Crucially, they would not have been entitled as next-of-kin had the applicant died at the date of the application to court, accordingly the cousins did not fall within the proviso to s 1(1)(b) and their own consent would not be required before approving the proposed arrangement for the variation of the trusts.

Knocker v Youle (1986)

An application was made to vary a settlement. The applicants were the settlor's son and daughter. Under the original terms of the settlement, income was directed to be paid to the daughter at 21, for her life. She had a general power to appoint those who would take after her. In default of appointment the fund would be held on trust for the settlor's four sisters in equal shares, and for the sisters' issue upon the death of any of the sisters. At the date of the application to court the question arose for consideration whether the court could grant its approval to the settlement on behalf of the sisters' numerous issue. They had not been made respondents to the application.

Held the court would not approve the arrangement varying the trusts at this time and the summons was adjourned. The children of the four sisters did not fall within any of the categories of person described in s 1(1) of the 1958 Act on whose behalf the court could give consent. They must give their own consent to the arrangement. Although their interests were very remote and contingent, they nevertheless had more than a mere expectation that they would acquire an interest under the trusts. As Warner J pointed out, 'a person who has an actual interest directly conferred on him or her by a settlement, albeit a remote interest, cannot properly be described as one who "may become" entitled to an interest' (see the wording of s1(1)(b), above).

9.2.1 Meaning of benefit

Re Weston's Settlement (1968) CA

The plaintiff had settled two trusts in favour of his children, but they were subject to certain tax disadvantages. In order to save tax the plaintiff moved with his children to Jersey and, claiming to be resident and domiciled there, he sought a variation of the trusts which would permit them to be exported to Jersey. This would involve the appointment of Jersey trustees and the transfer of the trust property to them.

Held the application would not be allowed. Lord Denning MR stated that 'the court should not consider merely the financial benefit to the infants or unborn children, but also their educational and social benefit. One of these things is to be brought up in this our England, which is still "the envy of less happier lands" ... The avoidance of tax may be lawful, but it is not yet a virtue ... if it really be for the benefit of the children, let it be done. Let them go, taking their money with them, but, if it be not truly for their benefit, the court should not countenance it'.

Note ————————————————————————————————————

Most variations are sought so as to secure tax-planning advantages. Charitable status also brings with it fiscal benefits, but before charitable status is granted a public benefit must nearly always be shown. It might be asked, therefore, whether there is a sufficient benefit to the public in the jurisdiction to vary trusts under the 1958 Act.

Re Tinker's (1960)

An application was made to vary a settlement. The applicant was the settlor, the respondents were his son and daughter, both of whom were beneficiaries under the settlement. The son would take an absolute interest in half the settled fund upon the settlor's death, or upon the son attaining 30, whichever first occurred. If the son died before that age his share would accrue to the daughter. The settlor had applied for the variation because he had not appreciated that, according to the terms of the settlement, if his son pre-deceased him, or failed to attain the age of 30, any children of the son then living would take no interest under the settlement due to the accruer in favour of the sister.

Held the judge refused to approve a variation whereby the accruer clause in favour of the sister would be removed. Such a variation would not be for the benefit of the sister's infant children and unborn issue. The judge was not persuaded by the argument that the proposed variation would yield a substantial non-financial benefit in the form of the family harmony that would flow from bringing the interests of the son's children in line with those of the daughter's children.

Re Remnant's ST (1970)

The testator of a will trusts provided by clauses in his will that any of his grandchildren practising Roman Catholicism at the date of his daughter's death would thereby forfeit any entitlement to the fund. According to the testator's definition, persons 'practice' Roman Catholicism if, *inter alia*, they have attended a Roman Catholic Church for worship at least once a year, or if they marry a Roman Catholic. An application was made to vary the trusts in several respects, including the removal of the forfeiture provision.

Held the court approved of the proposed arrangement for the variation of the trusts. Although the removal of the forfeiture provision carried the risk that certain family members, who would have taken in the event of forfeiture, might be financially worse off as a result of the variation, the variation could still properly be said to be for their benefit in the wider sense of that word, as tending towards familial harmony and freedom of marital choice. The fact that certain of the testator's expressed wishes had been defeated was said to be a 'serious but by no means conclusive consideration'.

Re T's ST (1964)

The applicant had a life interest in half of the trust fund; another quarter was held on trust for the applicant's daughter upon her attaining 21, and the final quarter was to pass to the daughter upon the applicant's death. the applicant sought the court's approval for an arrangement which would vary the trusts by placing the daughter's interest under protective trusts for her life. The application was made due to the daughter's allegedly immature and irresponsible attitude towards money.

Held the court refused to approve of the proposed arrangement, but approved an alternative proposal under which the vesting of the daughter's interest would be postponed until she attained 30. She would hold a protected life interest in the meantime.

9.2.2 Variation must benefit every beneficiary

Re Cohen's ST (1965)

The plaintiff was the only surviving son of the settlor. On the plaintiff's death the whole of the trust fund was to be held on trust for the settlor's grandchildren and their issue. An application was made to vary the trusts by inserting a fixed date in place of the plaintiff's death as a trigger for the grandchildren's trusts. It was improbable that the plaintiff would live beyond the fixed date. The variation was sought under s 1 of the 1958 Act and the court's consent was sought on behalf of the infant beneficiaries (defendants to the application) and on behalf of persons unborn who might become entitled under the trusts.

Held the court would approve the arrangement on behalf of the infant beneficiaries, but the court would not give the consent of persons unborn. In the event that the plaintiff might live beyond the fixed date, persons born after that fixed date would have had an interest under the original trusts but would not have an interest under the proposed new trusts. The court could approve of an arrangement varying the trusts only if every person who might become entitled under the trusts might reasonably be expected to benefit from the variation. Therefore the application to vary the trusts would not be approved in the instant case.

9.2.3   Risk of detriment

Re Holt's Settlement (1968)

The plaintiff, a life tenant under a trust, made an application to vary the trusts under which she held her interest. Under the proposed variation she would surrender half her income as life tenant, which income would be accumulated for her children. According to the original trusts her children were to take in remainder upon their attaining 21; under the proposed variation they would have to attain the age of 30 before their interests would vest in possession. Under the proposed scheme the variation would take place by resettling the income on new trusts with the new terms. The court was asked to approve the arrangement on behalf of persons unborn who might become entitled under the trusts.

Held in deciding whether or not to consent to the proposal on their behalf, the court was entitled to take the sort of risks that an adult beneficiary would have been prepared to take on their own behalf when considering whether to approve the variation. In the present case the variation would be allowed because the chance of a benefit and the risk of detriment was one which an adult beneficiary in the position of the unborn beneficiary would be prepared to take. *Re Cohen's ST* (above) was distinguished. In *Re Cohen's ST* the variation had been refused because the prospects of the unborn beneficiary would have been hopeless whatever events might have occurred.

Re Robinson's ST (1976)

An application was made to vary the terms of a settlement. If approved the new arrangement would carry with it the risk that the beneficiaries might suffer a loss due to certain tax liabilities.

Held approval would be given for the proposed variation provided that some of the infant beneficiary's income entitlement was set aside to purchase insurance cover against the risk of a large capital transfer tax liability.

9.2.4 Variation is permitted, resettlement is not

Re Ball's (1968)

An application was made to vary the terms of a settlement. Under the original terms the settlor had a life interest in the income of the fund, with the power to appoint his two sons (or their families) as beneficiaries in remainder. Neither family was to take more than half of the value of the fund under the power of appointment. Under the terms of the proposed new arrangement the two sons would be given life interests in half of the fund each, then their children would take in equal shares.

Held the new arrangement would be approved as the changes were likely to effect merely the detail of the trust and would not change it in substance. The arrangement could properly be described as a 'variation'. Megarry J stated that, 'the *substratum* of the original trust remains. True, the settlor's life interest disappears; but the remaining trusts are still in essence trusts of half the fund for each of the two named sons and their families'. An arrangement which alters the *substratum* of a trust may effect changes so extensive that the arrangement will not qualify as a 'variation'. Fundamental resettlements are not authorised under the 1958 Act.

Q Consider the facts of *Re Holt's Settlement*, above, was that a variation or a resettlement? Is the distinction between variation and resettlement a logical one?

Q Having reached the end of our consideration of variation of trusts do you think that the law in this area is primarily designed to ensure fidelity to the settlor's intentions or pragmatic derogation therefrom?

Part 4 Filling and fulfilling the office of trustee

---

10 Filling the office of trustee

10.1 General

Note ───

A trust will not fail even if all the trustees die. Nor will a trust fail if, for some other reason, the existing trustees become unfit, unable or unwilling to act. Traditionally this principle has been expressed in the maxim 'a trust does not fail for want of a trustee'.

───

10.2 The appointment of trustees

Trustee Act 1925 s 36(1)

Where a trustee ... is dead, or remains out of the United Kingdom for more than twelve months, or desires to be discharged from all or any of the trusts or powers reposed in or conferred on him, or refuses or is unfit to act therein, or is incapable of acting therein, or is an infant, then, subject to the restrictions imposed by the Act on the number of trustees –

(a) the person or persons nominated for the purpose of appointing new trustees by the instrument, if any, creating the trust; or

(b) if there is no such person, or no such person able and willing to act, then the surviving or continuing trustees or trustee for the time being, or the personal representatives of the last surviving or continuing trustee;

may, by writing, appoint one or more other persons (whether or not being the persons exercising the power) to be a trustee or trustees in the place of the trustee so deceased remaining out of the United Kingdom, desiring to be discharged, refusing, or being unfit or incapable, or being an infant, as aforesaid.

10.2.1 By persons nominated in the trust instrument

Re Wheeler and De Rochow (1896)

A marriage settlement nominated DeR for the purpose of appointing new trustees upon the happening of certain events, which events did not include a trustee becoming unfit to act in the trust. One of the trustees was declared bankrupt and was thus unfit to act as a trustee. DeR purported to appoint a new trustee in place of the bankrupt trustee.

Held the appointment should not have been made by DeR, but by the continuing trustees, according to Trustee Act 1893 s 10 (now Trustee Act 1925 s 36(1)). The events upon which a nominated appointer may appoint new trustees will include all the events listed in s 36(1) unless the trust instrument expressly or impliedly provides for a more limited list.

Re Power's Settlement Trusts (1951) CA

P was tenant for life under a settlement which nominated him as the person empowered to appoint new trustees in accordance with s 36(1). The three original trustees where still in office when P purported to appoint himself as an additional, fourth trustee.

Held the appointment was invalid. Subsection 36(1) only permits the appointment of new trustees in the event of a vacancy arising, which had not occurred in this case. And s 36(6), which authorises the appointment of additional trustees up to a maximum of four even when no vacancy has arisen, did not permit the nominated appointer to appoint himself. The crucial words 'whether or not being the persons exercising the power' which are found in s 36(1) do not appear in s 36(6).

10.2.2 Where the nominated appointer is an infant

Re Parsons (1940)

A settlement vested the power of appointing new trustees in the settlor during his lifetime and after his death in his son. After the death of the settlor the original trustee died and it fell to the son to appoint another, the son still being an infant. He purported to appoint his mother as sole trustee to fill the vacancy in the trust.

Held the appointment was invalid. Appointments made by infants would not be upheld if shown to have been made imprudently or against the interests of the infant. The appointment of the mother was invalid because she would have no compulsion to account to anybody, and her duty to the trust was bound to clash with her private interests.

10.2.3 Appointment by the current trustees

Note ———————————————————————————
See s 36(1) Trustee Act 1925 (10.2).

10.2.4 Appointment by the personal representatives of the current trustees

Note ───────────────────────────────────

See s 36(1) Trustee Act 1925 (10.2).

10.2.5 Appointment by the court

Trustee Act 1925 s 41(1)

The court may, whenever it is expedient to appoint a new trustee or new trustees, and it is found inexpedient difficult or impractical to do so without the assistance of the court, make an order appointing a new trustee or new trustees either in substitution for or in addition to any existing trustee or trustees, or although there is no existing trustee ...

Re May's WT (1941)

The testator appointed three trustees of his will trust. One of the trustees, his widow, happened to have been in Belgium at the date of the German invasion. The other two trustees took out a summons to establish whether they were empowered to appoint new trustees in her place.

Held the continuing trustees did not have the power to appoint new trustees, because there was nothing to suggest that the widow was 'incapable of acting' within the meaning of s 36(1) (which envisages, for example, mental or bodily incapacity). It would therefore be inexpedient, difficult or impractical to make an appointment without the assistance of the court. The court undertook to appoint a new trustee.

10.2.6 Factors guiding appointments by the court

Re Tempest (1866) CA

The will of Sir T appointed S and F as trustees of certain real estates. A codicil to the will appointed S, F and Lord C as trustees of certain charitable trusts. S predeceased Sir T Fleming and AT (Sir T's uncle) were empowered by the will to appoint new trustees of the real estates, but they could not agree upon a replacement trustee. Most of the beneficiaries concurred with AT's choice but F opposed it on the grounds that the proposed new trustee was connected to a branch of the family with whom Sir T had not been on friendly terms. The surviving trustees of the charitable trusts were, on the other hand, able to agree upon a replacement trustee of those trusts.

Held the trustee proposed by AT should not be appointed to the trusts. Certain principles were laid down to guide appointments by the court. First, if clear from the trust instrument, the court will have regard to the wishes of the person by whom the trust has been created. Secondly, the court will not appoint a trustee where some of the beneficiaries oppose the appointment, because of the risk that the trustee so appointed might breach his duty to act impartially as between all the beneficiaries. Thirdly, the court will ask itself whether the appointment of the particular person as trustee will impede the execution of the trust. The present case was disposed of on the second point. As regards the third, the judge made it clear that if the current trustees threatened to refuse to co-operate with a proposed new trustee this would not in itself be a ground for refusing to appoint the new trustee, but may be a ground to remove the current trustees from office.

10.2.7 Appointment of trustees by beneficiaries?

Re Brockbank (1948)
A will trust settled the testator's residuary estate upon trustees for his wife for her life and her children after her death. One of the trustees desired to be discharged from the trust and the beneficiaries wanted a bank to be appointed in his place. The retiring trustee was happy to appoint the bank but the continuing trustee refused to concur in the appointment. The retiring trustee joined the beneficiaries in taking out a summons requesting that the continuing trustee be required to concur in appointing the bank.

Held the beneficiaries had two options, either they must bring the trusts to an end (in accordance with the rule in *Saunders v Vautier* (9.1.1)), in which event they could re-settle the trust property on new trustees of their choice, or they must abide by the decision of the continuing trustee. The beneficiaries had no authority (under *Saunders v Vautier* or otherwise) to control the exercise by the trustee of his discretion. The first alternative, to bring the trusts to an end and to resettle them on new trustees, would attract tax disadvantages and would in practice not be advisable.

10.2.8 Limits on the number of trustees

Note ───
The maximum number of trustees permitted in private trusts of land is four, whereas for charitable trusts and trusts of pure personalty there is strictly speaking no upper limit to the number of trustees. As we saw above, s 36(1) Trustee Act 1925 legislates for the appointment of 'replacement' trustees, but where 'additional' trustees are appointed (beyond the original number of trustees) the maximum number of trustees post-appointment is limited to four (s 36(6) Trustee Act 1925).

10.3 Disclaimer of the trust

Note ───
A trustee is not obliged to accept the office of trustee. He or she may disclaim the office. If all the named trustees refuse to act the trust will gen-

erally result to the settlor (*Mallot v Wilson* (1901)). Sheer inactivity on the part of the trustee may amount to a disclaimer but the merest activity in service of the trust will be taken to be an acceptance of office, after which it will be too late to disclaim. It is recommended that trusts be disclaimed by deed.

Re Lord and Fullerton's Contract (1896) CA
A testator having real and personal property in England and abroad left his residuary estate to trustees upon trust for sale. One of the trustees disclaimed the trusts of the will except as to the property abroad. The remaining trustees sold land of the testator in England.

Held the disclaimer had no effect, and the disclaiming trustee was a necessary party to the conveyance. Partial disclaimer of the office of trustee is not permitted. If it were, purchasers of trust property from trustees would be unsure of the trustees' title to sell.

Note ———
Disclaimer can render a trust void *ab initio* ('from the start'). In *Re Lysaght* (1966) the testatrix settled the net residue of her estate on the Royal College of Surgeons as trustee for the charitable purposes of the college. The college threatened to disclaim the trusteeship unless certain conditions were removed from the gift. The court removed the conditions, stating that the gift would otherwise fail. The gift was applied *cy près* (see 7.6).

Q Does the judgment in *Re Lysaght* conflict with the principle that a trust does not fail for want of a trustee?

10.4 Retirement from the trust

Note ———
Retirement is the decision, made voluntarily, to relinquish the office of trustee. Trustees may retire whenever the trust instrument empowers them to do so, whenever the court consents to a retirement, or by obtaining the consent of all the beneficiaries (provided that the beneficiaries are *sui juris*). Apart from these instances, the Trustee Act 1925 details two modes of retirement.

10.4.1 Retirement under s 36(1) Trustee Act 1925

Note ———
A trustee who desires to be discharged may retire under this section provided that another trustee is appointed in his place. See 10.2 above.

10.4.2 Retirement under s 39(1) Trustee Act 1925

Note

This section applies where no new trustee will be appointed in the place of the retiring trustee.

Trustee Act 1925 s 39(1)

Where a trustee is desirous of being discharged from the trust, and after his discharge there will be either a trust corporation or at least two individuals to act as trustees to perform the trust, then, if such trustee as aforesaid by deed declares that he is desirous of being discharged from the trust, and if his co-trustees and such other person, if any, as is empowered to appoint trustees, by deed consent to the discharge of the trustee, and to the vesting in the co-trustees alone of the trust property, the trustee desirous of being discharged shall be deemed to have retired from the trust, and shall, by the deed, be discharged therefrom under this Act, without any new trustee being appointed in his place.

10.4.3 Liability of trustees after retirement

Head v Gould (1898)

This case concerned the marriage settlement of Mr and Mrs H, the settlement being on terms for their successive lives with powers of appointment in favour of any children they might have, which powers were never exercised. In default of appointment the fund would pass to any children they might have in equal shares upon their attaining the age of 21 or earlier marriage. A post-nuptial settlement was also made, by Mrs H, in similar terms. Mr H died leaving his widow and three children. One of the trustees of the marriage settlement retired and Mrs H appointed Mr C in his place. Mr C and Mr H were now the trustees of the marriage settlement, and some years later the retiring trustee of the post-nuptial settlement appointed them trustees of that settlement also. Mrs H got into financial difficulties and at her request the trustees discharged certain of her debts out of the trust funds by making a large cash advance. The trustees took securities for the advance, but the securities amounted to unauthorised investments. Further cash advances were made with some regularity until the whole of her entitlement had been advanced to Mrs H. In the event, the trustees handed the trusteeship over to Mrs H's daughter and to Mr G, a solicitor and family friend. After their appointment breaches of trust ensued and the interest of an infant beneficiary was lost.

Held the retired trustees would not be held liable for the breaches of their successors. Liability will only arise in such a case if the retired trustees are proven to have actually contemplated the breaches of trust which had occurred. It is not sufficient to show, merely, that the retirement facilitated the breach. In the present case the judge found that the retiring trustees did not believe, and had no reasonable ground for believing, that the trust would be anything but secure in the hands of their successors.

Re Boles (1902)
One of the trustees of a will trust retired from office by deed and with the consent of the continuing trustees. Twelve years later the continuing trustees sold land owned by the trust to the trustee who had retired. The question arose whether the sale was valid or should be set aside.

Held the sale was valid. A trustee may not retire with a view to doing that which would be a breach of trust had he remained a trustee, but if there is no evidence that the particular transaction was contemplated at the time of the retirement, there is nothing preventing the transaction from being carried out later. How much later was not specified, the judge holding, merely, that there must have been 'no idea' of a purchase at the date of retirement.

10.5   Removal of trustees

Re Lemann's Trusts (1883)
The testator's widow, one of the trustees of his estate, had become, through age and infirmity, incapable of executing the documentation necessary for the proper discharge of her duties under the trust.

Held the court had jurisdiction, under a statutory precursor to Trustee Act 1925 s 41, to appoint a new trustee in the widow's place.

Letterstedt v Broers (1884) PC
The plaintiff sought the removal of a corporate trustee on the grounds of various acts of 'misconduct and malversation' entered into with corrupt motive by the members of the corporation. The members were said to have, *inter alia*, invested in a particular business with a view to profiting from commissions which they had since received from the business; and which commissions were, in addition, said to have been wrongly inflated.

Held the trustee was removed from office. To warrant the removal of the trustees their acts or omissions must endanger the proper administration of the trust. Courts should exercise their jurisdiction according to the facts of each case with a view to meeting the beneficiaries' best interests. Lord Blackburn stated that the hostility of beneficiaries to their trustees was not of itself a reason for removing the trustees but was a factor to be taken into account, and that trustees who 'shew a want of honesty, or a want of capacity to execute their duties, or a want of reasonable fidelity' would be removed.

Re Henderson (1940)
The testator's widow and his niece were the sole beneficiaries of his estate, they were also the only trustees. Due to differences arising between them,

the widow stated her intention to retire from the trust, provided that the Public Trustee was appointed in her place. The niece concurred in this course of action. Later the widow added further conditions to her retirement, namely that the work of the trust be carried out in the Public Trustee's office and that independent solicitors be appointed. The niece took out a summons under s 41 requesting that the widow be replaced by the Public Trustee. The widow resisted the application.

Held the widow was removed from office and the Public Trustee appointed in her place. Bennet J acknowledged that the removal of trustees was a delicate matter and that whenever there is some dispute as to some fact alleged against a trustee the court should be reluctant to remove the trustee if they wish to continue in office. In the present case, however, there was no dispute as to the facts alleged. His lordship removed the widow because she had no reasonable grounds for changing her mind regarding the conditions attaching to her retirement. The Public Trustee was appointed because it was expedient to appoint a new trustee and impracticable to do so without the assistance of the court.

11 Fulfilling the role of trustee

11.1 Upon appointment

Note ————————————————

The new trustee is especially vulnerable, like a cricketer who has just come in to bat. The trustee ought promptly to become familiar with the terms of the trust, in order to identify all the beneficiaries and their respective entitlements. The trustee should also take steps to act on any suspicious circumstances, which may involve bringing a suit against other (perhaps retired) trustees of the trust, although only if there is a reasonable expectation that such action would prove fruitful. The trustee must also 'get in' any trust property which is not yet under their control.

Re Brogden (1888)

In this case a trustee failed to 'get in' certain monies due to the trust. Indeed, he waited so long before attempting to get the funds in that the trust suffered a loss of £17,250 (no small sum in 1888).

Held the trustee had breached his trust by failing to take action to get in the funds. He was obliged to sue for their recovery unless he had reasonable grounds for believing that an action would be fruitless. The burden rested on the trustee to show that such belief was reasonably held. The onus was on the trustee to show that the loss would have occurred despite his breach, and in the present case that defence had not successfully been made out.

11.2 The fiduciary nature of trusteeship

Note ————————————————

A fiduciary relationship is one in which the fiduciary owes to the other party a special duty to act in good faith. The fiduciary aspects of relationships such as employer/employee; director/company; agent/principal are defined by analogy to the relationship of trustee to beneficiary. The trust is the fiduciary relationship *par excellence*.

11.2.1 Conflict of interest and duty

Note

An important aspect of the fiduciary nature of trusteeship is that trustees must not put themselves in a position where there might be a conflict between their self-interest or duties to others, and their duties to the trust.

Williams v Scott (1900) PC

A purchaser of land brought this action against the vendor. The purchaser sought rescission of the contract of sale on the basis that the vendor had acquired his title by purchasing the land off a trust of which the vendor was trustee.

Held it would be inequitable to force the purchaser to complete the purchase, the vendor's title having been obtained through 'self-dealing' (see *Re Thompson's Settlement* (below)). The result would probably have gone in the vendor-trustee's favour had he purchased the land from the beneficiaries with their full assent, or if the vendor-trustee had completed a sale of the land to a third party in his capacity as trustee and had later purchased the land off that third party. However, neither of these answers to a complaint of 'self-dealing' could be made out on the facts of the present case, the trustee having purchased the land directly off the trust. Sir Ford North stated that the onus in such a case is on the trustee to show that the transaction is a 'righteous one'.

Re Mulholland's Will Trusts (1949)

The testator, M, leased land to a bank together with an option to purchase the freehold. M later appointed the bank and his widow to be the executors and trustees of his estate. Sometime later the bank exercised its option to purchase the freehold by giving notice to that effect. The beneficiaries brought an action seeking to have the conveyance set aside on the grounds that it had been made in breach of the bank's fiduciary duties.

Held the notice exercising the option to purchase the freehold did not create a new contractual relationship between the bank and the trust. The bank's contract to purchase had in essence arisen before the bank had been placed in its position as trustee. The bank would therefore be permitted to exercise the option.

Wright v Morgan (1926) PC

A trustee arranged to purchase trust-owned land from the other trustees of a will trust. He later retired from the trust and purchased the land at a price pre-determined by independent valuers. An action was brought by the beneficiaries seeking to set aside the sales and to call the trustee to account for the profits he had made from his position as trustee.

Held the sale was set aside. The trustees could not sell trust property to one of their number without a conflict of interest and duty arising. Viscount Dunedin held that whether the trustee had actually paid a fair or unfair price was irrelevant, 'the criterion ... is not what was done, but what might be done'.

Holder v Holder (1968) CA

The testator, H, had a younger son, V. V had held a tenancy in one of H's farms for some years. By H's will, V was appointed one of the executors of that farm and various other farms. After his father's death V purported to renounce his executorship in order to purchase the other farms (in fact the renunciation was formally ineffective). In due course the farms were obtained by V at public auction, whereby he contracted to purchase them at a fair price. However, upon failing to complete the purchase deed on time, V's elder brother, F, pressed the executors to re-sell the farms. They refused to do so. Eventually the sale of the farms to V was completed and the executors accounted to F for his share of the proceeds. Not being satisfied with this, F brought an action claiming rescission of the sale and a declaration that the farms should be re-sold with vacant possession. The judge held that because V's purported renunciation of his executorship had been ineffective V fell foul of the rule that a trustee must not purchase trust property off the trust. V appealed.

Held allowing the appeal, V had had only very limited dealings with the trust estate before his purported renunciation of the executorship, accordingly whatever he had learned about the properties he had learned in his capacity as tenant of one of the farms and not as trustee. The court held that 'in the very special circumstances of this case' there was 'in fact' no conflict between the trustee's duty to the trust and his self-interest.

Q Is the decision in this case consistent with the principle in *Wright v Morgan*, above, that a sale by trustees to themselves must be set aside if there 'might be' a conflict of duty and interest? It is generally accepted that the judgment in *Holder v Holder* should be restricted to the facts of that case.

Re Thompson's Settlement (1986)

The settlor, T, declared trusts of the sale proceeds of certain freehold properties which had been conveyed to trustees. At the date of the settlement the properties were let to a farming corporation of which T was the managing director. Other directors included T's sons, W and J, who were also trustees of the settlement. After T's death a meeting was held between W, J, their solicitor and the auditors of the farming corporation. At that meeting it was agreed that the corporation's tenancies of the various properties should be assigned to the businesses of W and J respectively, one business being a company, the other a partnership. The corporation was wound up without ever having formally consented to the assignments of the leases, and without having made any formal assignment of them. Some time later the family adopted a plan to distribute the properties amongst all the family members. In order to do this fairly it was necessary to make an accurate valuation of each of the properties. The valuations would be dramatically affected by W and J's leases if they were valid, the unencumbered freehold of the farm being more valuable than a freehold subject to a lease. W and J took out a summons to determine whether the tenancies would be voidable at the instance of a beneficiary even if the assignments had been fair.

Held according to the 'self-dealing rule' a trustee's purchase of trust property off the trust is voidable *ex debito justitiae* (out of a debt to justice). Accordingly such a purchase would be set aside if any beneficiary wished it to be so set aside. It would be no defence to such an action for the trustee to show that the purchase had been fair or even generous to the beneficiaries. Nor would it be a defence, on the facts of the present case, to argue that the leases had never, in fact, been trust property (but had been property of the corporation). Nor could it be argued that the leases had not been taken by W and J personally, but had been taken by the businesses controlled by them. (In spite of the fact that one of those, being a company, was an independent legal person.) The 'self-dealing' rule should not be narrowly construed, it is an application of the wider principle that trustees must not put themselves into a position where their duties and self-interests may be in conflict, or where their duties to one may conflict with their duties to another. The principle is applied strictly where a trustee concurs in a transaction which cannot be carried into effect without his concurrence and who has a personal interest in or owes a fiduciary duty to another in relation to the same transaction.

Note —————————————————————————————————

'Self-dealing' (purchases by trustees off the trust) should be contrasted with 'fair dealing' (purchases by trustees off adult beneficiaries). The latter transaction will not be set aside if the trustees can prove that they have taken no advantage of their position as trustees.

Sargeant and Another v National Westminster Bank Plc (1990) CA

A testator let a number of farms to his children which they worked as a partnership. He then appointed his children to be executors and trustees under his will. When one of the children died the surviving children exercised an option to purchase the deceased child's share of the partnership. Later they revealed plans to purchase the freehold of one of the farms of which they were tenants, and to sell the other freeholds. The administrators of the estate of the deceased child objected to these plans and argued that the surviving children would be in breach of their trust were they to sell, to themselves, the trust-owned freeholds of which they were trustees and under which they were tenants. The trustees sought a declaration that they would be entitled to sell the freeholds. This declaration was granted. The administrators appealed.

Held the trustees were in a position where their interest as tenants might conflict with their duties as trustees but they had not *put themselves* in that position. The trustees' rights as tenants pre-dated their duties as trustees and they would therefore be permitted to assert those rights. They must nevertheless endeavour to obtain the best price for the freeholds in order to fulfil their obligations to the trust.

11.2.2 The standard of care required of trustees

Speight v Gaunt (1883) CA

The testator, S, had been a 'stuff manufacturer' at Bradford. In his will he bequeathed his estate to Messrs G and W upon certain trusts for the benefit of Mrs S and her children. The trustees employed a stockbroker, C, to sell some securities forming part of the estate and to reinvest the proceeds in new securities. C was a broker of high repute. Having placed with the agent the securities to be sold, G made enquiries of C on many occasions as to when the new securities would be handed over to the trust. C gave excuses on these occasions. Eventually C declared his firm insolvent and was declared personally bankrupt. £15,275 of trust monies were lost. Mrs S brought an action seeking a declaration that G had breached his trust and seeking an order requiring him to account for the lost funds, together with interest at 4%.

Held the Vice-Chancellor gave judgment for the beneficiaries at first instance. This was overturned by the Court of Appeal. The judgment of the Court of Appeal was later affirmed by the House of Lords. In the Court of Appeal it was established that a trustee ought to conduct the 'business of the trust' in the same manner that an ordinary prudent man of business would conduct their own. Applying that test to the present case it was held that C had been properly appointed and that the trustee had acted prudently in his attempts to recover the trust property. Jessel MR stated: 'You are to endeavour as far as possible, having regard to the whole transaction, to avoid making an honest man *who is not paid* for the performance of an unthankful office liable for the failure of other people from whom he receives no benefit' (emphasis added).

Q What do you think is meant by the 'business of the trust'? Does the next case provide an answer?

Re Whiteley (1886) CA

Trustees had invested in a mortgage of a freehold brickfield on the advice of expert valuers, but the valuer's report had been based on wrong information. The trustees acted on the report in good faith but had not checked its accuracy by means of other inquiries.

Held the trustees had failed to act with ordinary prudence and would be liable to account for the losses to the trust together with interest at 4%. Lindley LJ stated that 'duty of a trustee is not to take such care only as a prudent man would take if he had only himself to consider; the duty rather is to take such care as an ordinary prudent man would take if he were minded to make an investment for the benefit of other people for whom he felt morally obliged to provide. That is the kind of business the ordinary prudent man is supposed to be engaged in'.

Note
See 8.3 for a standard of care proposed for pension fund trustees.

Jobson v Palmer (1893)

J, who was greatly in debt, conveyed nearly all his property to P to hold on trust for J's numerous creditors. Certain losses were caused to the 'trust property' in the hands of an agent, L, appointed by P to assist him. The question arose whether P should be judged according to the standard of the ordinary prudent man of business, or whether some higher standard should apply because P had been remunerated for performance of the trust.

Held trustees' liability is not increased by virtue only of the fact that they are remunerated. The principle in *Speight v Gaunt* should be applied to paid trustees despite the fact that the judges in that case had made express reference to the fact that the trustee in that case had been unpaid.

Buttle v Saunders (1950)

Trustees for sale of certain land had reached an advanced stage of their negotiations for the sale of the land to Party A when Party B made a higher offer. The trustees refused the higher offer, believing themselves to be bound by commercial morality to complete with Party A.

Held the trustees had wrongly assumed that they could act like an ordinary beneficial owner of property. The trustees had breached their duty to obtain the best price for the beneficiaries.

Re Rosenthal (1972)

A testator made a specific devise of a house to his sister, B. The residue of his estate he left to his wife, subject to his trustees first paying off his debts and testamentary expenses. The trustees transferred the house to B who sold it and emigrated to Israel without paying estate duty which was owing on the house. The trustees paid the duty out of the residue of the estate. The wife brought an action against the trustees seeking a declaration that the trustees should not have paid the estate duty out of her interest. The trustees sought to defend their actions by arguing that the estate duty was a 'testamentary expense' and could, therefore, be paid out of the residue.

Held the estate duty was not a 'testamentary expense'. The payment out of the residue was, accordingly, a breach of trust. The monies could not be recovered from B and so the question remained, where should the loss fall as between the plaintiff wife and the defendant trustees? It was held that the trustees must be liable even though they had acted in all other respects to the benefit of the estate, and had acted honestly throughout. As between an innocent beneficiary and a trustee in breach, the loss should fall on the trustee.

Re Waterman's WT (1952)

Lloyd's Bank had been appointed trustee by the will trust of the testatrix. The trust included a charging clause which permitted the bank to charge remuneration in accordance with its usual terms of business. In due course the bank deposited all the trust monies with itself, but failed over a number of years to make any investment of the monies. A summons was taken out for directions as to the proper administration of the trust.

Held the bank had shown a want of judgment, but it was not open to the court, on the summons in its present form, to find the bank liable for breach of trust. The judge did state, however, that 'a paid trustee is expected to exercise a higher standard of diligence and knowledge than an unpaid trustee, and that a bank which advertises itself largely in the public press as taking charge of administrations is under a special duty'.

Bartlett v Barclays Bank Trust Co Ltd (1980)

The settlor, B, had settled 99.8% of the shares in a private company ('BTL') on trust for his wife and issue. The trustee of the settlement was a Barclays Bank trust corporation. By 1960 B and his wife had both died and no member of B's family remained on the board of BTL. Neither did any members of the board regard themselves as representatives of the trust corporation. At various meetings the chairman of BTL put forward specific property development projects for the board's consideration, and without consulting the bank, invested heavily in two of the projects. One of these projects (at Guilford) made a substantial profit, but the other (at the Old Bailey, London) made a significant loss. The market value of shares in BTL fell causing a great loss to the trust. The beneficiaries brought an action against the trustee to make good the losses.

Held the bank was liable for breach of its trust. It had failed to act as an ordinary prudent person of business would have acted in relation to his own affairs. Moreover, a professional, corporate trustee such as the bank owed an even higher standard of care than that and would be liable to the extent that it failed to exercise the higher standard of care it professed to have. Brightman J did not refer to *Jobson v Palmer* but tacitly appeared to have accepted counsel's submission (based on *Jobson v Palmer*) that the fact of remuneration should not be a conclusive in determining the appropriate standard of care, but might well be a factor against granting the trustee relief (15.3.4) where a breach has been proven. A corporate trustee which is the majority shareholder in a company has a duty to ensure that it is represented on the board of the company and should ensure that it receives an adequate flow of information from the board. The trust company in the present case had failed to do so and had thus been unable to prevent the company's failed investment in the speculative property developments.

11.2.3 Liability limited by the trust instrument

Re Brier (1882) CA

Trustees had empowered an agent to collect certain debts. The agent collected the debts but failed to account for them to the trustees. The agent became insolvent and the debts were thereby lost to the trust. A clause in the trust instrument limited the trustees' liability to losses arising from the executors' own wilful default.

Held the presence of the clause limiting the executors' liability had the effect of shifting the burden of proof onto the plaintiffs to show that the loss was attributable to the trustees' default. This they had failed to do and the trustees were held not liable.

Rae v Meek (1889) HL

The defendant trustee was held liable for a positive breach of trust, but sought to rely upon a 'clause of immunity' contained in the trust deed.

Held the clause would not protect the trustee in this case. The trustee had acted honestly and with good motive, but he had nevertheless acted in direct violation of his trust. An exemption clause could not provide immunity for such a breach. Further, any clause which purports to exempt a trustee from liability will be ineffectual to protect a trustee against any consequences of gross negligence on his part, or of any conduct which is inconsistent with *bona fides*.

Hayim v Citibank NA (1987) PC

A testator made two wills, one dealing primarily with his American property, another with property outside of America (this latter was called the 'Hong Kong' will). The first defendant was executor and trustee of the American will, the second defendant was executor and trustee of the Hong Kong will. The plaintiffs directed the second defendant to sell a house in Hong Kong, where the testator's elderly brother and sister were living. The brother and sister were not entitled under either will to remain in the house and a sale of the house would have been for the benefit of the beneficiaries of the American will. Nevertheless, the first defendant directed the second defendant not to sell the house. When the house was eventually sold it had fallen in value, causing a loss to the beneficiaries of the American will.

Held on the question whether the second defendant was liable for delaying the sale of the house, there had been no breach of trust, because the second defendant owed no duty to the beneficiaries of the American will. On a proper construction of the trust, the second defendant was actually obliged to act on the instructions of the first defendant. As regards the liability of the first defendant, clause 10 of the American will expressly relieved the first defendant of any 'responsibility or duty' to the 'American' beneficiaries with respect to the house.

Bishop v Bonham (1988) CA

This case involved a chargee (mortgagee) rather than a trustee so-called. However, their Lordships drew a direct analogy between the two situations. The defendant had granted the plaintiff a charge over certain shares as security for a loan granted by the plaintiff. The terms of the charge permitted the plaintiff to sell the shares as he 'may think fit' in the event of the defendant defaulting in repayment of the loan. The defendant did in fact default and the plaintiff purported to sell the shares in accordance with the terms of the charge. However, the defendant refused to execute a transfer of the shares, considering the sale to be at an undervalue. The plaintiff brought the matter to court with a view to obtaining specific performance of the charge.

Held specific performance was refused. The sale was at an undervalue. Although the plaintiff had been expressly authorised to realise the security as he 'may think fit', such a discretion must be read as subject to the implicit limitation that it is to be exercised properly, within the limits of the duty of care imposed by the general law, that is to say, with the exercise of reasonable care to obtain a proper price.

Note ─────────────────────────────

Although the above cases illustrate that exemption clauses, and clauses limiting the trustee's duties, standards of care and liability, may not be used to exclude certain basic requirements of good faith which are essential to all trusts, it is nevertheless true that such clauses can be (and frequently are) used by professional trustees to lower (below the *Speight v Gaunt* standard) the standard of care owed by them. The rather peculiar result follows that professional trustees, who are paid and profess expertise, are frequently subject to a lower standard of care than that which applies to the non-professional trustee, 'who accepts, probably unpaid and sometimes reluctantly from a sense of family duty, the burdens of trusteeship', *per* Harman J, *Re Waterman's WT* (11.2.2).

12 Duties of trusteeship

12.1 Duty to act gratuitously

12.1.1 General

Bray v Ford (1896) HL

The case involved an action in libel and the appeal was based on the fact that the judge had misdirected the jury in some material aspect of the case. The case is referred to because of an important statement made by Lord Herschell in the course of his speech.

Held it is an inflexible rule of equity that a person in a fiduciary position is not entitled to profit from their position in the absence of express provision to the contrary in the trust instrument. The rule was said to be based on the consideration that 'human nature being what it is' there is a danger that a person in a fiduciary position might otherwise be swayed by self-interest rather than duty to the trust.

Note ──────────────────────────────────────

The duty to act gratuitously is derived from, or correlates with, the rule that trustees must not profit from their trust. In keeping with this duty trustees are not entitled, according to the general law, to be remunerated for their services. There is nothing, however, to prevent trustees from recovering their reasonable expenses from the trust fund.

12.1.2 Recovery of expenses incurred by trustees

Trustee Act 1925 s 30(2)

A trustee may reimburse himself or pay or discharge out of the trust premises all expenses incurred in or about the execution of the trusts or powers.

Hardoon v Belilios (1901) PC

H was the registered owner of certain shares in a bank. He held the shares for the benefit of the absolute beneficial owner, B. When the bank went insolvent the liquidator demanded certain payments of H. H paid these 'calls' made upon him in his capacity as legal owner of the shares.

Held a beneficial owner of property, being *sui juris*, must indemnify the legal owner of that property against expenses incurred by the legal owner in fulfilling the trust. It need not be shown that the beneficiary requested the incurrence of such expenses if they were a natural incident of the trust. Accordingly, B had to reimburse H for the expenses he had met in meeting the calls.

12.1.3 Remuneration of trustees

Re Chalinder & Herrington (1907)
By the terms of a will trust one of the trustees, a solicitor, was permitted to charge for 'all professional and other charges for his time and trouble'.

Held the clause would not permit the solicitor-trustee to charge for work which was not 'professional', even though it was work for which a solicitor could have charged a normal client.

Re Dover Coalfield Extension Ltd (1908) CA
D Co owned shares in another company (the Kent company). D Co placed these shares in the name of one of its directors, C. The intention was that C would represent the interests of D Co on the board of K Co. C executed a declaration of trust in favour of D Co to that effect. C was appointed a director of K Co and in due course received remuneration for his services to K Co. D Co sought a declaration that C held those profits on trust for D Co, as the profits had been acquired by virtue of C's fiduciary position.

Held the beneficiary (D Co) would not succeed in seeking an account for profits made by C in his capacity as a director of K Co as the profits had arisen from his appointment to a directorship made by K Co and had not arisen through the use of any property of D Co. Further, D Co would in any event be barred from claiming the profits because C had become a director of K Co at the request of D Co.

Williams v Barton (1927)
The defendant, B, was a trustee who worked for a firm of stockbrokers. He received commission for any work introduced by him. B therefore recommended to the other trustee of his trust that B's firm of stockbrokers should act for the trust. In due course the firm was appointed and B received his commission. Later, the plaintiff, B's co-trustee, claimed that B should account to the trust for the payment he had received.

Held B had received his commission by virtue of his trusteeship. He would therefore be required to account to the trust for the profits he had received.

Re Llewellin's WT (1949)
The testator, L, by his will empowered his trustees to appoint themselves as directors of a trust-owned company. Two of them did so and took out a summons to establish whether or not they were accountable to the trust for remuneration received by them in their roles as directors.

Held the trustees would be entitled to retain remuneration received in their capacity as directors of the trust-owned company. This was so notwithstanding the rule that a trustee must not profit from their trust, for that rule is subject to the expressed intention of the settlor or testator to allow remuneration. On the proper construction of the terms of the will trust L had clearly intended to allow his trustees to hold salaried offices as directors.

Note ——————————————————————————————————

The court has always had an inherent jurisdiction to award remuneration to trustees upon their appointment to a trust, but does this inherent jurisdiction extend to increasing the remuneration of existing trustees? This was one of the questions considered in the next case.

Re Duke of Norfolk's ST (1981) CA

A trust corporation ('SETCO') and an individual trustee, the trustees of a settlement set up in 1958, had, throughout the history of the trust, been called upon to devote increasing efforts to its good administration. The increased demands made upon them by the trust had arisen in large part due to the settlement of additional property upon the trust and changes in the tax laws. Accordingly, in 1977 the trustees applied to court for an order under its inherent jurisdiction authorising the trust corporation to claim remuneration at a level higher than that authorised by the trust instrument.

Held the court had inherent jurisdiction to authorise such increased remuneration if to do so would be in the interests of the good administration of the trust. It was nevertheless acknowledged that this involved balancing the proper administration of the trust against the fact that the trustee's office is essentially a gratuitous one. The court should have regard to the nature of the trust, the experience and skill of the particular trustees, the sums that they wished to charge compared with those of other trustees and all surrounding facts. The reason for such an extensive inquiry in determining whether or not remuneration would be in the interest of the good administration of the trust might be that such an inquiry should reveal whether or not the trustees will retire from the trust if they are not properly remunerated. The fact is that the choice facing the court is whether to increase the remuneration of a trustee who is familiar with the trust or to risk losing that trustee and appointing, instead, a new trustee who will probably insist on market-rate remuneration in any event. The present case was remitted to the Chancery Division to decide whether, on these principles, remuneration should be awarded in the present case.

Foster v Spencer (1995)

Trustees of a cricket club applied to be remunerated under the court's inherent jurisdiction for their past and future services to the club. They also sought the court's approval for an indemnity out of the trust funds in respect of certain expenses which they had incurred, and for interest thereon.

Held the trustees would be remunerated for their past services. There were no funds out of which they could have been paid at the time of their appointment and it had been impossible at that time to ascertain what they were letting themselves in for. Since then they had provided extensive service to the trust and to deny them remuneration for those services would be to unjustly enrich the beneficiaries at the trustees' expense. However, the judge refused to make an award of remuneration for future services as the task remaining to be performed in the execution of the trust did not call for any special expertise on the part of the trustees. The plaintiffs had said that they would be unwilling to continue if not allowed to charge, but the judge was satisfied that other persons existed who might be persuaded to undertake the trust for no remuneration. If the burden proved too onerous in the future a further application could be made to court. Applying *Re Duke of Norfolk's ST*, it could not be said that the continued service of the plaintiffs was necessary for the good administration of the trust. On the other claim, expenses were allowed but without interest.

12.1.4 The rule in *Cradock v Piper*

Note
Although trustees are not permitted to profit from their trust, there has existed for a long time an exception to that rule. The exception was laid down in the case of *Cradock v Piper* (1850). The rule permits a solicitor-trustee to be remunerated out of the trust fund for work done in litigation on behalf of himself and a co-trustee if the same costs would have been incurred through acting for the co-trustee alone. The ambit of the rule was extended in the next case below.

Re Corsellis (1887) CA

A next friend of an infant beneficiary made an application for maintenance of the infant. The two trustees of the trust were respondents to the application. One of the trustees, a solicitors' firm, sought to claim remuneration for acting in the application.

Held although the litigation in the present case was not hostile, but comprised a 'friendly' application in chambers on behalf of an infant beneficiary, it was quite proper, nevertheless, for the Rule in *Cradock v Piper* to apply to such a case. The solicitors' firm would be entitled to its fees.

12.1.5 Other illustrations of the duty to act gratuitously

Boardman and another v Phipps (1967) HL

B, a solicitor to a trust, attended the AGM of a company in which the trust had a substantial shareholding. Unhappy with the state of the company, B and one of the beneficiaries under the trust (the co-appellant) decided to launch a take-over bid personally for those shares in the company which were not already trust-owned. The inside knowledge of the company which enabled the appellants to make the take-over bid had been obtained at the AGM where they had been acting as proxies for the trustees. B wrote to the beneficiaries outlining his plans to take a personal interest in the company, thus giving them an opportunity to raise any objections they might have to his so doing. No objections having been made, the appellants proceeded with their take-over. In the event the take-over was highly successful and the value of all the shares in the company greatly increased in value. The trust profited, and so did the appellants. The present action was brought by P, a beneficiary under the trust, for an account of profits made by B in his fiduciary capacity as solicitor to the trust. The trial judge found as a fact that P had not been fully informed by B as to the precise nature of his plans.

Held (Viscount Dilhorne and Lord Upjohn dissenting) the appellants had placed themselves in a fiduciary position in relation to the trust and would therefore be accountable for the profits they had made on information obtained by virtue of their fiduciary position. However, they had acted honestly and openly throughout and their actions had yielded profits for the trust. They would accordingly be entitled to generous remuneration as reward for their work and skill.

Lord Hodson regarded the information obtained by the appellants as property of the trust and held them liable to account as constructive trustees for profits they had made thereon.

Lord Cohen, however, felt that information was 'not property in the strictest sense of that word'. In the event Lord Cohen held them liable to account because their personal profits had been made, not from property of the trust, but from opportunities gained from their positions of trust, that is, from the fiduciary roles into which they had placed themselves in relation to the trust.

Lord Guest's reasoning was similar to that of Lord Cohen.

Viscount Dilhorne, dissenting, stated that in his view the facts of the instant case did not disclose even a possibility of conflict between the personal interests of the appellants and those of the trust. Nor did he think that the information obtained at the AGM could be regarded as being property of the trust. The information was of no value to the trust because the trust had declined to take advantage of it. In the absence of any breach of duty or impropriety on the part of the appellants his Lordship refused to find them liable to account.

Lord Upjohn, dissenting, accepted that the appellants would have to give an account of their personal profits if their personal interests 'possibly may conflict' with the interests of the trust. However, he construed those words as meaning 'a real sensible possibility of conflict'. His

Lordship could not find any such possibility on the facts of the present case and accordingly held for the appellants.

Guinness Plc v Saunders (1990) HL

A committee of the board of directors of G plc authorised a payment of £5.2m to one of its members, S, for his part in a take-over bid being made by the company. G plc, having paid the monies to S, later sought to re-claim them on the basis that S had breached his fiduciary duty in failing to disclose a personal interest in the take-over.

Held although Article 2 of G plc's articles of association included 'any committee' within its definition of the board of directors it was clear from the proper construction of Article 91 that special remuneration could be awarded only by the board of directors proper, and not by a committee of that board. Neither could S retain the £5.2m under Article 100(D) as being remuneration for professional services. The services rendered by S were not rendered in a professional capacity, but as a member of the committee. The articles, therefore, on a true construction, did not authorise S to retain any part of the £5.2m. That being the legal situation, S sought to show that he was entitled in equity to an allowance for services rendered to G plc. This claim failed because in equity S, as a director, was treated as a trustee and would not be permitted to profit from his trust. The court was most reluctant to make an equitable award in circumstances where the articles of association confined to the board of directors the power to award remuneration.

O'Sullivan v Management Agency Music Ltd (1985) CA

When still an unknown artist, Gilbert O'Sullivan, a composer and per-former of pop music, signed management agreements with companies controlled by Mr Mills (M), a music agent. The terms of the agreements were not as favourable to OS as they would have been had he had inde-pendent legal advice. OS had naively trusted M and had failed to negoti-ate the agreements in the usual 'arm's-length' way. Nevertheless, the man-agement and marketing prowess of M's companies brought OS great suc-cess and the wealth that accompanies such success. In due course, howev-er, their working relationship deteriorated and ultimately OS brought an action against M and his companies, seeking to have the management con-tracts declared void on the basis that they had been obtained by undue influence. The trial judge set the contracts aside and ordered that M and his companies should account for profits made on the music of OS, togeth-er with compound interest on those profits. The defendants conceded that there had been undue influence on the part of M, but appealed against the companies' liability and against the remedies awarded against the compa-nies and against M.

Held the companies were subject to the same liability as M because they had been under the *de facto* control of M. It had therefore been proper to set aside all the contracts. However, in determining the appropriate remedy it was necessary to make allowance for the work done by the companies on behalf of OS. This meant that the companies would be allowed to retain a reasonable profit even though they, through M, had been in a fiduciary position in relation to OS. Further, the defendants would not be required to pay compound interest on their account of profits because some of the monies made by the companies had been used for the benefit of OS.

Note ───────────────────────────────────
As to the meaning of 'compound interest', see 15.1.5.

Note ───────────────────────────────────
The maxim 'he who comes to equity must do equity' was argued by counsel in *O'Sullivan* and appears to have informed their Lordships' judgment. The same maxim was expressly applied in the next case, a case which does not directly involve trustees' profits, but which illustrates the enormous potential of the flexible maxim.

Re Berkeley Applegate (Investment Consultants) Ltd (1989)

BA Ltd had gone into liquidation and its free assets were not sufficient to cover the expenses and remuneration of the liquidator. Accordingly, the liquidator applied to court for a determination of the question whether his expenses and remuneration might be met out of assets held by the company on trust for its clients.

Held the company, and not the liquidator, was trustee of the remaining assets, and the beneficiaries of that trust (the unpaid creditors of the company) were reliant upon the discretion of the court to enforce their equitable interests in the assets legally owned by the company. Accordingly, the liquidator was granted remuneration and expenses out of the trust property because of the rule that 'he who seeks equity must do equity'. If the liquidator had not administered the liquidation the task would have fallen to a receiver appointed by the court and such a person would have been entitled to claim his fees out of the trust assets. Accordingly, in granting equitable relief to the beneficiaries the court would also insist that the beneficiaries acted equitably towards the liquidator.

12.1.6 Bribes

Note ───────────────────────────────────
It was held by the House of Lords in *AG for Hong Kong v Reid* (1994) that persons in fiduciary positions who receive bribes to betray the interests of the persons to whom they owe fiduciary duties, are deemed by equity to hold the bribe (and any benefits flowing therefrom) on trust for the person who has been betrayed.

Reading v AG (1951)

R was a sergeant in the English army stationed in Cairo where he accompanied civilian lorries through security checkpoints in order to assist the transport of contraband goods. He was paid handsomely for his assistance.

Held R owed fiduciary obligations to the Crown and therefore had to account for any profits made through a breach of those obligations.

Q If, instead, the court had approached the facts of the above case by treating the sergeant's uniform as property held in trust by him for the Crown, could the case have been analysed as giving rise to a constructive trust, as opposed to a mere duty to account for unauthorised profits? (see 'Constructive Trusts' at Chapter 17, below).

12.2   The duty to provide personal service to the trust

12.2.1   General

Note

The traditional rule is *delegatus non potest delagatum* (a person to whom a role has been delegated may not delegate that role to another). In *Pilkington v IRC* (1964), HL, Viscount Radcliffe refined this rule by stating that 'the law is not that trustees cannot delegate: it is that trustees cannot delegate unless they have authority to do so'. Relevant 'authority' is provided in the Trustee Act 1925 and may be extended or altered by the terms of particular trust instruments.

12.2.2   Statutory authority to delegate

Trustee Act 1925 s 23

(1) Trustees ... may, instead of acting personally, employ and pay an agent, whether a solicitor, banker, stockbroker, or other person, to transact any business or do any act required to be transacted or done in the execution of the trust ... and shall be entitled to be allowed and paid all charges and expenses so incurred, and shall not be responsible for the default of any such agent if employed in good faith.

(2) Trustees ... may appoint any person to act as their agent or attorney for the purpose of ... administering any property ... subject to the trust ... in any place outside the United Kingdom or executing or exercising any discretion or trust or power vested in them in relation to any such property ... including the power to appoint substitutes, and shall not, by reason only of their having made such appointment, be responsible for any loss arising thereby.

(3) Without prejudice to such general power of appointing agents as aforesaid
–

(a) A trustee may appoint a solicitor to be his agent to receive and give a discharge for any money or valuable consideration or property receivable by the trustee under the trust ...

(b) A trustee shall not be chargeable with breach of trust by reason only of his having made such appointment ...

(c) ...

Provided that nothing in this subsection shall exempt a trustee from any liability which he would have incurred if this Act ... had not been passed, in case he permits any such money, valuable consideration, or property to remain in the hands or under the control of the banker or solicitor for a period longer than is reasonably necessary ...

Trustee Act 1925 s 25(1)

Notwithstanding any rule of law or equity to the contrary, a trustee may, by power of attorney, delegate for a period not exceeding twelve months the execution or exercise of any of the trusts, powers and discretions vested in him as trustee ...

Trustee Act 1925 s 30(1)

A trustee shall be chargeable only for money and securities actually received by him notwithstanding his signing any receipt for the sake of conformity, and shall be answerable and accountable only for his own acts, receipts, neglects or defaults, and not for those of any other trustee, nor for any banker, broker or other person with whom any trust money or securities may be deposited, nor for the insufficiency or deficiency of any securities, nor for any other loss, unless the same happens through his own wilful default.

Re Vickery (1931)

The executor (trustee) was a 'missionary ignorant of business affairs who inadvertently employed a rogue solicitor to wind up an estate. The beneficiaries requested the appointment of another solicitor but at first the defendant refused to do so, believing that the rogue solicitor, after repeated requests, was about to settle the matter. In the event the rogue solicitor made off with a large sum of money belonging to the trust.

Held the trustee was not liable for breach of trust. The words 'any other loss' in s 30(1) of the Trustee Act 1925 did not provide immunity for every breach of trust, but the subsection did cover the case, such as the present, where trust monies have been 'deposited' with an agent. Further, that a person is not guilty of 'wilful' default unless he is 'conscious' that he is committing a breach of trust, or 'reckless' to the possibility that he is committing a breach of trust. The judge effectively equated 'wilful default' with 'bad faith' in an attempt to reconcile the immunity enshrined in s 30(1) with the that contained in s 23(1). A trustee employing an agent to receive monies belonging to a trust will not be liable if the money is lost through the agent's misconduct, unless the trustee had has himself been guilty of wilful default.

Q Is the judge's decision consistent with a proper reading of s 30(1) and *all* the subsections of s 23? Does his decision have the effect of protecting 'honest fools'?

12.2.3 Delegation to agents and supervision of agents is subject to the general objective standard of care

Re Lucking's WT (1968)
The plaintiff was one of the beneficiaries under a will trust. L, the son of the testatrix, was the sole trustee of the trust and a beneficiary under it. Part of the trust property was a majority holding in a private company. In order to secure the profitable running of the company L appointed D to be a director of the company. Over time a practice was established whereby D sent blank cheques to L to be signed (two signatures were needed to authorise drawings on the company's account) to cover D's expenses. It became apparent to L that D was making withdrawals for his own ends, but L took no action to prevent this; on the contrary, L continued to sign D's blank cheques. The company's gross profits had increased under D's management, but so had its overdraft. D's personal indebtedness to the company eventually reached such a level that he was dismissed from his directorship. He was declared bankrupt while still owing £15,890 to the company.

Held L had failed adequately to supervise D's financial activities. He should have exercised the care of an ordinary prudent man of business. This would have meant ensuring that he had been represented on the board of the company. Having failed to do so he was liable to the other beneficiaries for the devaluation in the shares owned by the trust. The judge refused to apply the *Re Vickery* test of 'wilful default' on the basis that the facts of the present case did not fall within the categories of situation covered by s 30(1). There had been no 'deposit' of trust monies with D.

Note ————————————————————————————
Re Vickery has not been followed in any subsequent case. Although the 'result' in *Re Vickery* is generally acknowledged to have been a fair one, the technical reasoning of the judge has been subject to much criticism (in particular, see G H Jones (1959) 22 *Modern Law Review* 338).

12.2.4 Care in the choice of agents

Fry v Tapson (1884)

The trustees in this case had decided to invest in a mortgage of freehold land, such an investment being authorised under the terms of their trust. However, the trustees appointed a London-based valuer to value land in Liverpool, and what is more, the valuer was an agent of the proposed mortgagor and thus had a financial interest in inflating the value of the security. The valuer had been recommended by the trustees' solicitors. In the event the valuation turned out to have been inflated and the freehold proved to be inadequate security when, in due course, the mortgagor became bankrupt.

Held the trustees had not exercised sufficient care in their choice of agent. An agent should always be chosen to act within the agent's proper sphere of expertise, a London-based solicitor should not have been chosen to value a property in Liverpool. Further, the trustees had failed to consider the accuracy of the agent's valuation, but had accepted it at face value. Although it was not doubted that the trustees had acted honestly, they had failed to act as ordinary prudent persons of business would have acted in a business of their own and they would be liable, accordingly, to account to the beneficiaries for the losses caused through their lack of prudence.

12.3 Duty to exercise a sound discretion

Note

According to orthodoxy trustees' discretions are classified as being either 'dispositive' or 'administrative'. Dispositive discretions being those which relate to the disposition of the trust property (the main example is the discretion which characterises discretionary trusts, see 3.5.2), whereas administrative discretions are those which relate to the management of the trust (a major instance being the discretion as to how to invest trust property, see Chapter 13).

12.3.1 Where a dispositive discretion is expressly uncontrollable

Gisborne v Gisborne (1877) HL

Trustees held a fund upon trust for the maintenance of the testator's mentally infirm wife. The terms of the trust granted the trustees 'uncontrollable authority' as to how the fund should be applied. The care of 'lunatics' (the unfortunate label then applied to the mentally ill) normally lay within the powers of the court, and so a decree of the Court of Chancery had recorded the court's approval of the trustees' chosen course of action.

Held that part of the decree 'approving' of the trustees' course of action should be struck out. The court had no jurisdiction to approve or disapprove of that which was in the 'uncontrollable' discretion of the trustees.

Where trustees' discretion is qualified by words which make it 'uncontrollable', or by words of similar intent, it is to be without check by any superior tribunal, provided that the discretion was exercised in good faith. (This decision should now be read in conjunction with the rule in *Re Hasting's Bass*, see below.)

12.3.2 Where a dispositive discretion is not expressly uncontrollable

Re Roper's Trusts (1879)
A fund was settled upon trustees for certain infant beneficiaries. The income of the fund was to be paid by them to the mother of the infants, Fanny Keech. The will trust granted the mother discretion as to how the fund should be distributed amongst the children. The discretion was not expressed to be 'absolute' or 'uncontrollable'.

Held on finding that the mother had not exercised her discretion soundly the trustees were ordered to pay the income of the fund to the father of the infants to be distributed in his discretion.

Q Is this decision partly explicable as arising from paternalism based upon the relatively limited legal autonomy that women had in relation to property before the Married Women's Property Act 1882?

12.3.3 The rule in *Re Hasting's Bass*

Note
The rule in *Re Hastings' Bass* (1975), CA, is as follows: where by the terms of a trust trustees are given a discretion as to some matter under which they act in good faith, the court should not interfere with their action notwithstanding that it does not have the intended effect, unless (1) what is in fact achieved was unauthorised by the power conferred upon them, or (2) it is clear they would not have acted in the way they did had they not taken into account matters which they had taken into account and should not have taken into account, or had they not failed to take account of matters which they should have taken into account.

Mettoy Pension Trustees Ltd v Evans (1991)
M Ltd, a subsidiary of which used to manufacture the miniature toy cars known as 'Dinky Toys', had fallen victim to the recession and gone into liquidation. The pension funds of Mettoy employees were held by a trust corporation subject to rules governing the distribution of any surplus in the event of the company being wound up. The trust corporation had been appointed by the previous trustees and it was those trustees who had laid down the rules governing the distribution of surplus pension funds. In the event there was indeed a surplus in the pension fund at the company's winding up. However, the power to distribute the surplus was held by the trust corporation in a fiduciary capacity and thus could not be released to

the liquidator in order to be exercised by him. The result was that nobody had power to distribute the surplus and it therefore fell to the court to give directions as to the distribution. The question arose whether the appointment of the trust corporation, which had resulted in the confusion, had been a valid exercise of the trustees' discretion.

Held the trustees were not liable. There was no evidence to show that the trustees did not understand the effect of the rules, nor to show that they would have acted differently had they been informed that the rules for distribution had conferred a 'fiduciary power' on the trust corporation. In applying the rule in *Re Hastings' Bass* the judge held that three questions arose: (1) What were the trustees under a duty to consider? (2) Did they fail to consider it? (3) If so, what would they have done if they had considered it? The third question was 'all important' for it would not be enough to show merely that the trustees knew that what they were doing was in some way unsatisfactory. It must be shown that the trustees would, on the balance of probabilities, have acted differently.

Note ———————————————————————————

The rule in *Re Hasting's Bass* can be reconciled with cases such as *Gisborne v Gisborne* (above) because, although the courts will not interfere with the outcome of the exercise of a discretion over which they are expressed to have no control, the courts will intervene where, applying the rule in *Re Hasting's Bass*, there has been no valid process of discretionary decision-making at all.

12.3.4 There must be a conscious exercise of discretion

Wilson v Turner (1883) CA

Trustees of a marriage settlement had a power to apply the whole or part of the annual income of the trust towards the maintenance (see 14.1) of the child of the marriage as the trustees should in their discretion think fit. The trustees in fact paid the whole of the income of the trust fund to the child's father without exercising any discretion as to its application for the child's maintenance.

Held as the trustees had not exercised any discretion at all the father must be held liable to repay to the trust the entirety of the income he had received.

Re Locker's Settlement (1977)

The trustees of the settlement were empowered to distribute the income of the fund amongst a number of persons, and charitable (and other) institutions. Their discretion in this regard was stated to be 'absolute and uncontrolled'. Having accumulated all the income which had accrued since the inception of the trust (and having done so in breach of trust, but in accordance with the settlor's wishes) the trustees took out a summons for directions as to how the income ought to be distributed.

Held the court exercised its discretion to permit the trustees to remedy their breach by making a tardy distribution of the trust fund. A tardy distribution by the trustees was said to be closer to what the settlor had intended than a tardy distribution by somebody else at the court's direction. The court was able to exercise its discretion in this way despite the provision in the settlement granting the trustees an 'absolute and unfettered' discretion as to the distribution of the income. The court would not interfere with the exercise by the trustees of their discretion, but would interfere in cases, such as the present, where the trustees had failed to exercise their discretion at all.

12.3.5 Disclosure of reasons for decisions

Wilson v Law Debenture Trust Corp plc (1995)

W, a former employee of a company, had contributed to the company's pension scheme. When the company was sold to CMP, another corporation, W became a member of CMP's pension scheme. The defendant was the trustee of the CMP's scheme. By the terms of CMP's scheme the defendant trustee had a discretion to transfer into the new scheme such part of the assets of the original pension scheme as the trustee determined to be appropriate having taken actuarial advice. In the event the trustee transferred only a small part of the original pension fund into the new scheme. W issued a summons seeking disclosure of the trustee's reasons for exercising its discretion in the way it did.

Held the summons would be dismissed. Where a discretion is entrusted to a trustee by the trust instrument, the trustee is not required to give reasons for the exercise of the discretion. In the absence of disclosure of evidence that the trustee had acted improperly, whether from an improper motive, or through infringement of the rule in *Re Hastings' Bass*, the court would not interfere with the exercise of the trustee's discretion.

Note ——————
Trustees have to keep a diary-like record of the administration of the trust for production to new trustees (*Tiger v Barclays Bank Ltd* (1951) CA). Further, if a trustee deals with trust property *every* beneficiary has a right to see documents relating to that dealing, although it is doubtful that a beneficiary will be entitled to see documents which contain the trustees' reasons for exercising their discretions (*Re Londonderry's Settlement* (1964)). This is because trust documents are, in a sense, the property of the beneficiaries. However, a professional trustee may in certain circumstances raise professional privilege as a defence to a summons for disclosure of trust documents and in order to displace the privilege the beneficiaries must make out a *prima facie* case of fraud (*O'Rourke v Darbishire* (1920) HL).

13 The trustees' powers and duties of investment

13.1 The judicial definition of investment

Khoo Tek Keong v Ch'ng Joo Tuan Neoh (1934) PC

The terms of a will trust permitted the trustees to invest as they in their absolute discretion thought fit. The sole trustee made certain loans, for some he took security in the form of jewellery, for some he took no security at all.

Held the loans made without security could not qualify as 'investments' and were made in breach of trust. Lord Russell stated that 'loans on no security beyond the liability of the borrower to repay ... are not investments'. The secured loans were treated as proper investments in the absence of evidence to show that the security was insufficient.

Re Power (1947)

A will trust empowered the trustee (the Public Trustee in this case) to invest the trust fund 'in any manner in which he may in his absolute discretion think fit in all respects as if he were sole beneficial owner of such monies including the purchase of freehold property in England and Wales'. The testator's widow requested the trustees to purchase a freehold property as a residence for her and her children. The widow and children were the only beneficiaries under the will trust.

Held the terms of the will trust permitted freehold land to be purchased as an investment. But an 'investment' must, by definition, produce income, therefore the purchase of land for the beneficiaries to live in could not qualify as an investment.

Re Peczenik's ST (1964)

The terms of a settlement authorised the trustees to invest the trust funds 'in any shares stocks property or property holding company as the trustees in their discretion shall consider to be in the best interests of [the beneficiary]'. The question arose on the construction of this clause, whether the trustees were permitted to invest as they thought fit.

Held the clause should be given its natural construction. This would permit the trustees to invest in any 'property' capable of being treated as an investment. This would include income-producing property, but not property which is acquired merely for use and enjoyment. Further, trustees would not be permitted to invest on mere 'personal' security. In other words, a loan which is made on no security, apart from the debtors personal promise to repay, is not an investment.

Note

According to *Re Laing* (1899), loans on personal security will be permitted if the trust instrument in very clear and precise words expressly authorises investments of that nature.

13.2 Trustee Investments Act 1961

13.2.1 The permitted types of investment

Note

The Trustees Investments Act permits 'investment' in 'Narrower-Range Investments Not Requiring Advice' (First Schedule, Part I); in 'Narrower-Range Investments Requiring Advice' (First Schedule Part II); in, subject to s 2 of the Act, 'Wider-Range Investments' (Second Schedule), all of which are required to be made upon proper advice; or, finally, in 'Special-Range Property'. Investments within the first range include National Savings Certificates and deposits at the National Savings Bank. Included in the second are government-issued fixed-interest securities, debentures issued by UK companies, deposits with banks and building societies, and mortgages of freeholds and of leases with an unexpired term of at least 60 years. In the wider range are included unit trusts, shares in building societies and shares in certain companies. Companies falling within the wider range must be UK incorporated and listed companies with an issued and paid up share capital of at least £1m which have declared a dividend on all issued shares in each of the five preceding years. Investments within the 'Special Range' are those legal investments which the trustee is permitted to make outside the scheme of the Act by virtue of a special power in the trust instrument.

13.2.2 The relationship between the ranges of investment

Trustee Investments Act 1961 s 2

(1) A trustee shall not have power [under this Act] to make or retain any wider-range investment unless the trust fund has been divided into two parts (... the narrower-range part and the wider-range part), the parts being ... equal in value at the time of the division ...

(2) ...

(3) Where any property accrues to a trust fund after the fund has been divided ... then –

(a) if the property accrues to the trustee as owner or former owner of property comprised in either part of the fund, it shall be treated as belonging to that part of the fund;

(b) in any other case, the trustee shall secure, by apportionment of the accruing property or the transfer of property from one part of the fund to the other, or both, that the value of each part of the fund is increased by the same amount ...

(4) Where in the exercise of any power or duty of a trustee property falls to be taken out of the trust fund, nothing in this section shall restrict his discretion as to the choice of property to be taken out.

13.2.3 The requirement of diversification and the duty to take advice

Trustee Investments Act 1961 s 6

(1) In the exercise of his powers of investment a trustee shall have regard –

(a) to the need for diversification of investments of the trust, in so far as is appropriate to the circumstances of the trust;

(b) to the suitability to the trust of investments of the description of investment proposed and of the investment proposed as an investment of that description.

(2) Before exercising any power conferred by ... this Act to invest in a manner specified in ... this Act ... a trustee shall obtain and consider proper advice on the question whether the investment is satisfactory ... (3) A trustee retaining any investment made in the exercise of such a power ... shall determine at what intervals the circumstances, and in particular the nature of the investment, make it desirable to obtain such advice as aforesaid, and shall obtain and consider such advice accordingly.

(3) ...

(4) ... proper advice is the advice of a person who is reasonably believed by the trustee to be qualified by his ability in and practical experience of financial matters ...

(5) [the advice must be given, or subsequently confirmed, in writing].

Note ───

The duties contained within s 6 are merely detailed applications of the general standard of prudence which trustees must exercise in all the affairs of the trust (see 11.2.2). It follows that, even where a trust instrument expressly excludes the restrictive range of investments permitted by the Act, the provisions of s 6 will still apply.

13.3　Investment in mortgages

Trustee Act 1925 s 8(1)

A trustee lending money on the security of property on which he can properly lend shall not be chargeable with breach of trust by reason only of the proportion borne by the amount of the loan to the value of the property ... if it appears to the court –

(a) that in making the loan [the trustee acted upon the report of a person the trustee believed to be an independent and able surveyor or valuer]; and

(b) that the amount of the loan does not exceed two third parts of the value of the property as stated in the report; and

(c) that the loan was made under the advice of the surveyor or valuer expressed in the report.

Palmer v Emerson (1911)

Trustees invested trust money in a freehold mortgage, a portion of the freehold premises being used for the purposes of a butcher's business of 40 years standing. No independent valuation was made on behalf of the trustees before making the advance, instead they relied upon a three-year old valuation, made for a different purpose, by a local expert. The butcher's business subsequently failed, and the premises became much depreciated in value and wholly insufficient to pay the trust monies to the beneficiaries.

Held if mortgaged premises and a business carried out thereon are so inseparable that the discontinuance of the business may result in depreciation of the premises, trustees ought not advance more than half the proper value of the premises. However, the trustees in the present case would not be liable for breach of their trust because they had acted reasonably and ought to be excused. The pre-cursor to s 61 Trustee Act 1925 was applied (see 15.3.4) because s 8 of the Trustee Act does not impose upon trustees a statutory duty to make a valuation, but is a section relieving trustees of liability in certain circumstances.

Trustee Act 1925 s 9(1)

Where a trustee improperly advances trust money on a mortgage security which would at the time of the investment be a proper investment in all respects for a smaller sum than is actually advanced thereon, the security shall be deemed an authorised investment for the smaller sum, and the trustee shall only be liable to make good the sum advanced in excess thereof with interest.

13.4 Investment in land other than mortgages and long leases

Note ─────────────────────

The general rule is that trustees may not invest in land other than mortgages and leases for a term of 60 years or more. Trustees for sale of land are, however, an obvious exception to the general rule.

Law of Property Act 1925 s 28

Trustees for sale shall, in relation to land ... and to the proceeds of sale, have all the powers of a tenant for life and the trustees of a settlement under the Settled Land Act 1925.

Note ─────────────────────

The powers of investment contained in Settled Land Act 1925 include the power to invest in fees simple (s 73(1)(xi)).

Re Wakeman (1945)

Trustees for sale of land and personal property were directed, by the terms of a will trust, to sell the trust property and to invest the proceeds in the purchase of land. They took out an originating summons for directions as to whether such a course of investment would be permitted.

Held the trustees would have to satisfy the definition of 'trustees for sale of land' in the Law of Property Act 1925 s 28 in order to be permitted to invest in land. According to that definition, if they sold all the land to which they presently held the legal title they would no longer be 'trustees for sale of land' and would therefore have no authority to invest in other land.

Note ─────────────────────

It is common in practice to expressly include in the trust instrument wider powers of investment in land. This brings us to the next section.

13.5 Construction of trust instruments

Trustee Investments Act 1961 s 3(1)

The powers conferred by ... this Act are in addition to and not in derogation from any power conferred otherwise than by this Act ... (hereinafter referred to as a 'special power').

Re Harari's ST (1949)

In this case the trustees took out an originating summons to determine the proper construction to be placed upon an investment clause contained in the settlement of which they were trustees. The clause was in terms which purported to permit the trustees to invest 'in or upon such investments as to them may seem fit'.

Held the clause should not be restrictively construed. The words should be given their 'natural and proper meaning ... in their context'. Giving the words 'in or upon such investment as to them may seem fit' their true construction it was clear that the trustees had power to invest in any legal investments which they honestly believed to be suitable, even if their chosen investment was not an investment of a type authorised by the 'trustee range of investments'. (See, also, *Bishop v Bonham* (11.2.3).)

13.6 Applications for enlargement of investment powers

Note ──────────────────────────────────────
Trustee Investments Act 1961 s 15 authorises trustees to apply to court for an enlargement of their investment powers, so as to permit investment across a wider range of property types. Such applications should be brought under Trustee Act 1925 s 57 (9.1.2).

Re Kolb's WT (1962)
The trustees of a will trust took out a summons for directions as to the proper construction of an investment clause in the will. In the event of the clause being declared void they requested an extension of their investment powers to permit investment in fully paid ordinary shares and convertible debentures of certain companies. Some of the trust property was held by the trustees upon charitable trusts. The Attorney General, representing the charities, objected to the trustees' request for an extension of their investment powers.

Held the investment powers recently laid down by Parliament in the Trustee Investments Act 1961 should be treated as sufficient in the usual case. Those powers should be extended only in special circumstances. In the present case the court would not authorise an extension of investment powers; and would not do so, in any event, in the face of the Attorney General's objection.

Mason v Fairbrother (1983)
In 1929 the Co-operative Society settled a pension fund trust for the benefit of its members. The investment clause in the settlement deed permitted investments of only very restricted scope. By 1982 these investment powers were inappropriate to modern commercial conditions and to the great size of the fund. The trustees applied to court, seeking an extension of their powers of investment beyond those authorised by the 1961 Act. They argued that the court could authorise such an extension within its inherent

jurisdiction to compromise disputes as to the proper construction of trust deeds, or under s 57(1) Trustee Act 1925.

Held the proper interrelation between the investment powers contained in the 1929 settlement and the 1961 Act had given rise to a genuine area of dispute. The court had an inherent jurisdiction to resolve that dispute but it would not exercise its jurisdiction in the present case. What the trustees were seeking was not a compromised solution but the wholesale introduction of a totally new investment clause. However, the court would exercise its jurisdiction under s 57(1) Trustee Act 1925 to introduce enlarged investment powers. Special circumstances had been made out in the present case which justified the court's departure from the restrictive approach taken in *Re Kolb's WT* (1962). The court would therefore vary the investment provisions to permit investments beyond the scope of the 1961 Act.

Trustees of the British Museum v Attorney General (1984)

The trustees of the BM, a charity, applied to court for an extension of their investment powers. The question arose, therefore, whether the investment scheme set out in the 1961 Act was *prima facie* sufficient, or whether changes in the commercial environment and investment market meant that the provisions of the 1961 Act were now out of date.

Held in a large, well-supervised, well-advised trust such as the present, approval would be given for an investment scheme which went beyond the provisions of the Act, especially in view of the fact that the trust needed to raise funds in order to compete in an inflationary market for the purchase of museum exhibits. The decision in *Re Kolb's WT* should be interpreted in its historical context, coming, as it did, soon after the 1961 Act. *Re Kolb's WT* should not be followed, with the result that it would no longer be necessary to show 'special circumstances' in order to avoid the restrictive scheme of the 1961 Act. 'General' economic changes since 1961 would justify an enlargement of trustees investment powers in cases such as the present.

Steel v Wellcome Custodian Trustees (1988)

The trustees of a very large charitable trust (the fund was worth approximately £3,200m) applied to court for an extension of their investment powers. They wished to be permitted to invest as if they were beneficial owners of the property, although subject to the requirement that investments should be made upon expert advice and subject to certain guidelines as to suitable investments.

Held the extension of investment powers was approved as requested, the trustees would be permitted to invest in any kind of assets whatsoever. Hoffman J was persuaded by a number of factors: (1) general changes in investment practice since 1961, in particular an inflation-induced move towards shorter term investments such as shares; (2) the large size of the fund in the present case (600 times larger than that in the *British Museum* case, above); (3) the expert advice available to the trustees in the present case, namely four professional fund managers and a specialist firm to monitor their performance; (4) 90% of the fund, even with extended investment powers, was likely to remain invested in Wellcome plc, the judge was keen therefore to grant the trustees as much flexibility as possible as regards investments of the remaining 10%.

13.7 Over-cautious investment?

Note ——————————————————————————————
The motto of an ordinary prudent person of business, who is driven by the need to make profit, might be that one must 'speculate to accumulate'. The motto of a trustee, who is driven by the overriding duty to safeguard the trust fund, is quite different, it might be that one must 'select to protect'. However, where proper caution ends, and over-cautious neglect begins, is not easy to determine.

Nestle v National Westminster Bank plc (1993) CA
A testator died in 1922 leaving a fund worth approximately £54,000 on trust for various descendants. N, the testator's only granddaughter, became solely and absolutely entitled to the fund in 1986, at which time it was valued at approximately £270,000. N claimed that with proper investment the present value of the fund should have been more than £1m.

Held the bank had misinterpreted the powers of investment granted to it by the terms of the will trust and should have taken legal advice thereon. The bank should also have made regular reviews of the investments under its control. However, the plaintiff had failed to show that the bank's complacency had amounted to a breach of trust resulting in a loss to the fund. On that basis N's appeal was dismissed. Leggatt LJ held that a breach of duty will not be actionable unless it causes loss, and although 'loss' could include making a gain less than would have been made by a prudent person of business, N had failed to prove a loss in the present case.

Note ——————————————————————————————
See, also, *Re Waterman's WT* (11.2.2).

13.8 Political and ethical investment

Cowan v Scargill (1985)
One-half of the management committee of the National Coal Board's pension fund trusts brought an action against the members of the other half; the former having being appointed by the National Coal Board, the latter

by the National Union of Mineworkers (NUM). The committee members appointed by the NUM included Arthur Scargill, president of the union. The committee members were the trustees of pension funds worth approximately £3,000m, with a responsibility to invest £200m on an annual basis. Because the planned investment scheme included investments in overseas industries and in oil and gas, the union trustees refused to adopt the scheme. The union trustees justified their actions as being in the beneficiaries' best interests although they admitted that they had also been motivated by union policy. The National Coal Board trustees brought proceedings to determine whether the refusal of the union trustees had been in breach of trust.

Held the purpose of the trust was the provision of financial benefits, it was therefore the duty of the trustees to invest with a view to securing those benefits. The trustees must set their personal views to one side, although they could in rare cases take into account personal views unanimously held by the beneficiaries. In the present case the union trustees had put their political views before the best financial interests of the beneficiaries. Further, those financial benefits which might have arisen from the boycott of the overseas investments were held to be too vague and remote. They were, accordingly, in breach of trust for refusing to adopt the proposed investment scheme.

Harries v Church Commissioners (1992)

The Rt Rev Richard Harries, Bishop of Oxford, was one of the Church Commissioners. The Commissioners control and invest large sums of money on behalf of the Church of England, such funds being held under charitable trusts. The Bishop of Oxford, together with certain other Church of England clergy, brought proceedings against the other Commissioners, seeking declarations clarifying the Commissioners' obligation to invest in a manner compatible with Christian morality.

Held the declarations were refused. Charity trustees were required to invest with a view to securing the maximum financial return compatible with ordinary prudence. 'Christian morality' covered a range of divergent views which should not be accommodated if to do so would create significant financial prejudice to the funds. However, if some of those views could be accommodated without financial detriment, such an ethical investment policy would be proper. The Vice-Chancellor did acknowledge, that in rare cases the objects of the charity will be such that investments of a particular type would conflict with the aims of the charity and should be avoided for that reason. He gave, as one example, the investment of a cancer research charity in shares in tobacco companies. A major objection to granting the declarations in the present case was that the commissioners already followed an ethical investment scheme which excluded 13% of major UK listed companies. The scheme proposed by the Bishop would have excluded a further 24%.

14 Maintenance and advancement

14.1 Maintenance

Note ──────────

The court has a power to maintain infant beneficiaries under its inherent jurisdiction in cases of salvage and emergency (see 9.1.4, and see *Re Jones* (14.1.9)), and has a power to maintain infants under Trustee Act 1925 s 53 (9.1.3). Powers of maintenance can be expressly incorporated into trust instruments, too. In the absence of an express power, and provided that the trust instrument does not exclude it, the power of maintenance under s 31 Trustee Act will apply.

Trustee Act 1925 s 31

(1) Where any property is held by trustees in trust for any person ... then, subject to any prior interests or charges affecting the property –

(i) during the infancy of any such person, if his interest so long continues, the trustees may, at their sole discretion, pay to his parent or guardian, if any, or otherwise apply for or towards his maintenance, education or benefit, the whole or such part, if any, of the income of that property as may, in all the circumstances, be reasonable ...

(ii) if such person on attaining the age of [18 years] has not a vested interest in such income, the trustees shall thenceforth pay the income of that property and of any accretion thereto under subsection (2) of this section to him, until he either attains a vested interest therein or dies, or until failure of his interest:

Provided that [in deciding whether or not to maintain an infant] the trustees shall have regard to the age of the infant and his requirements and generally to the circumstances of the case, and in particular to what other income, if any, is applicable for the same purposes ...

(2) [During the infancy of the beneficiary the trustees shall accumulate surplus income by investing it and shall also accumulate income from the investments] ...

(3) This section applies in the case of a contingent interest only if the limitation or trust carries the intermediate income of the property, but it applies to a future or contingent legacy by the parent of, or a person standing in *loco parentis* to, the legatee ...

14.1.1 Gifts carrying the intermediate income

Note

See s 31(3), above. 'Intermediate income' is income arising on property during the intermediate period between the date when a contingent gift becomes effective (eg the date of the testator's death in the case of a will trust) and the date when the gift ultimately vests (ie the date when the contingency is met). Vested gifts typically carry the intermediate income, as do *inter vivos* contingent gifts (but see 14.2.6). It is important to remember, when considering the cases in this section, that death is not a contingency, it is a certainty. Note, also, that 'future' and 'deferred' gifts are the same thing!

14.1.2 Testamentary gifts

Law of Property Act 1925 s 175(1)

A contingent and future specific devise or bequest of property, whether real or personal, and a contingent residuary devise of freehold land, and a specific or residuary devise of freehold land to trustee upon trust for persons whose interests are contingent ... shall, subject to the statutory provisions relating to accumulations, carry the intermediate income of that property from the death of the testator, except so far as such income, or any part thereof, may be otherwise expressly disposed of.

Note

The following testamentary gifts are not directly covered by s 175.

14.1.3 Contingent bequest of residuary personalty

Re Adams (1893)

The residue of an estate was bequeathed in trust for such of the testator's sons and daughters as should attain 21 or, in the case of daughters only, marry before 21. Did the children's interests carry the intermediate income so that the children could be maintained out of the income on their interests?

Held maintenance would be permitted out of the income on the residue until the first child acquired a vested interest. North J did state, however, that such income should not be treated as intermediate income arising from the capital in which the infants had an interest. The income was not the infants' by right, but by default. As undisposed of income it had become part of the residue in which the infants had an interest. Accordingly, the infants had become contingently interested in the income, not because of their undoubted rights in the residuary capital, but because the income found itself in the residue by 'accident'.

14.1.4 Deferred residuary bequests of personalty

Re Oliver (1947)

O, the testator, set up a will trust of his residuary estate under which the trustees were obliged to invest the fund and to pay annuities to his widow, W, and daughters out of the income. If there was any surplus income after payment of the annuities, one-third of the surplus was directed to be added to the residue and held upon the ultimate trusts, the other two-thirds was to be paid directly to W. On the date of W"'s death the residuary estate was, by clause 7 of the will, directed to be divided into two equal parts and held on trust for O's two daughters (the 'ultimate trusts'). The question was whether the gifts to the daughters carried the intermediate income.

Held a gift expressly limited to take effect on a future date does not carry the intermediate income. The gift in the present case was just such a gift, being a vested gift limited to take effect at a future date, as opposed to an immediate gift on a contingent event. The latter would normally carry the intermediate income (see s 175, above). On the special facts of this case, however, the daughters could claim the income by virtue of clause 7. That clause had the effect of 'capitalising' the income as part of the ultimate residue (compare the similar reasoning in *Re Adams*, above).

14.1.5 Deferred devise of residuary realty

Re McGeorge (1963)

The testator, M, made certain gifts by a trust in his will. Amongst them was a devise of certain agricultural land to his daughter expressly deferred to take effect after the death of his widow. If the daughter pre-deceased M's widow the daughter's interest would pass to her children. A summons was taken out to determine, *inter alia*, whether the gift to the daughter carried the intermediate income, so that she could claim an interest under s 31(1)(ii) of the Trustee Act 1925.

Held Cross J affirmed *Re Oliver* (see above) for cases of personalty, but read s 175 (see above) as probably leading to a different result in cases of realty. The gift could, technically, be said to carry the intermediate income. However, the daughter's claim still failed. Section 31(1)(ii) had no application, for two reasons. First, because that section only applies to contingent gifts, which the present gift was not (it was a deferred vested gift). Secondly, because the deferral of the gift until the widow's death meant that the gift did not carry the intermediate income, the deferral amounting to an express contrary intention within s 69(2) (see below) which prevented s 31(1) from applying. Further, the gift was vested, but subject to possible defeasance during the widow's lifetime. Therefore, even if s 31(1) had applied, the income should have been accumulated for the benefit of persons who might become entitled upon a defeasance. The court ordered that it should be accumulated for 21 years or until the widow's death, if earlier.

14.1.6 Deferred-contingent bequests of residuary personalty

Re Geering (1962)

The income of the testatrix's residuary realty and personalty was held for her brother for his life, for the provision of an annuity. On his death the income was directed to be held on trust for certain named persons contingent upon their surviving the testatrix and the annuitant *and* attaining the age of 21 (or earlier marriage in the case of females). The gift was thus deferred *and* contingent. In the event the annuitant lived to a ripe old age and the trustees took out a summons for directions as to how they should distribute income (surplus to the annuity) to the expectant remainder beneficiaries.

Held the expectant beneficiaries were entitled to interests which had been deferred until the death of the annuitant (the brother), therefore their interests would, *prima facie*, not carry the intermediate income. Cross J drew a clear distinction between contingent gifts which are immediate and contingent gifts which are deferred. However, in the present case the precise words of the will (which established a gift of capital 'and the income thereof') had the effect, on a proper construction, of adding the income to the capital. The gift would, therefore, carry the intermediate income. However, s 31(1)(ii) would not permit the expectant beneficiaries to make a claim out of that income. This was because another clause of the will trust had the effect of excluding the effect of s 31(1)(ii) (see 14.2.6). That clause gave the trustees an express power to make payments to the capital beneficiaries out of, *inter alia*, the income of their contingent shares which would otherwise have been accumulated. Such a provision, the judge held, was quite inconsistent with a general provision (s 31(1)(ii)) that any beneficiary who has attained 21 is entitled as of right to be paid the income of his contingent share.

14.1.7 Deferred contingent devises of residuary realty

Q No case has decided the question whether such a gift would carry the intermediate income, do you think it should?

Note ———
The wording of s 175 is not clear on this point. In coming to your conclusion, bear in mind the following: (1) deferred *vested* devises do not carry the income; (2) one aim of the 1925 legislation was as far as possible to bring the law of realty into line with the law of personalty; (as to which, see the case of *Re Geering* (14.1.6)).

14.1.8 Contingent or deferred pecuniary legacies

Re Raine (1929)

Shortly after the 1925 legislation came into force, the question arose as to the proper construction of s 175 LPA 1925. In particular, it was asked whether contingent or deferred pecuniary legacies would carry the intermediate income. The section refers only to 'bequests' and 'devises'.

Held the omission of any reference to 'legacies' in s 175 was crucial. The pre-1925 law must be treated as still applying to such a gift. According to the pre-1925 law contingent or deferred pecuniary legacies *prima facie* did not carry the intermediate income. There were, however, certain established exceptions to this rule.

Note ────────────────────────────────────

For the remainder of this section it is intended to consider each of the exceptions to the general rule in *Re Raine*.

14.1.9 The first exception to the general rule

Note ────────────────────────────────────

See Trustee Act 1925 s 31(3), above.

Re Abrahams (1911)

The testator bequeathed £15,000 to each son living at his death who should attain the age of 25, and a further £15,000 to each son who should attain 30. Upon a summons to determine whether the legacies carried interest:

Held inasmuch as the legacies were made contingent upon events having no reference to the infancy of the legatee, the case fell within the general rule that contingent legacies do not carry the intermediate income, and did not fall within the exception to that rule giving to an infant the interest on a legacy from a parent or person in *loco parentis* ('in the place of a parent'). The *'loco parentis'* exception is based on the presumed intention of the testator to make income available to maintain an infant, no such presumption could be made in the present case in the face of the testator's clear intention to make the legacy contingent upon the legatee reaching mature adulthood.

Re Jones (1932)

The testator, J, left legacies of £1,850 to each of his infant children upon their attaining the age of 25. J made no provision for the maintenance of the children during their infancy.

Held where a testator, being the parent (or in *loco parentis*) of an infant, gives a legacy to that infant, contingently on his or her attaining an age other than the age of majority (now 18 – Family Law Reform Act 1969 s 1), and makes no provision for maintenance, it is within the discretion of the

145

court, under its inherent jurisdiction, to order the interest on the legacy to be applied in maintaining the legatee until the legacy vests.

14.1.10 The second exception to the general rule

Re Churchill (1909)

A testatrix left the residue of her estate to trustees on trust for sale, with directions to pay certain pecuniary legacies out of the proceeds. The legacies were to be paid to various younger relations upon their attaining 21 or, in the case of females, their marriage, if earlier. However, the will trust also gave the trustees the power 'to apply the whole or any part of the share to which any beneficiary hereunder may be contingently entitled in or towards the advancement in life or otherwise for the benefit of such beneficiary whether male or female and whether under the age of 21 or not'. One of the potential legatees, the great-nephew of the testatrix, applied by a next friend to be maintained out of the income on the legacy during his infancy.

Held interest was payable on the legacy and therefore the trustees were able to maintain the infant beneficiary out of that income. The present case came within an established exception to the rule that pecuniary legacies do not carry the intermediate income. That exception applies where the testator has *shown an intention* that the legatee should be maintained 'as part of his bounty'.

Re West (1913)

The testatrix, W, bequeathed a legacy to her grand-niece, A, if she should attain the age of 21, but so that the trustees should be free to apply the whole or any part of it in or towards her maintenance and education. W also made provision for the maintenance and education of A out of other funds. A was now 13.

Held (distinguishing *Re Churchill*) that, W having made provision for the maintenance and education of A out of other funds, the legacy only carried the income from the time A reached 21.

> Note ────────────────────────────────
> You should recall, also, that the existence of other funds is a factor that the trustees should take into account when considering whether to exercise their discretion to maintain under s 31(1) (14.1).

14.1.11 The third exception to the general rule

Re Medlock (1886)

A testator bequeathed £750 to trustees upon trust to pay and divide the same among three people contingently upon their surviving him and attaining 21. If none got a vested interest the fund was to fall into residue.

Held a definite fund had been segregated by the will from the rest of the estate. In such a case the legatee will be able to claim the intermediate income produced by the separate fund.

14.1.12 Apportioning the income of a class gift

Re Joel's (1967)

In exercise of a power of appointment granted by his father's will, a son appointed a fund to be held on trust for such of his grandchildren as should be living 21 years from his death, or should by that date have attained 21 or married. If more than one grandchild qualified they were to take in equal shares. The trustees took out a summons to determine *inter alia* (1) how the income and outgoings should be apportioned on the birth of new grandchildren, and (2) how, on the death of a grandchild before obtaining a vested interest, the investments representing accumulations (under s 31(2) Trustee Act) on such grandchild's contingent share should be allocated.

Held on the first question it was held that if there is a gift to a class contingent upon its members attaining a certain age, the class closes (provisionally) when the first person attains that age. The trustees may then maintain that beneficiary out of the income attributable to their notional share. If a new beneficiary is born later the class is re-closed, again on a provisional basis, and a fresh allocation of notional shares is made. Income and outgoings of the fund should at all times be apportioned between each beneficiary's share in accordance with the provisions of the Apportionment Act 1870. The trustees should, therefore, apportion on an equitable basis. On the second question, it was held that in the event of the death of a grandchild the accumulations on that grandchild's share should be added to the general capital of the fund, notwithstanding that a grandchild born subsequently would thereby acquire an interest in capital arising from income which had accrued before he was born.

Re Delamere's ST (1984) CA

Trustees of a settlement executed a deed of appointment under which the income of the trust was to be held on trust for a number of infant beneficiaries 'in equal shares absolutely'. On appeal the beneficiaries contended that they were individually entitled to claim an equal share in the income from the fund.

Held the income on the fund was indefeasible. The beneficiaries would not be entitled to shares of the income, together they were absolutely entitled to the 'whole' of it.

14.2 Advancement

Note
The power to apply capital for the advancement of a beneficiary may be granted by the express terms of the trust instrument and may replace or modify the statutory power of advancement. If there is no express power the statutory power will apply, provided that there is no express intention to the contrary (see 14.2.6). The statutory power of advancement is found in s 32 Trustee Act 1925. As to the general exercise of the discretionary power of advancement, see *Re Hasting's Bass* and *Mettoy v Evans* (12.3.3).

Trustee Act 1925 s 32(1)

Trustees may at any time ... apply any capital money subject to a trust, for the advancement or benefit, in such manner as they may, in their absolute discretion, think fit, of any person entitled to the capital of the trust property ... notwithstanding that the interest of such person is liable to be defeated by the exercise of a power of appointment or revocation, or to be diminished by the increase of the class to which he belongs:

Provided that –

(a) the money so paid or applied ... shall not exceed altogether in amount one-half of the presumptive or vested share or interest of that person in the trust property; and

(b) if that person is or becomes absolutely and indefeasibly entitled to a share in the trust property the money so paid out or applied shall be brought into account as part of such share; and

(c) no such payment or application shall be made so as to prejudice any person entitled to any prior life or other interest, whether vested or contingent, in the money paid or applied unless such person is in existence and of full age and consents in writing to such payment or application.

Note
Unlike the statutory power of maintenance, the statutory power of advancement is not restricted to infant beneficiaries.

14.2.1 'Advancement and benefit'

Molyneux v Fletcher (1898)
Trustees made a payment to a beneficiary out of her presumptive share in the capital of the trust fund, purporting to make the payment with a view to her 'advancement in life'. Payments of this sort had been expressly authorised by the terms of the trust, but the particular payment had been made in the full knowledge that the sums paid to the beneficiary would be used to pay a debt owed by the beneficiary's husband to one of the trustees.

Held although the trustees had a sole discretion as to how payments should be made for the advancement of the beneficiaries, the payment in the present case had been made in breach of trust because it could not possibly be considered to be a payment which would advance her in life.

Re Collard's WT (1961)

Clause 7 of a will trust provided a power of advancement in the following terms: 'I declare that the statutory power of advancement of capital given to my trustees by s 32 of the Trustee Act 1925, shall apply to the trusts hereof as if incorporated herein save that no such advancement shall be made to or on behalf of any beneficiary for the purpose of acquiring a share or interest in any business'. The question arose whether the trustees could exercise the power of advancement by conveying a trust owned farm to the beneficiary. The beneficiary was at the time working the farm. The intention behind the proposed conveyance was to avoid the payment of estate duty which would have been payable had the farm passed to the beneficiary on the death of his mother, who was also a beneficiary.

Held the trustees would be permitted to convey the farm to the son by way of exercise of the power of advancement. There were two arguments supporting this conclusion. First, the trustees could have advanced the beneficiary by paying capital monies to him, and the beneficiary could then have bought the farm with the capital monies. Therefore, to avoid this circuitous result, the farm would be directly conveyed to the beneficiary. Secondly, clause 7 of the will did not prohibit the conveyance, because the purpose of the conveyance was to give the beneficiary the benefit of a tax advantage, it was not to give the beneficiary a share in a business.

Re Clore's ST (1966)

The father of a trust beneficiary had established a charitable foundation to which the beneficiary felt morally obliged to contribute. It would have been more tax efficient for the donation to be made through an exercise of a power of advancement in favour of the beneficiary, than for it to be made out of the beneficiary's private funds. The trustees sought the court's approval to make a capital payment to the beneficiary for this purpose.

Held the payment would be a proper exercise of the power of advancement. The beneficiary was morally bound to make the donation. He would benefit financially from making the donation out of the trust fund rather than from out of his private monies.

Hardy v Shaw (1975)

Trust-owned shares were transferred to trust beneficiaries to enable them to have a controlling interest in the company from which they earned their livelihood. The question was whether such a transfer could properly be described as a payment made under the power of advancement.

Held the word 'advancement' was not to be construed narrowly, as being restricted to a gift establishing a young person in life or, in the case of an older person, a gift for the purpose of meeting some particular need, but as including any gift whereby the donor made some permanent provision for the donee. Accordingly, the transfer of shares to the beneficiaries in the present case was a payment 'by way of advancement'.

14.2.2 Advancement by resettling capital

Re Wills' WT (1958)
The trustees, in purported exercise of a express power in the will trust, executed a deed appropriating certain investments to the share of residue to which one of the beneficiaries, M, was contingently entitled. M was employed in active military service and there was a real risk that he might not reach the contingent age of 25. The deed of resettlement recited that the investments should be held on certain trusts for M's twin sons on their attaining 21, and if they failed to attain that age, then on the original trusts applicable as if the deed had never been executed. On a summons to determine, *inter alia*, whether the deed was a valid exercise of the express power of appointment.
Held it was. The simple resettlement was for the benefit of the twins because of the real risk that M might die before attaining the age of 25. Trustees may validly make advancements by way of resettlements if the particular circumstances of the case warrant such a course as being for the benefit of the beneficiaries.

Pilkington v IRC (1964) HL
A will trust directed trustees to hold the income of the testator's residuary estate upon protective trusts for his nephew and nieces. Should a nephew or niece die, their share was to be held on trust for such of their relations as the trustees might appoint. In default of appointment the income was to be held for their children at 21. In due course the trustees wished to exercise the power of advancement for the benefit of the child of one of the nephews, so as to avoid estate duties. They proposed to make the advancement by settling the child's share in a new settlement under which the child could be maintained out of income until she reached the age of 21; thereafter she would be absolutely entitled to the income until the age of 30, whereupon she would be entitled absolutely. If she should die before the age of 30 her share was to be held on trust for her children at 21, and in default of that it would pass to the nephew's other children. The question before the court was whether the trustees could exercise their power of advancement in the proposed manner.
Held the advancement would have been permitted, even though the terms of the new settlement would have created the possibility of persons

benefiting under the new settlement who would not have benefited under the terms of the original settlement. The main consideration must be to ensure that the advancement is for the benefit of the primary beneficiary, it did not much matter that new incidental beneficiaries might be created.

Viscount Radcliffe stated that 'advancement or benefit' means 'any use of the money which will improve the material situation of the beneficiary. It is important, however, not to confuse the idea of "advancement" with the idea of advancing money out of the beneficiary's expectant interest. The two things have only a casual connection with each other'.

The proposed resettlement was not void as breaching the rule against delegating basic discretions, because the trust instrument expressly permitted such a delegation (see 12.2.1). However, on the particular facts of the present case the advancement could not be permitted as the resettlement would infringe the rule against remoteness of vesting. In considering the rule against remoteness of vesting the power of advancement was held to be analogous to special powers of appointment, which are effective at the date of the instrument which creates the power. It was a clear possibility that the ultimate beneficiaries under the proposed resettlement would not take a vested interest until more than 21 years after the execution of the instrument of resettlement.

14.2.3 Consent of persons with prior entitlement

Note ──
See Trustee Act 1925 s 32(1)(c), above.
──

Re Beckett's Settlement (1940)
The question was whether the objects of a discretionary trust were persons 'entitled to any prior life or other interest vested or contingent' within s 32(1)(c). If they were, they would have to give their consent before an advancement could be exercised in favour of a beneficiary under the settlement.

Held the objects of a discretionary trust do not have prior 'interests', they have a mere 'hope' of benefiting from the trust. In the present case, therefore, their consent was not required before advancing beneficiaries under the settlement.

Henley v Wardell (1988)
According to s 32(1)(c) of the Trustee Act 1925, before a payment is made to advance a beneficiary under a trust, written consent must be obtained from any person with a prior entitlement under the trust. In the present case the testator had granted his trustees an 'absolute and uncontrolled discretion' to advance capital. The question was whether this removed the requirement that consent should be obtained from persons with prior

interests. The trustees had already exercised the power in the face of objections from a person with a prior entitlement.

Held the requirement for consent would still apply, despite the testator's attempt to enlarge the trustees' power of advancement. The testator's enlargement of the trustees' power should be limited, on the facts of the present case, to enlarging the trustees' discretion as to the amount to be paid by way of advancement. The judge acknowledged that a discretion which could only be exercised subject to a consent could not be said to be 'uncontrolled'. Nevertheless his Lordship held that the single word 'uncontrolled' was not enough to bear the weight the trustees had attempted to put on it.

14.2.4 Exhausting the power to make an advancement

Re Marquess of Abergavenny's Estate Trusts (1981)

Trustees exercised their discretionary power of advancement in full, paying over to the beneficiary the entirety of one-half of his share in the trust fund. The remainder was invested and greatly increased in value. At a later date the beneficiary took out a summons for directions as to whether the trustees would be permitted to make further advancements, which, combined with payments already made, would total one-half of the present value of the fund.

Held the power had been totally exhausted on its initial exercise. The fact that the value of the remainder of the fund had now increased did not justify a fresh exercise of the power.

14.2.5 The fiduciary nature of the power of advancement

Re Pauling's ST (1963) CA

A marriage settlement was made in 1910 to provide an income for a wealthy lady who had married a husband of moderate means. Subject to the provision of this income, the fund was to be held for the children, or remoter issue, of the family. Many years later the husband wished to purchase a house, but the family was not as wealthy as it once had been. Counsel advised that the purchase monies could be obtained by paying capital from the fund to the children under the power of advancement. The children could then resettle the funds on their mother for life and for themselves thereafter. The children had all become adults in recent years. In due course the trustee (Coutts & Co, a bank) paid over the price of the house to the adult children by way of advancement. However, rather than resettling the property in accordance with counsel's advice, the purchase monies were used to purchase the house direct, which was conveyed to the father and the mother. The bank knew what was going on, and that the children had not taken independent legal advice. In future years and months a number of further payments were made by the bank in purported exercise of the power of advancement, and on many of these occasions the monies were used by the parents for their own purposes. The present action was brought by the four children against the trustee bank, seeking an account of the monies which had been paid over to them, supposedly for their advancement. In its defence the bank sought to rely upon the consent of the beneficiaries, the Limitation Act, *laches* and acquiescence and it sought to be relieved from liability under s 61 of the Trustee Act 1925 (see 15.3.4 for the detail of these defences).

Held the power of advancement must be exercised only if the exercise will be for the benefit of the beneficiaries in whose favour the power is exercised. This placed a duty on the bank to refuse to exercise its power of advancement if it had notice that, after previous payments by way of advancement, the monies had not been used for the purpose for which the payment had been made. The beneficiaries' apparent consent would be no defence if the bank ought reasonably to have known that the beneficiaries were acting under the undue influence of their parents. The presumption of undue influence of a parent over a child can continue for a short time beyond the child's attaining majority. On this basis the bank was held liable to account to the beneficiaries. However, relief was granted under s 61 (15.3.4) in relation to some of the advancements, but not others. The Limitation Act would not apply because the beneficiaries had future interests which had not yet vested in possession, therefore they did not yet have a cause of action which could be the subject of a time-bar (see 15.2.1). Their interests could not be said to have vested in possession upon the payment over, in breach of trust, of capital monies by way of 'advancement'. The doctrine of 'laches' could not apply because the Limitation Act, though not applicable in the instant case, applied generally to actions of this sort. Acquiescence had not been established on the facts.

Finally, it is worth noting that the Court of Appeal emphasised the fiduciary nature of the power of advancement. Namely that, when considering an exercise of the power, the trustees must weigh, against the benefit to the beneficiaries in whose favour the power is exercised, the interests of other beneficiaries entitled under the trust.

14.2.6 The powers contained in Trustee Act 1925 ss 31 and 32 are subject to express contrary intention in the trust instrument

Trustee Act 1925 s 69(2)

The powers conferred by this Act on trustees are in addition to the powers conferred by the instrument, if any, creating the trust, but those powers, unless otherwise stated, apply if and so far only as a contrary intention is not expressed in the trust instrument, if any, creating the trust, and have effect subject to the terms of that instrument.

Re Ransome's WT (1957)

The testatrix, R, directed her trustees to hold some shares on trust to apply dividends, as the trustees shall deem fit, towards the education of certain great-grandchildren, any surplus income on the shares to be accumulated until the youngest great-grandchild should reach 21. Upon the first great-grandchild reaching 21 the trustees were directed to hold the shares and accumulated income on trust for all living great-grandchildren on that side of the family. In the event that no great-grandchild should actually attain 21 the fund was directed to be held on other trusts. Upon reaching the age of 21 the only great-grandchild claimed to be absolutely entitled to the fund and to the income thereon.

Held the great-grandchild was not so entitled. As regards the income on the fund, it was held that s 31(1)(ii) Trustee Act 1925 would not apply so as to entitle the great-grandchild to the income. This was because the words of the trust, requiring the accumulation of income, evidenced a contrary intention for the purposes of s 69(2) Trustee Act 1925. The fact that the direction to accumulate breached the rule against excessive accumulation (5.3), and was therefore partially invalidated, did not alter the judge's holding that the direction evidenced an intention contrary to the operation of the power in s 31(1) to apply income.

Inland Revenue Commissioners v Bernstein (1961) CA

A settlor had directed that the income on his settlement should be accumulated during his lifetime, thereafter to pass, with the capital fund, to his wife and children. The Inland Revenue brought the present action to recover tax which it claimed was chargeable on income which the wife could receive on capital paid to her under the statutory power of advancement.

Held by directing that income should be accumulated the settlor had made clear his intention that a capital sum should be built up for the future benefit of his wife and children. This intention to provide a capital sum in the future was incompatible with the operation of the statutory power of advancement. It followed that the statutory power must be treated as having been excluded in accordance with s 69(2) Trustee Act 1925. In the absence of a power of advancement, the Inland Revenue's claim must fail.

15 Breach of trust: defences and relief

15.1 Trustees' liability for breaches of trust

15.1.1 General

Note ───────────────────────────────────
'The basic right of a beneficiary is to have the trust duly administered in accordance with the provisions of the trust, if any, and the general law' *per* Lord Browne-Wilkinson in *Target Holdings v Redfern* (1995), see below.

Target Holdings Ltd v Redferns (a firm) (1995) HL
The defendants were a firm of solicitors acting on behalf of a mortgagor (an established client) and a mortgagee on the creation of a mortgage. The defendants held the loan monies on trust for the mortgagee but paid them over to the mortgagor before the mortgage had been completed. This was in breach of trust. The mortgagee sued the firm of solicitors. In their defence the solicitors argued that they had committed only a technical breach of trust and that the plaintiff had not suffered any loss because the solicitors had acquired the mortgages to which the plaintiffs were entitled.

Held In the Court of Appeal it had been held that when the trustees (solicitors) paid away the trust monies to a stranger they came under an immediate duty to reinstate the trust fund, and that an inquiry into whether the breach of trust actually caused loss to the trust fund was unnecessary, the causal connection being obvious. The House of Lords reversed this. A common sense view of causation should be applied, with the full benefit of hindsight. Applying this test the defendant was not liable, because the plaintiffs would have suffered the same loss even but for the defendant's breach of trust.

Lord Browne-Wilkinson emphasised the difference between actions for compensation, for an account and for specific restitution. If specific restitution of the trust property is not possible, then the liability of the trustee is to pay sufficient compensation to the trust estate to put it back to what it would have been had the breach not been committed. His Lordship also distinguished traditional trusts (eg 'to A for life and to B in remainder') from bare trusts in commercial contexts. But he noted that when a traditional trust has come to an end it is, on the question of compensation, very similar to a bare trust in a commercial context.

155

Note ──

After *Target Holdings v Redferns* it appears that the beneficiary of a bare trust in a commercial context should be compensated more or less by analogy to a common law award of damages. In other words, the beneficiary should be put in the position they would have been in had the breach not occurred. Where the trust is of a more traditional type, however, (eg 'to trustees on trust for A for life and to B and C in remainder equally') compensation to individual beneficiaries is more problematic. In such a case the first duty of the trustees is to fully reinstate the trust fund, even where there is a risk that individual beneficiaries may be over-compensated as a result.

Note ──

To appreciate the potential inter-relationship between the three remedies of 'specific restitution', 'compensation' and the 'account of profits', consider the following hypothetical scenario: If a trustee of a traditional-type trust has misapplied property belonging to the trust he will be immediately liable to make *specific restitution* to the trust fund by reinstating the asset of which he has deprived it. If that property has been, let us say, destroyed, the trustee will be liable to *compensate* the trust for the loss of that property. Further, suppose that the trustee had been paid to destroy the property, or had earned income on the property before its destruction, he will be liable to *account* to the trust for the unauthorised profits that he has made from his position as trustee.

15.1.2 Specific restitution

Re Massingberd's Settlement (1890) CA

The settlement trustees sold authorised investments and reinvested the proceeds in unauthorised mortgages.

Held the trustees would be required, if the beneficiaries so requested, to replace the original investments with investments of a similar type, even though the value of such investments had risen since the trustees' breach, and despite the fact that the trustees had already reinstated the monies which had been misapplied in the unauthorised mortgages. The beneficiaries were entitled to elect to recover either the value of the authorised investment at the date of the writ, or (where possible) to recover the specific asset which had been sold, even where that asset had since risen in value. In the present case the trustees were required to repurchase the original authorised investment which they had misapplied, even though it was now worth more than it had been worth at the date of misapplication.

15.1.3 Compensation for loss

Note ──

See *Target Holdings v Redferns*, above.

Re Bell's Indenture (1980)
The trustees of a traditional-type trust misapplied nearly £30,000 of the trust fund with the knowledge and assistance of H, a partner in a firm of solicitors acting for the trustees.

Held loss to the trust fund should be assessed at the date of the judgment, not at the date of the writ nor at the date of the breach of trust. Nevertheless, even if it appears in retrospect that, as a result of the breach of trust, the tax liability of the trust has been reduced, the trustee will not be able to claim the benefit of such reduction and will not be entitled to set it off against the amounts due from him to the trust.

Note ──
Although compensation should be assessed at the date of the court's judgment, with the full benefit of hindsight, it should not be reduced by application of common law notions of remoteness of damage or unforeseeability of damage.
──

15.1.4 Account for profits

Note ──
See *Boardman v Phipps, O'Sullivan v MAM* and *Guinness v Saunders* (12.1.5).
──

15.1.5 Liability to pay interest

Wallersteiner v Moir (1975) CA
M, a minority shareholder in a company, sent a circular letter to the other shareholders in which certain allegations were made against W, a director of the company. W sued M for libel. M, in his counterclaim, sought declarations that W had been guilty of fraud, misfeasance and breach of trust. The judge at first instance gave judgment for M, in the absence of any defence from W. The judge also awarded interest on the judgment. W then appealed to the Court of Appeal on the basis that there had been no jurisdiction to award interest.

Held the court had an inherent equitable jurisdiction to award interest where a fiduciary had improperly profited from their position. In the present case the interest rate was fixed at 1% above the minimum bank lending rate. It was further held that the court's equitable jurisdiction to award interest would extend in the appropriate case to making an award of compound interest. So, for instance, the court might consider an award of compound interest in a case where the trustee had used misapplied trust funds for the purposes of his own business. The aim of an award of compound interest is to ensure that the trustee retains no unauthorised profit from his breach of trust, the award should not be used as a means of punishing the trustee.

157

Note

Simple interest is a sum calculated, usually on an annual basis, on the capital monies due from the trustee to the trust. Compound interest is calculated annually by adding to the capital the simple interest which has arisen during the previous year. Compound interest for the following year is calculated on the compound sum of capital and simple interest. The following year accumulated compound interest is added to capital, and the process repeated. It is, essentially, interest on interest.

15.2 Defences

15.2.1 Limitation Act 1980

Limitation Act 1980 s 21

(1) No period of limitation prescribed by this Act shall apply to an action by a beneficiary under a trust, being an action –

(a) in respect of any fraud or fraudulent breach of trust to which the trustee was a party or privy; or

(b) to recover from the trustee trust property or the proceeds of trust property in the possession of the trustee ...

(2) ...

(3) [Subject to provisions elsewhere in this Act] an action by a beneficiary to recover trust property or in respect of any breach of trust ... shall not be brought after the expiration of six years from the date on which the right of action accrued.

For the purposes of this subsection, the right of action shall not be treated as having accrued to any beneficiary entitled to a future interest in the trust property until the interest fell into possession ...

Limitation Act 1980 s 28(1)

... if on the date when any action accrued for which a period of limitation is prescribed by this Act, the person to whom it accrued was under a disability, the action may be brought at any time before the expiration of six years from the date when he ceased to be under a disability or died (whichever first occurred) notwithstanding that the period of limitation has expired.

Limitation Act 1980 s 32(1)

... where in the case of any action for which a period of limitation is prescribed by this Act, either –

(a) the action is based upon the fraud of the defendant; or

(b) any fact relevant to the plaintiff's right of action has been deliberately concealed from him by the defendant; or

(c) the action is for relief from the consequences of mistake;

the period of limitation shall not begin to run until the plaintiff has discovered the fraud, concealment or mistake (as the case may be) or could with reasonable diligence have discovered it.

Note ───
There are a number of situations where the Act does not apply. These include (1) where a beneficiary brings an action in relation to a fraudulent breach of trust; (2) where the trustee still holds trust property in breach of trust; (3) where the trust is charitable.

15.2.2 Fraud

Note ───
See s 21(1)(a), above.

Thorne v Heard (1895) HL
This case did not involve trustees as such, but it concerned the trust-like situation where a first mortgagee sells land the subject of the mortgage and holds some of the proceeds for the benefit of a second mortgagee who also had an interest in the land before it was sold. In this case the trouble began when the first mortgagee employed the services of a solicitor to conduct the sale of the mortgaged land. The solicitor sold the land and accounted to the first mortgagee for their part of the proceeds of sale, however the solicitor failed to account to the second mortgagee for their part of the proceeds. The solicitor dishonestly kept those monies to himself. Normally the second mortgagee would immediately seek recovery from the first mortgagee, by suit if necessary. In this case the second mortgagee did not go to court because they did not realise that a cause of action had arisen in their favour against the first mortgagee. The solicitor had craftily kept the cause of action hidden from the second mortgagee by paying off the interest on the second mortgage out of his own money, thus giving the impression that the second mortgage was still subsisting. He was able to do this successfully because he happened also to be the agent of the second mortgagee. The second mortgagee did not discover the fraud until 14 years later, only then did it bring an action to recover the monies from the first mortgagee.

Held the action was time-barred under the Statute of Limitations (a precursor to the Limitation Act 1980). The statute would not be disapplied as it could not be shown that the monies continued to be in the hands of the first trustee, neither could it be shown that the first trustees had been privy to the concealment of the cause of action. The concealment had not been carried out by the defendants, but by a third party, the solicitor.

15.2.3 Where the trustee still holds trust property

Note ————————————————————————————
See s 21(1)(b), above.

Wassell v Leggatt (1896)

A husband forcibly deprived his wife of certain monies which he knew had been left to her personal use by the terms of a will. Only after her husband's death were proceedings commenced to recover the monies.

Held the husband had constituted himself a trustee of the monies and accordingly the Statute of Limitations could not be raised to bar proceedings by his wife against the executors of his estate.

Re Howlett (1949)

A son was entitled, during his infancy, to the rents and profits arising out of premises which had devolved to him on his mother's intestacy. However, his father, the administrator of the estate, occupied the premises for his own purposes and had never paid any rent to the son. After his father's death the son brought an action against his estate for an account of the unpaid rents.

Held many defences were considered. As to the defence that the son's claim was time-barred under the Limitation Act 1939, it was held that the father had continued in his breach of trust by his continuing to hold trust property and therefore his estate would not be entitled to raise the time-bar as a defence (see now Limitation Act 1980 s 21(1)(b)). An account to the son was ordered out of the father's estate.

15.2.4 Charitable trusts

Note ————————————————————————————
As to charitable trusts, generally, see Chapter 7.

Attorney General v Cocke (1988)

The Attorney General brought an action for an account against the trustees of a charitable trust. The defendant trustees sought to show that the Attorney General was time-barred from bringing the action.

Held the Limitation Act 1980 s 21(3) had no application to a case such as the present. First, because a charitable trust has no beneficiary, as such, capable of bringing an action which could be time-barred. Secondly, because the writ had not alleged a breach of trust, nor had it sought to recover property owing to the trust.

15.2.5 Time-bars by analogy to the act

Thomson v Eastwood (1877) HL

An express will trust gave a legacy to a person who in the event never received it. The intended legatee became insolvent, released the legacy and then died. Only at a much later date were proceedings brought to enforce the legacy on behalf of the legatee's only son. The action sought payment of the legacy, together with interest thereon covering the period of delay in payment.

Held the Statute of Limitations would not apply to bar the action for payment of the legacy. The statute had no application to the case of an express trust. Payment of the legacy was ordered. However, interest on the legacy was not paid. The Limitation Act did not apply to an express trust for a legacy, yet where the beneficiary or his representative had allowed a very long time to elapse without attempting to enforce the trust, equity would, when enforcing it, apply, as to interest on the legacy, the principle of the statute.

Note ————————————————————

Limitation Act 1980 s 36(1) states that the time limits under the Act may be 'applied by the court by analogy', to bar equitable relief of a sort which would have been time-barred under the Act in comparable legal proceedings.

15.2.6 *Laches*

Note ————————————————————

The doctrine of *laches* bars an action by reason of the 'staleness' of the claim. This defence can only be resorted to in situations where the Act does not apply either expressly or by analogy. The word *laches* has its root in the Latin *laxus*, meaning 'loose'. Even today we might describe as 'lax' a person who acts in a tardy manner.

Re Sharpe (1892) CA

The liquidator of an insolvent company brought an action against one of the former directors of the company, seeking to recover monies which had been paid (in the form of interest payments) to the shareholders of the company in the years prior to its insolvency.

Held the directors were to be treated as being in the position of trustees, accordingly the defendant could not raise the Statute of Limitations as a bar to the action. Neither would the action be barred as a 'stale demand'. Lindley LJ held that 'a defence based on staleness of demand renders it necessary to consider the time which has elapsed and the balance of justice or injustice in refusing relief'. In the present case the relevant period of delay in bringing the action was calculated to be around two and a quarter years, which his Lordship did not consider long enough to raise the defence of *laches*.

15.2.7 Where a beneficiary instigates, requests or consents to the breach of trust

Somerset v Earl Poulett (1894) CA
Trustees of a settlement committed an innocent breach of trust when they invested in an under-secured mortgage. One of the beneficiaries had consented in writing to investing by way of mortgage, the question therefore arose whether the trustees should for that reason be indemnified by the beneficiary for the consequences of their breach.

Held where a beneficiary has instigated, requested or consented to an investment which amounts to a breach of trust, that beneficiary will be liable to indemnify the trustee for any liability to the other beneficiaries arising from that breach. And as against that beneficiary, the trustees in breach will have an absolute defence to any action or claim arising from the breach. When considering whether a beneficiary had instigated, requested or consented to a breach of trust it is necessary to show that the beneficiary was *sui juris* and had full knowledge of what they were consenting to, but it is not necessary to show that they knew that the investment was, in law, a breach of trust. If, however, the beneficiary has instigated, requested or consented to an investment which is not of itself a breach of trust the beneficiary will not be liable if the trustee proceeds to make that investment with a lack of ordinary prudence. In the present case the beneficiary had consented to an investment within the terms of the trust and the trustees would therefore be liable in full.

15.2.8 Where the beneficiary acquiesces in the breach

Note ───────────────────────────────────────
See *Holder v Holder* (1968) (11.2.1).

15.3 Relief from liability

15.3.1 Set-off

Note ───────────────────────────────────────
The general rule, as laid down by the Lord Chancellor in *Dimes v Scott* (1828), is that where trustees make a gain for the trust through one transaction they may not set those gains against losses made on another transaction carried out in breach of their trust. In such a case trustees will be liable to remedy their breach of trust in the usual way and will not be able to claim the benefit of a 'set-off'.

But see *Bartlett v Barclays Bank Trust Co* (11.2.2). In that case the shares in a trust-owned company fell in value due to inadequate supervision of the company by the trustees. The shares had decreased in value due to two speculative property investments undertaken by the company, one of which resulted in a profit, the other of which resulted in a loss. The trustees were permitted to set-off the gain made in one investment against the loss in the other. This allowance did not infringe the principle in *Dimes v Scott*, because the two property investments had arisen as a result of a *single* overall breach of trust.

15.3.2 Contribution

Bahin v Hughes (1886)

There were two trustees and the management of the trust was left in the hands of one of them. Following a breach of trust resulting in a loss to the fund the two trustees were sued by the beneficiaries for an account. The 'passive trustee' claimed a right of indemnity against the 'active trustee'.

Held the trustees were equally liable to the beneficiaries. The trustee who had been 'passive' was liable for breach of trust in failing adequately to supervise and participate in the activities of the 'active trustee'.

Note
The 'passive trustee' in *Bahin v Hughes* was not jointly and severally liable for the breach committed by the 'active trustee', she was liable for her own, quite distinct, breach of trust. Trustees will, however, be jointly and severally liable for each other's breaches of trust where they are all parties together in carrying out a joint breach of trust (*Bishopsgate Investment Management v Maxwell (No 2)* (1994)).

Civil Liability (Contribution) Act 1978

Under this Act the court may 'apportion' liability between trustees who are 'jointly and severally liable' for the same breach of trust, according to whatever is 'just and equitable'.

15.3.3 Indemnity

Note
A trustee who is liable to the beneficiaries for breach of trust may claim an indemnity from a co-trustee if that co-trustee: (1) is a solicitor-trustee whose controlling influence over the other trustees resulted in the breach (see *Re Partington* below); or, (2) committed the breach fraudulently; or, (3) exclusively benefited from the breach.

Re Partington (1887)
A solicitor-trustee had a controlling influence over his co-trustee, the testator's widow. The widow made an unauthorised investment in breach of her trust.

Held the solicitor-trustee had misled the widow into making the investment. He would therefore have to indemnify the widow against her liability to the trust.

Note ─────────────────────────────────────

It will not be presumed that a solicitor has a controlling influence (*Head v Gould* (1898)).

Chillingworth v Chambers (1896) CA
The parties to this action were trustees of the same trust. The plaintiff was also entitled to a share as a beneficiary under the trust. Together the trustees made certain authorised investments which proved to be inadequate. They were declared jointly and severally liable to account for the resultant loss to the trust.

Held the whole of the plaintiff's share as a beneficiary under the trust must be used, to whatever extent was necessary, to remedy the consequences of the breach of trust. The co-trustees of the trustee-beneficiary were said to have a 'lien' over the share of the trustee-beneficiary, because the co-trustees had never had a hope of benefiting from the breach, and because the trustee-beneficiary could not be heard to assert a claim to his beneficial share under the trust until such time as he had remedied the breach of trust.

Re Towndrow (1911)
A trustee who was entitled to a specific legacy under the trust of which he was a trustee misappropriated part of the residue of the trust fund. The residuary beneficiaries brought an action seeking to make good their loss out of the trustee's legacy, which had since been assigned to a third party.

Held the legacy and the residue were held upon entirely separate trusts, therefore the residuary beneficiaries could not take advantage of the principle that a trustee who had caused a loss to his trust could not assert his entitlement to a share in the trust fund. The trustee's assignees took the legacy free from any equitable charge or lien in favour of the residuary beneficiaries.

15.3.4 Relief under s 61 Trustee Act 1925

Trustee Act 1925 s 61
If it appears to the court that a trustee, whether appointed by the court or otherwise, is or may be personally liable for any breach of trust ... but has acted honestly and reasonably, and ought fairly to be excused for the breach of trust

and for omitting to obtain the directions of the court in the matter which he committed the breach of trust, then the court may relieve him either wholly or partly from personal liability for the same.

Marsden v Regan (1954) CA

The defendant, the executrix of a will, committed a *devastavit* (a misapplication of the deceased's estate, usually by paying legacies before debts). She had acted, throughout, on the advice of her solicitor and sought to be excused from liability on the basis that she had acted honestly and reasonably and ought fairly to be excused.

Held that part of the judgment at first instance, in which the judge held that the defendant should be granted relief from liability, was upheld. The mere fact that she had acted on her solicitor's advice would not of itself justify relief, but on the facts it had been reasonable for the trustee to follow her solicitor's advice. The more difficult question was whether she 'ought fairly' to be excused. Evidence showed that she had paid off all the deceased's business creditors apart from the landlord of the premises, without whose premises there would not have been any business at all. The Court of Appeal held that this question was a matter for the judge's discretion, and there being no evidence that the judge had misdirected himself on that question, their Lordships chose not to disturb the conclusion of the judge at first instance that she should be granted relief.

Q Could it be argued that s 61 introduces, by the back door, a tort-like test of reasonableness into the determination of trustee liability? You should recall that the usual standard applied to trustees is that of 'prudence', not 'reasonableness' (see 11.2.2).

15.3.5 Impounding the beneficiary's interest

Trustee Act 1925 s 62(1)

Where a trustee commits a breach of trust at the instigation or request or with the consent in writing of a beneficiary, the court may, if it thinks fit ... make such order as to the court seems just, for impounding all or part of the interest of the beneficiary in the trust estate by way of indemnity to the trustee or persons claiming through him.

16 Resulting trusts

16.1 General

Note ————————————————————————

The 'sulting' in 'resulting' shares a common Latin root with the 'sault' in 'somersault'. To 're-sult' means, quite literally, to 'jump back'. The etymology is highly informative. Take, first, the simple case where B delivers an asset to a stranger, A, in circumstances where A has given nothing in return and B has not specified upon what terms the transfer was made. We cannot tell to whom the asset belongs. Equity is said to 'abhor' such a vacuum in beneficial ownership and therefore presumes that the asset, although held by A, has 'jumped back' to B under a resulting trust. Take, secondly, the simple case where B delivers an asset to A, to be held on trust by A for a specific purpose. If that trust fails for some reason, perhaps because the purpose has become impossible to perform, who, in equity, will own the asset? Again, equity sees a resulting trust as the solution to the vacuum in beneficial ownership, and treats A as a trustee for B. According to orthodoxy the first example illustrates a presumed resulting trust and the second illustrates an automatic resulting trust.

16.2 Presumed resulting trusts

16.2.1 The presumption of resulting trust on a voluntary conveyance

Note ————————————————————————

Where property (other than land) is transferred for no consideration to a person other than the wife or child of the transferor, the transferee is presumed to hold the property on a resulting trust for the transferor. This presumption of a resulting trust is theoretically based upon the presumed intentions of the transferor, but can also be seen as an application of the maxim that 'equity will not assist a volunteer' (see 4.2). The transferee, having given no consideration, is a mere volunteer. That the presumption does not arise in the case of a voluntary conveyance of land is laid down in the Law of Property Act 1925 s 60(3).

Fowkes v Pascoe (1875) CA

Mrs B purchased certain stock in the joint names of herself and P, the son of her daughter-in-law. On the same day she purchased more of the same stock in the joint names of herself and a lady companion. Mrs B's will left the residue of her estate to the daughter-in-law for life, thereafter for P and his sister equally.

Held the presumption of a resulting trust had been rebutted by evidence that a gift had been intended. Mellish LJ could think of no other reason why Mrs B, who already owned £5,000 worth of the stock in her own name, should invest £250 in the joint names of herself and P on the same day as investing £250 in the joint names of herself and her companion. The facts were not consistent with an intention to subject the stock to trust.

Re Vinogradoff (1935)

Mrs V made a gift of £800 worth of stock into the joint names of herself and LJ, a granddaughter. On the question whether the property belonged to LJ after Mrs V's death:

Held it did not. The presumption of resulting trust applied and so the stock belonged to Mrs V's estate.

Q How can the presumption of a resulting trust be reconciled with the fact that in cases like *Re Andrew's* (see 3.2.1) a gift will be presumed unless there is sufficient evidence that the donor intended a trust?

16.2.2 The presumption of advancement

Note

Where a voluntary conveyance is made to the wife, fiancée or child of the transferor, or where the transferor is in *loco parentis* ('like a parent to') the transferee, there is a presumption that the transferor has made a gift for the advancement of the transferee. This presumption rebuts the presumption of a resulting trust. However, the presumption of advancement can itself be rebutted if there is evidence that the transferor did not in fact intend to make a gift to the volunteer transferee. However, to rebut the presumption of advancement this evidence must be such that the court may take it into account.

Gascoigne v Gascoigne (1918)

Mr G purchased a leasehold in the name of his wife, Mrs G, with a view to protecting the lease from his creditors. Mrs G claimed the property as her own on the basis of the presumption of advancement. Mr G brought the present action against her to recover the property.

Held Mr G could not rely upon evidence of his own fraud in order to rebut the presumption of advancement. The maxim *ex turpi causa non oritur actio* ('no action may be founded upon a wrong') was applied.

16.2.3 Purchase money resulting trust

Lloyds Bank v Rosset (1991) HL
Mr R had received a loan to buy a derelict house on the understanding that the house should be in his name alone. Mrs R did a limited amount of work towards the renovation of the house, in particular she helped with the interior decorations. However, the vast bulk of the work was carried out by contractors employed and paid for by Mr R. Following matrimonial problems, Mr R left home, leaving his wife and children in the premises. The loan which Mr R had taken out was not, in the event, repaid. Consequently, the bank brought proceedings for possession. Mr R raised no defence to that action, but Mrs R did resist. She claimed to have a beneficial interest in the house under a trust.

Held to succeed Mrs R would have to show that there had been some agreement (arising from express discussions between herself and her husband) that they were to share the property beneficially in equity. In the absence of evidence of such an agreement, a trust would not arise in her favour unless she had made direct contributions to the purchase price or mortgage repayments.

Note ────────────────
Lord Bridge, who delivered the leading speech, appeared at times unclear as to whether a constructive trust or a resulting trust would arise in such a case. The better view is that a resulting trust is, analytically, the more appropriate here.

16.3 Automatic resulting trusts

Note ────────────────
For an introduction to the nature of this form of resulting trust see 16.1 above.

Vandervell v Inland Revenue Commissioners (1967) HL
In 1958, V, the controlling director and shareholder of VP Ltd, decided to give 100,000 shares in VP Ltd to the Royal College of Surgeons to found a chair in pharmacology. The shares were currently held by V's bank under a bare trust for V. Accordingly, V directed the bank to transfer 100,000 shares to the RCS. It was intended that the RCS should keep the shares for a limited period only, and should relinquish them after receiving £150,000

income on the shares by way of dividends. To ensure that the RCS did not keep the shares forever the RCS, upon receipt of the shares, executed an option in favour of a trustee company set up by V. The terms of the option provided that the RCS must transfer the shares to the trustee company upon receipt of a payment of £5,000 from the trustee company. By 1961 the RCS had received over £150,000 in dividends from the shares and so the trustee company exercised the option to repurchase the shares for £5,000. The present action was brought by the IRC to recover tax from V which had been assessed on the dividends for the period between 1958 and 1961. The question therefore arose whether V had owned the shares during the period in which the dividends were declared. The IRC argued that V, in directing the bank to transfer the shares to the RCS, had tried to dispose of his equitable interest in the shares, but had failed to do so because the disposition had not been made in writing and therefore had failed to satisfy the formality requirement in s 53(1)(c) LPA 1925 (2.2.1).

Held s 53(1)(c) did not apply to these facts. That section only applied to cases where the equitable interest in property had been disposed of independently of the legal interest in that property. The object of s 53(1)(c) was to prevent hidden oral transactions in equitable interests which might defraud other parties (such as the Inland Revenue). In cases, such as the present, where the equitable owner had directed his bare trustee to deal with the legal and equitable estates simultaneously, s 53(1)(c) had no application. However, the decision in the present case ultimately went in favour of the IRC for other reasons. Three out of the five law lords held that the option had been held by the trustee company upon unspecified trusts. According to the maxim 'equity abhors a vacuum', the option could not be permitted to merely 'remain in the air', their Lordships therefore held that the benefit of the option must have been held by the trustee company under a resulting trust for V. In failing to specify trusts of the option, V had failed to divest himself of his equitable interest in the option, it followed that he had also failed fully to divest himself of his equitable interest in the shares which were the subject of the option. In the result, therefore, V was liable to pay tax on the dividends declared on the shares.

Re Vandervell's Trusts (No 2) (1974) CA

In 1965, V executed a deed transferring to the trustee company all or any right, title or interest which he might have in the option (see *Vandervell v IRC*, above), to be held by it on trust for V's children according to the terms of an existing settlement. V died in 1967. His executors brought this action against the trustee company, claiming that V had owned the shares for the period between 1961 and 1965. The IRC was joined to the action and sought to recover tax from V's estate for the period between 1961 (when the option was exercised) and 1965 (when V executed the deed divesting himself entirely of his equitable interest). The trustee company claimed that the shares should be treated as belonging to the children's settlement.

Held upon the exercise of the option by the trustee company in 1961, using £5,000 from the fund of the children's settlement, and in accordance with the company's intention, and V's evinced intention, that the shares should be thereafter held for the benefit of the children's settlement, the trustee company did indeed hold the shares on the trusts of the children's settlement. Accordingly, the shares did not form part of V's estate and his estate could not be taxed for the period 1961 to 1965. Lord Denning MR stated that when the option was exercised the 'gap in the beneficial ownership' came to an end. The resulting trust under which the shares had previously been held for the benefit of V ceased to exist upon the exercise of the option and the registration of the shares in the name of the trustee company. Following *Milroy v Lord* (see 4.3.1), V and the trustee company had, after the exercise of the option, 'done everything which needed to be done to make the settlement of these shares binding upon them'. Lord Denning MR stated, further, that even if V had retained an equitable interest in the shares after the exercise of the option he would have been estopped from asserting his entitlement to those shares as against his children. He could not claim to own the shares after having done everything possible to give them away to the trustees of the children's settlement.

Note ────────────────

There are arguably several points of inconsistency between the judgment of Lord Denning MR and the reasoning of the House of Lords in *Vandervell v IRC*. For example, Lord Denning MR held that in 1961 V intended to divest himself, and did indeed divest himself, of his equitable interest in the shares, despite the fact that V had not realised, until the decision of the House of Lords in *Vandervell v IRC* that he had any equitable interest in the shares!

Q Does the distinction between presumed and automatic trusts appear to you to be a logical one to make? In which category would the trusts in the following cases belong? *Morice v Bishop of Durham* (6.1); *Re Gillingham Bus Disaster* (6.6); *Re Abbott* (3.2.1); *Re Osoba* (1.2.4); *Re West Sussex* (6.6).

17 Constructive trusts

Note ──────────
There is an ongoing debate as to whether constructive trusts are created by the courts, or merely recognised by the courts. In other words, do constructive trusts arise by way of remedy, or in the nature of an equitable 'right' (See *Re Sharpe*, below). Another burning question is the nature of the obligations and liabilities of a constructive trustee (see *Lonrho plc v Fayed (No 2)*, below). In particular, when a stranger is held liable 'as a constructive trustee', does this give the 'beneficiary' of the trust a proprietary right against property held by the stranger, or merely a right against the stranger personally? (see 17.4).

17.1 Constructive trusts of land

Bannister v Bannister (1948) CA
D agreed to sell her cottage at an undervalue to her brother-in-law, P, in reliance upon P's oral assurance that D would be able to live in the cottage rent-free for the rest of her life if she so desired. P later attempted to evict D.

Held P held the house on constructive trust for himself and for D for her life.

Protheroe v Protheroe (1968) CA
A leasehold was bought in the name of Mr P, Mrs P having contributed the deposit out of her own monies. Mr P paid the purchase expenses and the mortgage instalments on the property. Ten years later, the parties having separated, Mr P paid a lump sum for the freehold of the property. Mrs P claimed an equal share in the freehold. Mr P argued that her interest should be limited to her interest in the leasehold.

Held Mrs P was entitled equally to the freehold of the property subject to the prior reimbursement to the husband of his payments under the mortgage and the legal expenses he had incurred in connection therewith. Following the case of *Keech v Sandford* (1726), Lord Denning held that there was a long established rule of equity that a trustee of a lease, who purchases the freehold reversion to that lease, automatically holds the freehold subject to the same trusts as the lease. This trust was a form of constructive trust.

Peffer v Rigg (1977)

Title to the land was registered. Mr P and Mr R purchased a house as an investment and in order to accommodate a relative. The house was registered in Mr R's sole name, but it was agreed that he would hold the legal title on trust for himself and Mr P as tenants in common in equal shares. This arrangement was confirmed by an express deed of trust at a later date. On their divorce, Mr R transferred the house to Mrs R for £1, as part of the divorce settlement. Mrs R was, accordingly, registered as sole proprietor. She was fully aware, throughout, of the trust in favour of Mr P. Unfortunately, Mr P had failed to protect his interest on the register and so the question arose whether Mrs R was bound by his interest.

Held (inter alia) Mrs R had known that the property she had received was trust property. She would therefore be liable as a constructive trustee, on normal trust principles, to account to the plaintiff for his share of the property.

Q A prequisite to the creation of an express trust is proof that the settlor certainly intended to create a trust. How central is the settlor's intention to resulting and constructive trusts?

17.2 Constructive trusts: rights or remedies?

Re Sharpe (a bankrupt) (1980)

Mr S, Mrs S and an elderly aunt, J, lived together in leasehold premises which were held in the name of Mr S. J had contributed the majority of the purchase price of the lease. In providing the money, J had been told that she would be permitted to reside in the premises for so long as she wished. Upon Mr S being declared bankrupt, the trustee in bankruptcy took out a summons for possession of the premises.

Held possession was denied. J did not have an interest in the land under a resulting trust because she had given her money by way of loan, not gift. The terms of the loan gave her the contractual right to reside in the premises until the loan had been repaid, but such a right would not bind the trustee in bankruptcy. However, J's right of occupation did confer on her a right in the property under a constructive trust. Browne Wilkinson J acknowledged that he had recognised J's constructive trust interest because 'to hold otherwise would be a hardship to the plaintiff'. He stopped short, however, of treating 'constructive trusts' as a mere remedy which the court could impose to address injustice: 'it cannot be that the interest in property arises for the first time when the court declares it to exist. The right must have arisen at the time of the transaction in order for the plaintiff to have any right the breach of which can be remedied'.

17.3 The obligations of a constructive trustee

Lonrho plc v Fayed (No 2) (1992)

The plaintiff, a large shareholder in Co A, had given an undertaking to the Secretary of State for Trade and Industry that it would not acquire more than 30% of the shares in Co A. It therefore sold it's shares in Co A to Co B, hoping thereby to be released from its undertaking, so as to enable a future takeover of Co A. However, having received the shares in Co A, Co B went on to acquire more than 50% of the shares in Co A. The plaintiff *was* subsequently released from its undertaking, but by then it was too late to acquire a majority shareholding in Co A. The plaintiff claimed, *inter alia*, that Co B held the shares in Co A on trust for the plaintiff because they had been acquired by the fraud of Co B.

Held a contract obtained by fraudulent misrepresentation is voidable, not void, even in equity. The representee (the plaintiff) may elect to avoid it, but until he does so no fiduciary relationship arises and the representor (B Co) cannot be a constructive trustee of the property transferred pursuant to the contract. Even if a constructive trust is established, 'it is a mistake to suppose that in every situation in which a constructive trust arises the legal owner is necessarily subject to all the fiduciary obligations and disabilities of an express trustee' *per* Millet J. In the present case there was no constructive trust because the plaintiff had demonstrated only that the company might have been acquired by fraud, it had not shown that it would be unconscionable for its interest to be denied.

17.4 Strangers as constructive trustees

Note ──────────────────────────────

A 'stranger' is any person who has not been expressly appointed as a trustee to a trust and is not a beneficiary thereunder. Strangers who frequently have dealings with trusts include solicitors, stockbrokers, bankers, company directors and other agents. Actions against strangers have become very popular, especially in cases where the principal trustee is for some reason (often insolvency) not worth suing.

Note ──────────────────────────────

The liability of a stranger who has held, but no longer holds, any property subject to the trust (and who, perhaps, has never held property subject to the trust at all – see 'knowing assistance', below), may nevertheless be liability 'as a constructive trustee'. So, for instance, the stranger will potentially be liable, like an express trustee, to account for trust monies which had at one time been in his hands, and to pay compound interest on those sums. It is important to grasp, however, that in such a case the liability is merely 'analogous' to that of a trustee. The beneficiary's claim against the stranger is merely a claim against the stranger personally. Unlike the claim of a beneficiary against a trustee who still holds trust property, it will not rank ahead of the claims of other personal creditors in the event of the stranger's insolvency.

17.4.1 Trustees *de son tort*

Note ————————

In *Mara v Browne* (1896) Smith LJ stated that '... if one, not being a trustee and not having authority from a trustee, takes upon himself to inter-meddle with trust matters or to do acts characteristic of the office of trustee, he may thereby make himself what is called in law a trustee of his own wrong – ie a trustee *de son tort*, or, as it is also termed a constructive trustee'.

17.4.2 Knowing receipt and knowing assistance

Note ————————

Liability for knowing assistance has now been superseded by liability for dishonest assistance (see *Royal Brunei Airlines v Tan*, below).

Barnes v Addy (1874)

A, the sole surviving trustee of a trust wished to appoint B to be sole trustee of one-half of the fund. A solicitor advised against the appointment but nevertheless prepared the deed of appointment according to A's instruction. B's children brought the present action against A, and against the solicitor.

Held as the solicitor had no knowledge of, or any reason to suspect, a dishonest design on A's part, and as he had not received the trust property, the action against him would be dismissed. 'Those who create a trust clothe the trustee with a legal power and control over the trust property, imposing on him a corresponding responsibility. That responsibility may no doubt be extended in equity to others who are not properly trustees, if they are found either making themselves trustees *de son tort*, or actually participating in any fraudulent conduct of the trustee to the injury of the *cestui que* trust. But ... strangers are not to be made constructive trustees merely because they act as the agents of trustees ... unless those agents *receive* and become chargeable with some part of the trust property, or unless they *assist* with knowledge in a dishonest and fraudulent design on the part of the trustees' (emphasis added).

Selangor United Rubber Estates Ltd v Cradock (1968)

The plaintiff company was in liquidation and the present action was in fact brought by the Board of Trade on the company's behalf. C had persuaded a bank to pay a banker's draft to him out of a company's account, supposedly to finance a take-over of that company. C intended to receive monies from the company which would more than repay the draft. The take-over having been completed, the new board of directors issued a cheque in favour of a third party by way of a loan. This third party then endorsed the cheque over to C who was accordingly able to repay the original draft at the bank. It was never suggested that the bank had acted dishonestly in assisting C to illegally purchase the company's shares with the company's own monies.

Held the bank was liable as a constructive trustee based on its knowing assistance in C fraudulent breach of his fiduciary duty.

Carl Zeiss Stiftung v Herbert Smith & Co (1969) CA

This action was brought against one of the United Kingdom's largest solicitors' firms alleging that fees which the firm had received from a West German company comprised property which the West German company held in trust for an East German company. Both of the German companies had been involved in litigation to decide which was entitled to the property.

Held the solicitors' firm had actual knowledge of the claim made by the East German company, but knowledge of a claim that a trust existed was not enough to found liability as a constructive trustee on the basis of knowing assistance.

Belmont Finance Corp Ltd v Williams Furniture Ltd (1979) CA

The plaintiff claimed that the defendant company had knowingly assisted in the misappropriation, by some of Belmont's directors, of monies belonging to Belmont. The plaintiff sought to fix the defendant with liability as a constructive trustee.

Held the action could not succeed with the pleadings in their present form as there had not been a specific allegation that the defendant had been aware of the dishonest nature of the misapplication of the monies.

Baden v Société Generale (1983)

The plaintiffs (Baden and others) were liquidators of various investment funds. They brought this action to recover their clients' monies which the defendant bank had misapplied by transferring them electronically to a Panamanian bank. The monies had been dissipated after their arrival at the Panamanian bank.

Held the defendant was not liable as a constructive trustee on the basis of 'knowing assistance' because it did not know *at the time* of the transfer to Panama that the former directors of the investment fund had been involved in a dishonest and fraudulent design. Peter Gibson J stated that there are four elements to liability for 'knowing assistance'. (1) existence of a trust (which need not mean a 'formal' trust); (2) existence of a dishonest and fraudulent design on the part of the trustee of that trust; (3) the assistance by the stranger in that design; and (4) the knowledge of the stranger. 'Knowledge' for this purpose can comprise any one of five different mental states: (i) actual knowledge; (ii) wilfully shutting ones eyes to the obvious; (iii) wilfully and recklessly failing to make such inquiries as an honest and reasonable man would make; (iv) knowledge of circumstances which would indicate the facts to an honest and reasonable man; (v) knowledge of circumstances which would put an honest and reasonable man on inquiry.

Re Montagu's ST (1987)

The 11th Duke of Manchester brought this action against the trustees of a family settlement set up by the 10th Duke, claiming that they had breached their trust in releasing certain trust assets to the 10th Duke, despite knowing that they were subject to the settlement. Action was also brought against the 10th Duke who, on the advice of his solicitor, had sold some of the property. It was sought to show that the 10th Duke was liable as a constructive trustee of the assets.

Held the trustees were liable for breach of trust, having transferred the properties to the 10th Duke. However, the 10th Duke was not liable as a constructive trustee because, even if he had known about the trust at some time in the past (which was not shown) there was no evidence to show that he now remembered about it. He could not be liable for 'knowing' receipt or assistance if he had genuinely forgotten that which he might once have known.

Agip (Africa) Ltd v Jackson and others (1989)

A senior officer of A Ltd innocently signed a payment order which was then forged and used by a fraudulent accountant in the employ of A Ltd. The accountant took the order to a Tunisian bank, who in turn requested a payment from Lloyds Bank plc, in accordance with the terms of the order. Lloyds Bank then made a payment over to the defendants' account, believing that it would be reimbursed by the recipient's New York bank. In doing so Lloyds took a delivery risk, as the New York bank had not yet opened for business. By the time the plaintiff had discovered the fraud it was too late to stop the payment; neither could a refund be obtained from the defendants. The defendant claimed that they had acted innocently throughout and that the Tunisian bank, and not the plaintiff, was entitled to bring the action.

Held the defendants were not liable for 'knowing receipt of trust property in breach of trust' because some of the defendants had never received any of the property at all, and those that had received the property had not received it for their own benefit. However, they would be liable for 'knowing assistance in a dishonest and fraudulent design'. Millet J stated that 'the true distinction is between honesty and dishonesty, and not between various levels of knowledge'. Applying this test to the defendants, it was held that their indifference as to the true state of affairs was not honest behaviour. (As to the 'tracing' issues raised by this case see 18.1.) Incidentally, Millet J, speaking *obiter*, distinguished cases where a person has received for his own benefit trust property transferred to him *in breach of trust* (a proper case of 'knowing receipt'), from cases where a person, usually an agent, receives trust property *lawfully* and then proceeds to deal with it in a manner inconsistent with the trust (a case of 'inconsistent dealing'). In both cases the stranger will be liable to account as a constructive trustee.

Lipkin Gorman (a firm) v Karpnale Ltd (1992) CA

Cass, a partner in a firm of solicitors (the plaintiffs), had used monies from the firm's client account in order to gamble at the 'Playboy' casino (run by the first defendant, Karpnale Ltd). In addition to the action brought against the casino, the firm sued the bank, alleging that it had knowingly assisted in Cass's dishonest and fraudulent design.

Held (Nicholls LJ dissenting) the bank's duty to pay cheques signed in accordance with its mandate had to be performed without negligence and given that there had been no finding of negligence there could not be, on the present facts, a finding of liability as a constructive trustee.

Eagle Trust plc v SBC Securities Ltd (1992)

The defendant company had underwritten the finance for a take-over bid being undertaken by the plaintiff company. The chief executive of the defendant company had then arranged to sub-underwrite its liability. The present action was brought by the plaintiff to recover monies which the chief executive had fraudulently used to clear personal, and other, debts arising out of the sub-underwriting arrangements. The plaintiff sought to fix the defendant with liability as a constructive trustee on the basis that it should have been aware that the executive would draw on the plaintiff's monies in order to clear his debts, and that the defendant should at least have made enquiries as to how the executive had managed to pay off his debts.

Held in a commercial transaction where the defendant had received, but no longer held, misapplied funds, it had to be shown that the defendant had known that the monies had been misapplied in order to fix them with liability as a constructive trustee on the basis of 'knowing receipt' of trust property. 'Knowledge' in this context meant actual knowledge or wilfully shutting ones eyes to the obvious or wilfully and recklessly failing to make inquiries such as an honest and reasonable man would make. In short, knowledge, and not merely technical 'notice', had to be proven. As Vinelott J pointed out, 'a man may have actual notice of a fact and yet not know it. He may have been supplied in the course of a conveyancing transaction with a document and so have actual notice of its content, but he may not in fact have read it'. It was stated further, *per curiam*, that it would not be possible to fix liability for 'knowing assistance' in a fraudulent breach of trust unless dishonesty or 'want of probity' could be shown on the part of the defendant. On the facts of the present case, there was no ground for making the defendant liable as a constructive trustee. The statement of claim was accordingly struck out.

Cowan de Groot Properties Ltd v Eagle Trust plc (1992)

Certain directors of ET plc sold company-owned properties at a gross under-value to P Ltd, a wholly-owned subsidiary of CGP Ltd. Consequently ET plc refused to complete the sale of one of the properties, and were sued by P Ltd. ET plc counterclaimed that CGP Ltd was liable as a constructive trustee for knowingly assisting in the ET plc's directors' fraudulent breach of trust.

Held the breach had arisen out of a standard commercial transaction and therefore CGP plc would only be liable if it had actual knowledge of the fraudulent breach of trust, or had wilfully shut its eyes to it, or had wilfully and recklessly failed to make the sort of enquiries that an honest and reasonable person would have made. Its directors would not be required to have made enquiries as to why the properties were being offered at a very low price. The line should be drawn at the point where the price in question was indicative of dishonesty on the part of the directors of the vendor company, regard being had not only to the market value, but also to the terms and mode of sale. On that basis the defendant was not liable as a constructive trustee.

Polly Peck International plc v Nadir (1992) CA

The administrators of PPI brought the present action against Nadir, the controlling shareholder of PPI, who, they claimed, had misapplied PPI funds. They also brought further action against the Central Bank of Northern Cyprus, through whose accounts the monies had passed. They sought to fix liability as a constructive trustee on the bank.

Held the fact that the Central Bank knew that PPI was exchanging large sums of money into foreign currencies was not enough to put the bank on enquiry as to whether there had been improprieties in the nature of a breach of trust. The bank should have concluded that the monies belonged to Nadir or to the group of companies to which PPI belonged, but there was no basis on which to infer that the bank ought to have known that the monies were specifically PPI monies. The real question was whether the bank should have been 'suspicious of the propriety of what was being done'. On that basis the bank was not liable as a constructive trustee for 'knowing assistance'.

Royal Brunei Airlines Sdn Bhd v Philip Tan Kok Ming (1995) PC

An insolvent travel agency owed monies (ticket receipts) to the plaintiff airline, and held those monies on an express trust for the airline. The present action was brought against the principal director/shareholder of the travel agency. The plaintiffs sought to fix the defendant with liability as a constructive trustee on the basis of the defendant's knowing assistance in a dishonest and fraudulent design. The 'design' was the use of the airline's monies by the travel agency for its own business purposes in breach of the trust under which those monies were held.

Held the defendant would be liable on the basis of his dishonest assistance in, or procurement of, the breach of trust. Lord Nicholls observed disapprovingly that courts had restrained themselves within the 'straitjacket' of Lord Selborne's *dictum* in *Barnes v Addy* (see above), with the result that liability for 'knowing assistance' had been confined to cases where the original trustee had been dishonest. His lordship considered the hypothetical case of an innocent trustee who is deceived into breaching his trust by a dishonest stranger and asked whether it could be right for the stranger to escape liability in such a case. His conclusion was that the emphasis should be switched from the state of the trustee's mind to that of the stranger. Liability should not depend upon the *'Baden'* categories of knowledge (which his Lordship suggested should be forgotten), but upon whether the stranger had himself been dishonest. His Lordship made it clear that whereas dishonesty is a necessary and sufficient ingredient of accessory liability for breach of trust, "knowingly' is henceforth better avoided as a defining ingredient'. An objective test of dishonesty should be adopted, although his Lordship appeared prepared, in determining 'dishonesty' to consider the stranger's 'personal attributes ... such as his experience and intelligence, and the reason why he acted as he did'.

Brinks Ltd v Abu-Saleh and Others (No 3) (1995)

B Ltd were the victims of a massive gold bullion heist in which a principal actor had been one of its own employees. In gross breach of his fiduciary duties to B Ltd, the employee had provided a key and photographs to the robbers. Another man, Mr E, had carried £3m of the stolen cash to Zurich and in the instant case Brinks claimed that his wife, who had accompanied her husband to Zurich, should be held liable in equity for assisting in the employee's breach of trust.

Held in order for Mrs E to be liable in equity as an accessory to a breach of trust it was necessary for her to have given relevant assistance in the knowledge of the existence of the trust or, at least, of the facts which gave rise to the trust.

Q In this recent case Rimer J has attempted, it seems, to re-introduce 'knowledge' as a defining ingredient of this head of liability. Was he right to do so, or is it sufficient for 'knowledge' to simply be one factor which informs the more important question whether the stranger was dishonest or not?

17.4.3 Should procurement of a breach of trust be a tort?

Note

It has long been accepted that procurement of a breach of contract is an actionable tort, a fact to which Lord Nicholls expressly refers in *Tan*. It might seem surprising, then, that he did not discuss the possibility of tortious liability for accessories to a breach of trust. The possibility was rejected by the Court of Appeal in the recent case of *Metall und Rohstoff AG v Donaldson Lufkin & Jenrette Inc* (1989) because the area was 'adequately covered' by *Barnes v Addy*. Now that *Tan* has removed the 'straitjacket' of *Barnes v Addy* could it be time to introduce tortious liability, rather than trust-like liability, for accessories to a breach of trust? Put another way, does it not seem odd that strangers can become liable 'as constructive trustees', even though they have never held or controlled trust property?

Part 6 Tracing and equitable remedies

18 Tracing

> **Note** ──────────────────────────────────
> Tracing is not a remedy, it is a technical process of following property through a series of transactions. If A successfully traces his property into the hands of B it may be that A will then be able to assert a right against B and the court might remedy the breach of this right by requiring some or all of the property to be returned to A. This ultimate remedy is known as restitution, and it is frequently the case that restitution is ordered on the basis that B is a constructive trustee of the property.

18.1 Tracing at common law

> **Note** ──────────────────────────────────
> According to the orthodox view, a clear distinction must be drawn between tracing at common law and tracing in equity. After reading this chapter you may agree with the growing number of academics who believe this distinction to be without principled justification.

18.1.1 Property must be identifiable at every stage

Banque Belge pour L'Etranger v Hambrouck (1921) CA
H, a cashier, stole monies from his employer, BB. H paid them into a new bank account. He later made certain withdrawals and made payments to S, with whom he was living, S then paid these monies into her own deposit account. She spent the majority of the balance of this account. Only £315 remained in S's account at the date of the court hearing.

Held the bank was entitled to trace its money. The £315 could be identified as the product of, or substitute for, the original money.

Agip (Africa) Ltd v Jackson and others (1990)
For the facts see 17.4.2.

Held due to the fact that there had been no mixing of the plaintiff's funds with funds of another person, the plaintiff would normally have been able to trace at common law. (Tracing at common law fails if the claimant's monies have at some stage been mixed with the defendant's monies or the monies of some other party.) However, the plaintiff would not be entitled to trace at common law in the present case because the monies had been transferred 'telegraphically' between the banks. Had a physical fund changed hands between the various banks and companies common law tracing would have been possible because a physical asset, representing the plaintiff's monies, would have been identifiable at every stage. As Millet J observed, 'nothing passed between Tunisia and London but a stream of electrons'. Nevertheless, his Lordship held that this would not be an answer to the plaintiff's (alternative) claim to be able to trace in equity (see below) into any property still being held by the defendants. The fraudulent accountant had owed the plaintiff a fiduciary duty, thus a fundamental prerequisite to tracing in equity had been established. It was further held that the defendants would be personally liable to account as constructive trustees for monies which the plaintiff had been unable to trace. This was because the defendants had knowingly assisted in a misapplication of the plaintiff's property (see 14.4.2).

18.1.2 Defences to the restitutionary claim based on common law tracing

Note ───
When a claimant attempts to trace at common law into funds or assets held by X it will be a defence to the ultimate restitutionary remedy for X to show that they have given contractual consideration for the funds or assets, or that they have altered their position in good faith in reliance upon the receipt of the funds or assets.
───

Lipkin Gorman (a firm) v Karpnale Ltd (1992)
For the facts see 17.4.2.

Held the casino was liable under the common law action for money had and received. Further, because it could not show that it had given consideration for the monies it had received (gambling contracts being legally unenforceable), the club had been unjustly enriched and would have to account to the solicitors firm for trust monies received by it. However, the club did not have to pay back all the money which it had received; it was entitled to pay a sum net of winnings which it had paid out. This is because, by paying the winnings, the club had altered its position in good faith.

18.1.3 Recent consideration of unjust enrichment and the change of position defence

South Tyneside Metropolitan Borough Council v Svenska International plc (1995)

Shortly after the plaintiff local authority had entered into an interest swap agreement with the defendant bank, the House of Lords declared that participation in such arrangements was outside the powers of local authorities. Accordingly, the bank refused to continue with the commercial arrangement. At the cessation of the arrangement the bank owed the authority nearly £700,000. The local authority brought the present action to recover money had and received, on the basis of the defendant's unjust enrichment. The defendant sought to show that it had a defence on the grounds that it had changed its position in good faith due to the receipt of the monies.

Held (1) the bank had been unjustly enriched; and (2) on the facts of the present case the bank could not rely upon the defence of change of position. As to (1) Clarke J stated that there had been unjust enrichment of the bank because it had received money which in equity belonged to the council and which both law and equity said should be repaid to the payer. His Lordship rejected the bank's argument that it had not been unjustly enriched because it had made a loss on the transaction as a whole or because it had entered into a transaction which proved to be void. As to (2) his Lordship held that the bank could not rely upon this defence because to do so would be to permit the bank to rely, not upon the receipt of money, but upon the validity of a void transaction.

18.2 Equitable tracing

Note ———

Successful tracing at common law leads to a mere personal claim against the defendant. In contrast, successful tracing in equity leads to a right in specific property held by the defendant. The distinction becomes of utmost importance in the event of the defendant's insolvency. The plaintiff with a mere personal claim against the defendant must join the queue of the defendant's unsecured creditors, whereas the plaintiff with a proprietary right against the defendant's funds or assets will rank ahead of the defendant's general creditors (see 8.2).

18.2.1 Limitations on the right to trace in equity

Re Diplock (1948)

The executors of a will trust had distributed the residuary estate amongst a vast number of charities. However, the House of Lords later established that the original bequest had been invalid (see the *Chichester* case, 7.1). The plaintiffs brought an action against the executors, which was compromised. They then brought the present actions against a number of the charitable institutions to which monies had been paid by mistake. The beneficiaries had two types of claim: first, a claim *in personam* which every under-paid legatee has against over-paid beneficiaries or strangers to the estate; secondly, claims *in rem*, that is, tracing claims in equity.

Held the claim *in personam* could, in principle, succeed against a volunteer such as the charities in the present case, however, the beneficiaries must first bring an action (as they did) against the executors who were responsible for the mistaken payment to the charities. The sums recovered from the executors should be applied rateably to reduce the liability of the charities. The charities would not have to pay interest on the sums owed to the beneficiaries. The claims *in rem* (equitable tracing) also succeeded, even though the funds into which tracing had been carried out had been mixed by innocent parties (the charities). However, the charities were under no obligation to give priority to the plaintiffs' claims. The charities would be entitled to assert their own claims to the mixed funds (of their monies and the plaintiffs' monies) to the extent that it would not be unconscionable to do so.

It was stated that equity will not permit a plaintiff to trace into property which has been purchased by the defendant in good faith and without notice of the plaintiff's rights (see 1.1). Nor will equitable tracing be permitted where it would be inequitable. So, for instance, equitable tracing would not be permitted, in the present case, into property held by those innocent volunteers (charities) which had changed their position in good faith on account of the receipt of the property.

Boscawen v Bajwa (1995) CA

The registered proprietor of a property charged it to a building society and exchanged contracts for the sale of the property to purchasers who had obtained a mortgage offer from a bank. The bank transferred cash to the purchaser's solicitors for the sole purpose of completing the purchase. The purchaser's solicitors transferred the money to the vendor's solicitors who then paid it on to the building society in repayment of the vendor's mortgage arrears. The building society duly discharged the charge and forwarded the title deeds of the property to the vendor's solicitors. However, the sale fell through. Later, the plaintiff, who was a judgment creditor of the vendor, obtained a charging order absolute against the property. The question was whether the plaintiff's charge had priority to the equitable claim of the bank.

Held as the bank's money could be traced into the payment to the building society and had been used towards the discharge of the latter's charge, the bank was entitled to a charge on the property by way of subrogation to the rights of the building society to the extent that the money had been used to redeem the charge and in priority to any interest of the plaintiff. Millet LJ rejected the plaintiff's claim, based upon *Re Diplock* (see above), that the vendor and the bank had both contributed to the discharge of the building society's charge, and should therefore be entitled to the property in proportion to their contributions, thus allowing the plaintiff to assert its charge against the vendor's part. The present case, his Lordship declared, was very different to *Re Diplock*. In that case an innocent volunteer had mixed trust monies with its own monies. In the present case the vendor and his solicitors were not innocent volunteers, although it was true that their actions fell short of dishonesty (because the vendor had relied upon the solicitors, and the solicitors had honestly believed that completion was imminent). The vendor must have known that any monies received by his solicitors would represent the balance of the proceeds of sale due *on completion*. He cannot possibly have believed that he could, at one and the same time, retain possession of the property and use the proceeds of sale. Had he thought of the matter at all, he would have realised that the money was not his to mix with his own and dispose of as he saw fit. This was not wholly innocent behaviour and it followed that the more favourable tracing rules which are available to an innocent volunteer who inadvertently mixes trust money with his own could not be relied upon by the plaintiff in the present case.

Chase Manhattan Bank NA v Israel-British Bank (London) Ltd (1981)

The plaintiff bank paid £2m to the defendant bank by mistake. When the defendant bank obtained a winding up order the plaintiff bank sought to trace in equity to recover the sums that had been paid by mistake.

Held the plaintiff had retained an equitable property right in the monies and would be able to trace in equity because that equitable right bound the conscience of the defendant bank. The fund to be traced need not (as was the case in *Re Diplock*) have been the subject of fiduciary obligations before it got into the wrong hands. It is enough that (as in *Sinclair v Brougham* (18.2.2)) the payment into wrong hands itself gave rise to a fiduciary relationship.

Note ───────────

It is clear that for equitable tracing to succeed the property which is being traced must at some time have been held by the defendant or his predecessors in a fiduciary (trust-like) relationship.

Note ───────────

Equitable tracing will not be permitted where the plaintiff's property has been dissipated or destroyed (*Borden (UK) Ltd v Scottish Timber* (1981) CA).

18.2.2 Tracing into mixed bank accounts, mixed funds and assets bought with mixed funds

Note

If a trustee places £10,000 of trust A into a current account which already holds £10,000 of trust B, and later withdraws £10,000 and spends it on a luxury cruise, who can claim the £10,000 left in the account. According to the rule in *Clayton's Case* (1816) the first payment into a current account is deemed to correspond to the first payment out of the account. The beneficiaries of trust B will be able to claim the £10,000. Subsequent cases have sought alternatives to the manifest unfairness which flows from a strict application of the rule.

Re Hallet's Estate (1880) CA

A solicitor mixed trust monies with monies in his personal bank account. When the solicitor died the beneficiaries under the trust sought to trace into the solicitor's estate. The balance in his personal account was not sufficient to satisfy the beneficiaries and other creditors.

Held the beneficiaries were successful with their equitable tracing claim. The general rule is that when a trustee disposes of trust property the beneficiary can take the proceeds of sale, and if the proceeds have been reinvested in new property the beneficiary can take the property or elect to treat the property as security for the amount of trust monies laid out in its purchase. But where, as here, a trustee has mixed trust monies with his own the beneficiary can no longer elect to take the property, because it no longer represents pure trust monies, but is the exchange product of a mixed fund. The beneficiary can still, however, assert an equitable charge over the property for the value of the trust monies employed in the purchase of the property. Relying on the rule in *Clayton's Case* (see above) Mr H's general creditors attempted to defeat the beneficiaries' claim to the property bought with the mixed fund by arguing that, because the trust monies had been paid into the mixed account first, they must be deemed to have been withdrawn first from the account. Jessel MR firmly rejected this argument. It is a 'universal law', he declared, that a trustee cannot be heard to say, against a beneficiary, that something has been done in breach of trust, when the facts can be read so as to show no breach at all. Accordingly, the trustee (solicitor) must be presumed to have withdrawn his own money first from the account.

Sinclair v Brougham (1914) HL

A building society was wound up leaving insufficient funds to satisfy the claims of all the customers, creditors and shareholders.

Held applying *Re Hallet's Estate*, the assets remaining after the payment of external creditors must be treated as belonging to the depositors and shareholders equally, so that individuals could claim a rateable portion of the assets according to the amount they had deposited or invested with the building society. The rule in *Clayton's Case* was not applied as it was not likely to achieve 'substantial justice'.

James Roscoe (Bolton) Ltd v Winder (1915)

A company sold its business to W and one of the terms of the sale was that W would account to the company for certain sums received by him in satisfaction of the company's book debts. In fact, when W received the payments which should have been used to clear the company's debts, he paid them instead into his own private account. He then used the mixed monies from his account for his own private purposes, leaving a total balance, at its lowest, of only a few pounds. At a later date W paid several hundred pounds into his account. Later still W was declared bankrupt. The company brought the present action against the trustee in bankruptcy to recover the monies representing their book debts.

Held the company could not trace into the final balance of W's account, but would be restricted to tracing into the balance of the account at its lowest level, when it stood at only a few pounds. This conclusion was reached by extension of the principle established in *Re Hallet's* that a trustee must be deemed to use his own monies first, with the result that the plaintiff's claim must be presumed to be restricted to the lowest intermediate balance of the mixed account. This presumption could have been rebutted if W's later payments into his account had been expressly 'ear-marked' by W as being for the benefit of the company.

Barlow Clowes International Ltd (in liquidation) v Vaughan (1992) CA

An investment company went into liquidation leaving insufficient funds to satisfy the claims of all its investors. The judge at first instance held that investors should be able to trace into the funds on a 'first in, first out' basis, following the rule in *Clayton's Case*.

Held on appeal. The 'first in, first out' rule was a rule of convenience only and should not be applied in the present case because it would result in injustice and there was a practical alternative method of distribution, namely to allow the investors to claim shares of the fund *pari passu* ('in proportion to') the size of their original investments.

Bishopsgate Investment Management Ltd (in liquidation) v Homan (1995) CA

The liquidators of the plaintiff company brought an action to try to establish an equitable tracing claim into the bank account of one of the insolvent Maxwell companies. The plaintiff's monies had been paid into the bank account, but the account had later become overdrawn.

Held the tracing claim must fail. It was not possible to trace through an account which had been overdrawn at the time of the payment into the account, or had gone overdrawn at a later date.

18.2.3 Tracing into profits made on assets acquired with mixed funds

Re Oatway (1903)

A trustee mixed trust monies with the monies in his own private account and used the mixed fund to purchase shares as a personal investment. Later the balance of his personal account was dissipated. The beneficiaries sought to trace into the shares bought with the mixed fund.

Held the beneficiaries were permitted to trace in equity into the shares. They were granted a charge over the shares for the full amount owing to the trust (even though the shares were in fact at that time inadequate security for the charge).

Re Tilley's WT (1967)

The testator's widow (who was the executor of the testator's will trust) mixed the trust monies with her own. After the death of one of the beneficiaries (the testator's daughter) her administrators brought the present action for an account against the estate of the widow who had also died in recent years. At her death the widow's account had been heavily overdrawn.

Held tracing could not succeed on the facts, because the widow had paid in the beneficiaries' monies in reduction of her overdraft. Ungoed Thomas J accepted *obiter* that if a trustee deliberately uses a mixture of trust money and his own money to buy property in his own name, the beneficiary should be permitted to adopt the purchase 'and claim a share of any resulting profits' to the extent to which the property had been bought with trust monies.

19 Equitable remedies

19.1 The equitable remedy of specific performance

Note ───

Specific performance is an equitable remedy, granted by order of the court, which requires the defendant to do that which he has contracted to do in law. The plaintiff has no absolute right to the remedy, like all equitable remedies it is awarded in the court's discretion. So, for instance, if a plaintiff has substantially breached a term of a contract they will not be awarded specific performance of that contract against the defendant, for 'he who comes to equity must come with clean hands'. Further, specific performance will not be awarded when the remedy at common law (damages) is adequate. For this reason a number of specific performance cases relate to land, for all land is unique and damages are presumed not to be an adequate compensation for breach of contract to convey land.

───

Hutton v Watling (1948)

W's contract to sell a dairy business to H contained the following provision: 'in the event of H wishing at any future date to purchase the property in which the business is situated H has the option of purchase at a price not exceeding £450'. Seven years later H purported to exercise the option. W resisted on the ground (*inter alia*) that the option was void for perpetuity (see 5.1). H sought specific performance of the option.

Held the jurisdiction to grant specific performance of a contract for the sale of land is founded not on the equitable interest in the land which the contract is regarded as conferring upon the purchaser, but on the simple ground that damages will not be an adequate remedy. In other words, specific performance is merely an equitable mode of enforcing a personal obligation with which the rule against perpetuities has nothing to do.

Beswick v Beswick (1968) HL

Mr B gave his coal merchant business to his nephew, in consideration of which the nephew agreed to maintain Mr B's widow after Mr B's death in the sum of £5 per week. In due course Mr B died and his widow sought to enforce the nephew's promise.

Held their Lordships granted the equitable remedy of specific performance of the contract in favour of the widow, because the defendant had received the whole benefit of the contract and as a matter of conscience the court would ensure that he carried out his promise so as to achieve 'mutuality' between the contracting parties. However, the widow could not enforce the contract in her own person, but only in her capacity as Mr B's personal representative. The doctrine of privity of contract would not permit her to sue in her own right. Lord Reid acknowledged that had the case involved a trust for the benefit of Mrs B, as opposed to a contract for her benefit, she would have been entitled to sue in her own person. However, counsel for Mrs B did not argue that there was a trust, and so their Lordships restricted their deliberations to the contract issue. The fact that the widow was suing in her husband's place meant that common law damages would have been merely nominal (the husband, being dead, had suffered no real loss) therefore, damages being inadequate, specific performance was ordered.

Q Can you see how the enforcement of trusts can be distinguished from specific performance?

19.2 Equitable injunctions

Note ————————————————————————————

The typical equitable injunction is almost, one might say, a court order for specific non-performance. Equitable injunctions typically order the defendant to refrain from doing such and such a thing, although they can be used to require the defendant positively and actively to undo a particular act (eg to demolish a house which should never have been built). The former, and more usual, type of injunction is said to be 'prohibitory', the latter, 'mandatory'. Injunctions may be perpetual or interlocutory (temporary injunction orders made before the final hearing of the matter). Like all equitable remedies the injunction acts *in personam* (see 1.1) and thus will not bind third parties.

Supreme Court Act 1981 s 37

(1) The High Court may by order (whether interlocutory or final) grant an injunction ... in all cases where it appears to the court to be just and convenient to do so.

(2) Any such order may be made either unconditionally or on such terms and conditions as the court thinks just.

(3) The power of the High Court under subsection (1) to grant an interlocutory injunction restraining a party to any proceedings from removing from the jurisdiction of the High Court, or otherwise dealing with, assets located within the jurisdiction shall be exercisable in cases where that party is, as well as in cases where is not, domiciled, resident or present within that jurisdiction.

19.2.1 The *quia timet* injunction

Note ———————————————————————————

The court will order an injunction to restrain a threatened infringement of the plaintiff's legal rights, and is especially likely to do so where the defendant has infringed the plaintiff's rights in a similar manner in the past. *Quia timet* means literally 'because he fears'.

Redland Bricks Ltd v Morris (1970) HL

R Ltd had excavated a pit near M's land, causing M's land to slip into the pit. The judge at first instance accepted evidence that further slipping was likely to occur and granted a *quia timet* injunction against R Ltd requiring R Ltd to restore support to M's land.

Held R Ltd appealed successfully against the injunction on the basis that it had not specified what R Ltd was required to do in order to support M's land. Their Lordships stated certain principles governing the grant of injunctions. In particular, that a mandatory injunction should only be granted where the plaintiff shows a 'very strong probability upon the facts that grave damage will occur to him in the future ... it is a jurisdiction to be exercised sparingly and with caution but in the proper case unhesitatingly'.

Hooper v Rogers (1974) CA

R bulldozed a deep track through land supporting H's farmhouse. The track exposed the land to erosion by the weather and threatened an eventual collapse of H's farmhouse. H brought an action for a *quia timet* mandatory injunction to provide support for the farmhouse (in fact H claimed damages in the place of the injunction in order to effect the repairs himself).

Held the mandatory injunction was ordered, there being no evidence that any other step would produce an equitable result. The degree of probability of future injury was not an absolute standard. The aim of the injunction should be to achieve justice between the parties in all the circumstances.

19.2.2 The *Mareva* injunction

Note ———————————————————————————

This form of injunction is designed to prevent a defendant from dissipating assets in order to defeat a judgment of the court. The injunction is effective *in personam* against any person made a defendant to proceedings in an English court, and is not defeated by the mere fact that the assets subject to the injunction are based outside the jurisdiction of the English court, although the order is usually used to prevent assets from being taken outside the English jurisdiction.

Mareva Compania Naviera SA v International Bulkcarriers SA (1975) CA

MCV owned a ship, the *Mareva*, which they let to IB on a charter bound for the Far East. IB subsequently sub-chartered the vessel to the president of India on a voyage charter to India. The Indian High Commission paid £174,000 into IB's London Bank. Out of these monies IB paid two instalments of the fees they owed to MCV, but failed to pay a third instalment which had fallen due. The judge at first instance granted an injunction against IB in favour of MCV, with a view to preventing dissipation of the balance of monies in the London Bank.

Held (*per* Lord Denning MR) the injunction was upheld on the basis that 'it is only just and right that this court should grant an injunction'. His Lordship stated that if IB should have any grievance about the injunction when they came to hear of it, they would be permitted to apply to court to attempt to have it discharged.

Derby & Co Ltd v Weldon and others (Nos 3 & 4) (1990) CA

The plaintiff sought a *Mareva* injunction against a number of defendants, including a Panamanian company and a Luxembourg company, neither of which appeared to have any assets within the UK.

Held the purpose of the *Mareva* injunction was to prevent frustration of a court order and, although normally confined to assets within the jurisdiction, could be used in relation to foreign assets, subject to the ordinary principles of international law. Because the injunction operated *in personam* (against the defendant personally) it did not offend against the principle that courts should not make orders to take effect in foreign jurisdictions. Their lordships did suggest, however, that the existence of sufficient assets within the jurisdiction would be an excellent reason for refusing a world-wide injunction.

Re BCCI SA (No 9) (1994)

The BCCI group of banks collapsed as the result of fraud on the grand scale. A world-wide *Mareva* injunction was granted to the liquidators against a director and an employee of BCCI with a view to making them personally liable for the losses which (it was alleged) had resulted from their fraud.

Held the injunction was granted. Generally the plaintiff who is granted a world-wide *Mareva* injunction must undertake not to engage in vexatious proceedings against the defendant in arbitrary locations throughout the world, but liquidators were in a special position and need not give an undertaking or obtain the court's consent before initiating proceedings in foreign jurisdictions. However, liquidators would be required to give an undertaking if, as here, it seemed *prima facie* oppressive that they would be free to initiate foreign proceedings.

Lord Chief Justice's Practice Direction as to the Standard Form Order for a Worldwide *Mareva* Injunction (1994)

... The terms of this order do not affect or concern anyone outside the jurisdiction of this court until it is declared enforceable or is enforced by a court in the relevant country and then they are to effect him only to the extent that they have been declared enforceable or have been enforced *unless* such person is: (a) a person to whom this order is addressed or an officer or an agent appointed by power of attorney of such a person; or (b) a person who is subject to the jurisdiction of this court and (i) has been given written notice of this order at his residence or place of business within the jurisdiction of this court and (ii) is able to prevent acts or omissions outside the jurisdiction of this court which constitute or assist in a breach of the terms of this order.

Mercedes-Benz AG v Leiduck (1995) PC

M advanced $US20m to L to facilitate the sale of cars in the Russian Federation by a Monaco incorporated company controlled by L. In breach of the agreement L then misappropriated the monies and applied them in favour of a Hong Kong incorporated company controlled by him. A Monaco court ordered L to be taken into custody and froze those of L's assets which were within the Monaco jurisdiction, but could make no order as to the assets in Hong Kong. Consequently, M applied *ex parte* ('without joining the 'defendant' as a party') in the relevant Hong Kong court for a world-wide *Mareva* injunction restraining the defendant from dealing with the Hong Kong assets pending final resolution of the Monaco action. The question was whether the Hong Kong court could grant a *Mareva* injunction against a foreigner who was out of the Hong Kong jurisdiction, in support of an action underway in a foreign court. The defendant's arguments amounted to this: that his assets were in Hong Kong, so the Monaco court could not reach them, and that he was in Monaco, so that the Hong Kong court could not reach him.

Held the majority held that, whatever its precise status the *Mareva* injunction is quite a different kind of injunction from any other, that it was in fact *sui generis*, and that it could not stand independently of a cause of action within the court's jurisdiction. Lord Nicholls, dissenting, stated that '... as the world changes, so must the situations in which the courts may properly exercise their jurisdiction to grant injunctions ... jurisdiction must be principled, but the criterion must be injustice. Injustice is to be viewed in the light of today's conditions and standards, not those of yesteryear'.

19.2.3 *Anton Piller* injunction

Anton Piller KG v Manufacturing Processes Ltd (1976) CA

AP Ltd, a German Company, claimed that MP Ltd, its English agent, had been passing on confidential information to certain of AP's rival German companies. AP Ltd applied for an interim injunction to permit, *inter alia*, entry of MP's premises to inspect documentation and to remove documentation to the custody of AP's solicitors. AP undertook to issue a writ forthwith to support the action for breach of confidence and AP was granted its injunction. MP appealed.

Held the appeal was allowed. Lord Denning MR held that in very exceptional circumstances, where the plaintiff has a very strong *prima facie* case to show that the defendant has caused or will cause very serious damage to the plaintiff, and where there is clear evidence that the defendant possesses vital evidence which might be disposed of so as to defeat justice, the court could by order permit the plaintiff's representatives to enter the defendant's premises to inspect and remove such material. The order could in such very exceptional circumstances be made *ex parte* (ie without the defendant's presence at the hearing). The order so made is made, not under the statutory Rules of the Supreme Court, but under the court's inherent jurisdiction. If such an injunction is granted the plaintiff must act carefully and with full respect for the defendant's rights.

Columbia Picture Industries Inc v Robinson (1986)
CPI sought an *Anton Piller* injunction against an alleged 'video pirate' (a person who, according to the judge, 'manufactures and trades in video cassettes which infringe the copyright in cinematographic films'). On one issue the dispute ultimately came down to the films 'For Your Eyes Only' and 'Star Wars'. The AP order was sought to authorise entry to the defendant's house and to premises owned by companies controlled by him. Scott J gave some important guidelines on the application of *AP* orders.

Held the decision whether an AP order should be granted required a balance to be struck between the plaintiff's civil remedies for infringement of its rights and the requirement of justice that the defendant be not deprived of his property without a hearing. Therefore the injunction should be limited to the preservation of articles or documents which might otherwise be destroyed or concealed. Thus the plaintiff's solicitors should photocopy confiscated documentation and return the originals to their proper owner. If there is some dispute as to the proper ownership of certain items, such as alleged pirate tapes, they should not be retained by the plaintiff or his solicitor, they should be passed, subject to an undertaking that they be produced in court, to the defendant's solicitor. Where an AP order has been executed in an excessive and oppressive manner the court may order aggravated damages against the plaintiff and possibly, since solicitors executing such orders do so as officers of the court, exemplary damages.

Index

197